Jan 04 2016

Tommy Lasorda

MY WAY

Tommy Lasorda

MY WAY

Colin Gunderson

TRIUMPH
BOOKS

This book is available in quantity at special discounts for your group or organization. For further information, contact:

Triumph Books LLC
814 North Franklin Street
Chicago, Illinois 60610
www.triumphbooks.com
@TriumphBooks

Printed in U.S.A.
ISBN: 978-1-62937-071-2
Design by Patricia Frey
Page production by Sue Knopf
Photos courtesy of AP Images unless otherwise indicated

Dreams are often thought impossible to reach.
When my wife, Silvie, married me,
she fulfilled one of my dreams.
When she gave birth to our son, Vincent,
she fulfilled another one of my dreams.
Because of her patience, belief, support, and love
throughout the process of writing this book,
she has fulfilled another one of my dreams.

Thank you, Mahal.
To you, I dedicate this book.

CONTENTS

Foreword *by Joe Torre* .xi

Introduction. xiii

1. Self-Confidence 1

2. Hard Work. 21

3. Competitiveness 43

4. Determination 57

5. Winning. 77

6. Family 97

7. Laughter. 115

8. Patriotism. 133

9. Love for the Dodgers 153

10. Dodger Royalty 171

11. Dodger Realeza. 189

12. Loyalty 207

13. My Favorite Tommy Stories 219

Acknowledgments. 237

Sources. 239

FOREWORD

In June of 1995, the St. Louis Cardinals—the team I played for from 1969 to 1974 and a club I had managed since 1990—told me that they were bringing another manager on board. From a professional standpoint, it was a tough time. I loved the city of St. Louis and the fans. I also wondered whether I'd ever get another chance to manage in the major leagues. It felt like I was at a crossroads in my career.

One of the first people to call me up was Tommy Lasorda. "Don't worry about it," he bellowed. "This is a blessing in disguise." I'm not sure that I believed him, but I appreciated the encouragement. He also told me something that his father had told him many years ago: "If you're so concerned with the door that just closed behind you, you'll never see the door that will open in front of you."

Months later, I got the surprise of a lifetime when the New York Yankees called in pursuit of a general manager. Soon enough, their focus shifted, and George Steinbrenner made me his manager. Tommy's words from his father proved prophetic—a new door opened, and it presented the best opportunity of my career. At the age of 55, I had a chance to implement my philosophy with a team capable of winning the World Series.

My first year with the Yankees turned out to be the final season in the dugout for Tommy Lasorda, who had an incredible 21-year run as the manager of the Dodgers. I'd always respected Tommy as a fellow National League manager, especially because we believed in many of the same attributes that managing required: communication, trust, teaching, and motivation. But his phone call—at a time in my career when I needed a jolt of energy—

was very meaningful to me, and it was an act that further heightened my regard for him.

Our paths continued to cross over the years. Before Game 3 of the 2000 World Series, Tommy and his Olympic gold medal–winning Team USA had the ceremonial first pitch honors. Before the start of the game against the crosstown-rival Mets, Tommy said hello—and pointed out that Bobby Valentine and Mike Piazza, both of whom were in the opposite dugout, were two of his favorite people. Tommy's reminder—prior to such a big game for us—made me laugh, but I admired his loyalty to his dear friends.

Tommy and I have much in common. We both appreciate fine Italian food, and we share many favorite restaurants. We have both been honored at the Ellis Island Family Heritage Awards. Many years ago in my native Brooklyn, there was a field dedicated in my honor. During the ceremony, I looked up and saw Tommy out in the crowd. He was in town for a Dodgers series against the Mets. I was touched that he took the time to be there. I can relate to the many people who have experienced Tommy's kindness.

When I became the Dodgers manager before the 2008 season, it was an honor to fill the chair once held by Tommy and his predecessor, fellow Hall of Famer Walter Alston. I was fortunate to follow in their footsteps in the summer of 2014, when I joined that great tandem as a member of the National Baseball Hall of Fame. After the ceremony, Tommy gave me the patented "Lasorda hug" and told me that my life would never be the same. Standing among the ranks of Tommy and all the Hall of Famers in Cooperstown was an extraordinary experience.

I was a rare Giants fan in Brooklyn as a kid, but Tommy Lasorda played a huge part in helping me understand why Dodger blue is so special. After reading this book, I believe you will understand why Tommy has been such a tremendous goodwill ambassador for Major League Baseball, throughout a lifetime of service to his beloved Dodgers and our national pastime as a whole.

—Joe Torre

INTRODUCTION

It was my first year working as Tommy Lasorda's assistant. We were sitting in Booth 6 in the Vin Scully Press Box at beautiful Dodger Stadium, the "House That Walter Built" and Tommy nicknamed. As we peered down at some of the greenest grass known to man, Tommy told me something fans have heard him say millions of times over the years: "Dodger Stadium is Blue Heaven on Earth. If you want to get to heaven, you have to go through Dodger Stadium first."

It was his booth, just a few boxes over from where Vin Scully—baseball's poet laureate, the Voice of Summer—has enlightened and entertained fans for decades and next to Jaime Jarrin's perch, who did the same *en Español*. To the left of his booth was the owner's box, where Walter O'Malley and his son, Peter, would host the Dodger Nation, entertaining guests and fans alike with the utmost respect and consideration.

Tommy and I would sit there to watch his beloved Dodgers play. He would survey the field and its players like Grant surveyed Richmond and Gettysburg. I would look at his face and see the memories roaring past his eyes, a lifetime serving the game he loved, the fans who loved his team, and his players whom he loved like sons. I would imagine him remembering sitting in the top deck as a scout in the 1963 World Series against the Yankees, telling his wife that one day he would be managing the Dodgers in the World Series. "She thought I was crazy, but 14 years later I was sitting in that dugout managing the Dodgers in the 1977 World Series against the Yankees," he would say, echoing the same determination that helped him accomplish that feat.

I would imagine him remembering his *paisan*, Frank Sinatra, singing "The Star Spangled Banner" on Opening Day in '77, Tommy's first as manager. "He promised me that when I became manager he would sing the anthem, and by golly he did," Tommy would say, his prideful eyes mirroring the blue of Sinatra's.

I would imagine him remembering Dusty Baker hitting a home run in the final game of the '77 regular season, his 30th, putting the Dodgers in the history books. "If you think back through the history of baseball about all those great Yankee teams and sluggers, that we were the first team to have four players hit 30 or more in one season..." Tommy would say, trailing off with the same amazement he had watching Baker's ball sail over the wall.

I would imagine him remembering Bob Welch face Reggie Jackson in the '78 World Series in a nine-pitch at-bat that ended when Welch, the rookie, struck out Reggie, the slugger. "That was by far the greatest duel I've ever witnessed."

I would imagine him remembering being a coach in the 1980 Midsummer Classic, the only All-Star Game ever held at Dodger Stadium. "The National League had an eight-game winning streak going and there was no way I was going to let that go under our watch," he would say with the same aggression he carried into every game he managed.

Giving the ball to an unknown pitcher from Mexico on Opening Day in '81 and sparking Fernandomania. "The first word he learned in English was *million*," Tommy would say of Valenzuela, with a hearty chuckle.

Jerry Reuss outdueling Nolan Ryan in the '81 division series. "Jerry pitched an outstanding game. It was a tremendous game."

Steve Garvey playing his 1,000th consecutive game. "I don't commend hard work. I expect it."

Beating the Yankees in the 1981 World Series after losing to them in '77 and '78. "For three years I would lay my head on the pillow and pray to God and say, 'Dear Lord, if you see it clear to let the Dodgers play in another World Series, please, let it be against the Yankees.'"

The Bulldog, Orel Hershiser, beating the Mets in the only Game 7 in Dodger Stadium history to punch their ticket to the '88 Fall Classic. "I put the whole ball of wax on the Bulldog," he would say, bragging like a proud father does of his son's accomplishments.

Hershiser's scoreless inning streak surpassing Tommy's old roommate's, Don Drsydale. "Hershiser didn't want to break the record but Donnie wanted him to. That record may never be broken."

And of course that magical swing from Gibby's bat in Game 1 of the '88 Series, a moment that has gone down in history as the greatest World Series home run, one that propelled the Dodgers past the A's for the championship. "Nobody thought we could beat the Mighty Mets. Nobody thought we could beat the team that won 104 games, but we believed," he would say, getting his players or anyone else listening to believe what he believed all along.

I asked him if he missed managing. He looked at me with that weathered face and said, "I miss it every single day."

• • •

I worked for the Dodgers as Tommy's assistant and press coordinator for 12 years. As I would learn during those remarkable years, yes, he missed the glory of victory and even the agony of defeat, though he hated to lose. What he really missed was the sum of those parts, the camaraderie he had with his players. He loved his players like sons and relied on them. Like any father does, he taught them. He taught them not just lessons about the game of baseball but about life itself. His knowledge was gained through a lifetime of experience, turned into sage advice. His impact on his players was profound on and off the field.

The interconnectedness of Tommy's lessons are like pitching and hitting. Self-confidence fuels a major league work ethic, a ferocious competitiveness, and unwavering determination. All of those are characteristics of winners. All of those are necessary to win in baseball.

The age-old question is whether chemistry helps you win, or if winning builds chemistry. That might be a more enduring debate than the Ted Williams–Joe DiMaggio "who is the greatest hitter?" debate. However, Tommy's teams won, and the Dodgers were a family. They won together and laughed together.

All of those characteristics are part of the Dodger Way, part of why we all love baseball.

The Italian word *narratore* means storyteller, which is something Tommy certainly is. He has been telling stories for decades about himself and his players, and now it is time to turn the tables. This book aims to pay tribute to Tommy Lasorda by getting some of his former players, and a few of his close friends, to tell their favorite Tommy stories, and to use those stories to highlight his life's work and the lessons he taught.

He taught the Dodger Way, his way. As you will see in the following pages, that is exactly what Tommy did for his players, and for millions of friends and fans who have had the privilege and honor of interacting with Tommy and being influenced by his wisdom.

CHAPTER 1

SELF-CONFIDENCE

"You gotta believe!"

He said it. He said it time and again. He said it so much that people may have gotten worn out, either because they already believed him or because they would never believe him.

He said it even though it was never supposed to happen, but it did. His roster was not a championship one. Filled with aging stars, journeymen, and rookies, with a few athletes sprinkled amongst the group of ballplayers, it happened because he said it, and kept saying it, because his will was one to never admit defeat, to never surrender to doubters, to never accept anything but the best from himself and his players, even if they didn't think they were of that caliber. That was his way, and it was the Dodger Way.

"I said it because I believed it, and I wanted my players to believe it. You gotta believe!"

He said it in May of '88 when the Dodgers outlasted the Phillies in a game on the road. They scored a run in the first, but the Phillies tied it. They led 4–1 in the sixth, but Don Sutton gave up two runs. They tacked on a run for a 5–3 lead, but Tim Crews gave up three runs in the seventh. The Dodgers answered, but Jesse Orosco blew a 7–6 lead. Finally, they scored three runs in the top of the ninth and Jay Howell pitched two scoreless innings for a 10–8 victory. Steve Sax hit two home runs, doubled, and scored on a sacrifice fly to the shortstop. Yes, the shortstop.

"You gotta believe!"

He also said it when the Mets completed a three-game sweep at Dodger Stadium, amidst a bunch of bad blood. Fernando Valenzuela didn't make it out of the second inning, giving up five runs. The night before, a Dwight Gooden fastball hit Alfredo Griffin in the hand and broke it, which kept Griffin out two months. The Mets led 5–0 in the sixth inning when David Cone just missed hitting Pedro Guerrero with a fastball. The next pitch was a slow curve that hit Guerrero on the shoulder. Enraged, Guerrero threw his bat at Cone and barely missed him. After games and series like that, Tommy would holler it loud enough for the entire locker room to hear.

"You gotta believe, boys!"

He said it that July when the Dodgers swept a doubleheader over the Giants at Candlestick Park. They won the first game 7–3. Between games, Giants manager Roger Craig told reporters it was the most important game of the season. Despite being in late July, the temperature was 49 degrees when the second game started at 9:08 PM. The game was tied 4–4 entering the ninth. Both teams scored a run, and entering the 10th it was tied 5–5. This was near the end of the road trip from hell—17 games in 14 days in four cities—and now extra innings. In the 11th, the Dodgers scored the go-ahead run on a balk.

"You gotta believe!"

He said it in August when Kirk Gibson looped a single into left field that tied a game against Montreal. On a 1-1 pitch, Gibson stole second base. On the next pitch, Expos reliever Joe Hesketh bounced a pitch in the dirt that got past the catcher. Gibson raced to third base, never slowed down, sprinted home, created a cloud of dust with his slide, and scored the game-winning run.

"That-a-boy, Gibby! You gotta believe!"

He also said it that September, as the Mets beat the Dodgers, yet again. The Mets won the night before, 8–0. In this game, Gibson stole second base but felt a burning sensation in the back of his leg. This was the start of the problems that would bother him into October. Gibson was tough, but he was buoyed by Tommy's confidence.

"You gotta believe, Gibby. You'll be okay."

He said it even after Reds pitcher Tom Browning threw a perfect game to beat the Dodgers 1–0 that September. He said it when Orel Hershiser pitched his fifth consecutive shutout. And he said it when the Dodgers clinched the division in San Diego.

Fernando Valenzuela lasted only three innings. Brian Holton pitched the fourth. Holton, Ricky Horton, and Tim Crews each got an out in the fifth. Alejandro Pena pitched the next three innings. Down 2–0, John Shelby and Tracy Woodson homered to tie the game at 2–2. In the eighth, Alfredo Griffin reached on an error, Steve Sax bunted him over, and Mickey Hatcher singled home the winning run. Hatcher was only playing because Gibson was nursing his leg. Jay Howell pitched the ninth. Sax caught the final out to clinch the division and start the celebration.

And celebrate they did, because they believed it would happen, even though it wasn't supposed to.

But Tommy said it long before that. He said it in his clubhouse meetings during spring training, when he would take his players to lunch, and in letters he wrote them during the off-season. He said it to himself at home getting ready for the day, in hotel rooms across the country before speeches; he said it to anyone in need of motivation. He said it before the season even started, on a promotional tour of Los Angeles, telling fans, "Get your tickets now because we'll be dancing in the streets of Los Angeles in October! You gotta believe that the Dodgers are the greatest team in Major League Baseball!"

That is Tommy Lasorda's mantra, his belief that winning isn't about being the best, but believing you are the best.

"It's not always the strongest man who wins the fight, or the fastest man who wins the race; it's the one who wants it more than the other guy."

Tommy would preach about the importance of desire, and that desire is only fulfilled when you believe in yourself. "Self-confidence is the first step toward success. If you believe it, you can achieve it."

"How bad do you want it?" he would thunder. "How much of a price are you willing to pay?"

Success to him, his mission, was to win the World Series every year, and he never let his players forget that. It all started with them believing they would win the World Series.

"If you believe you are championship team, you will practice like a championship team. If you practice like a championship team, you will play like a championship team. And if you play like a championship team, that's exactly where you will finish."

That was the tone he set, the expectation he had for his team and its players. That was the expectation in 1988 in Vero Beach when the Dodgers reported for spring training. Nobody thought it would happen but him, and he refused to let anyone else who wore the Dodgers uniform think differently.

He said it so much that the players started to believe, too. It became the team's mantra because it was Tommy's first. It carried them through the season and into October when they were to play the Mighty Mets in the National League Championship Series. He said it even though the Dodgers had lost 10 of 11 against the Mets that year. He said it even though they were down 2–1, in New York, even though they were facing Doc Gooden in Game 4 with his blistering fastball, his 9–1 regular season record, his 1.31 ERA. He said it even though Gooden had handled them in Game 1.

Getting on the bus to go to the Shea Stadium, he knew things had to change. "If we lose today we are in deep, deep trouble." Deep indeed. But he also knew that anyone on that team could be a hero on any given day. That was the character of the team, because each and every one of them believed. Who would it be today? Who would step up? Who would have the will to rise to the occasion? He believed that person would be a Dodger. It would be somebody whom he could affect, somebody that had been listening to him preach about belief all year long, or maybe just today.

Would it be Saxy? Would it be Hatch? Maybe T-Bone, hopefully Gibby, or maybe even Jeff Hamilton? Maybe.

The Dodgers jumped out to a 2–0 lead when John Shelby singled in Sax and Hatcher. The Mets countered with a two-run bomb by Darryl

Strawberry, followed by a solo shot by Kevin McReynolds. The Mets scored again in the sixth and Gooden retired six of the next seven batters he faced, giving the Mets a two-run lead going into the top of the ninth.

But Tommy kept saying, "You gotta believe!" The Dodgers had just one win and 60 losses while trailing after seven innings in postseason games. "You gotta believe." Pacing back and forth in the visitors' dugout, clapping. "You gotta believe." John Shelby waited in the on-deck circle as Gooden warmed up. "You gotta believe, you gotta believe."

Unbelievably, Shelby walked. "John was a Bible hitter: thou shalt not pass." One of baseball's golden rules is to never let the leadoff hitter get on base, a rule Gooden broke. "That was almost a miracle. Who ever would have thought this guy would walk him? He had him 0-2."

All the while Mike Scioscia, the Dodgers catcher, Tommy's field general, his eyes and ears on the field, was in the on-deck circle. "You gotta believe, Sciosc," Tommy hollered from the dugout. As Shelby ran to first base, Gooden shook his head in disbelief at the walk. Scioscia was not a power hitter. He had hit only 35 home runs in eight and a half big league seasons. Gooden knew that, and he also knew what Tommy knew—that Scioscia the catcher could think like a pitcher.

"Mike was an outstanding receiver," said Tommy. "He could handle pitchers as good as any catcher who ever played for me." To Gooden, that meant Scioscia was going to take the first pitch, since the previous batter had just walked. That's how pitchers think, so that's how Scioscia should think, too.

Gooden leaned in, gripped the ball with his fingers across the seams, let a little spit out onto the mound, came set, and with the high leg kick fired his signature fastball. But Scioscia wasn't thinking the way Gooden assumed he would. Scioscia was sitting on a first-pitch strike, a pitch he hit over the fence, one that yanked Gooden's neck as he watched it fly, that evened the score, that changed the course of the NLCS, that validated Tommy.

"You gotta believe!"

As Scioscia rounded third, Joey Amalfitano gave him a slap on the backside. As Scioscia crossed home plate and came back to the dugout,

Tommy gave him the Lasorda hug. As the scoreboard changed to reflect the new score, so did the attitude about the Dodgers' chances; some people started to believe.

Back in the dugout, and in Tommy's mind, this was no shock. They were supposed to win. They were supposed to believe. Somebody was going to be the hero, and it happened to be Mike Scioscia.

"Mike wasn't exactly a home run hitter, but when he did hit home runs, they were of great consequence. He hit home runs off great pitchers, and only players who know how to win do that. Only players who know how to be successful do that."

Tommy also knew what kind of player Scioscia was. He knew Scioscia was tough—just ask Jack Clark after he piled into him and nearly knocked him unconscious. He knew Scioscia was a winner.

He had known this about Scioscia for a long time. By 1988 Scioscia had been a Dodger for nine years, and had been a minor league Dodger for the previous four, learning the Dodger Way. Of course, it is the job of the minor league coaching staff to teach young players the game, to teach them the Dodger Way of playing baseball. Scioscia though, was indoctrinated even before he met any of the minor league coaches. Tommy knew this, because he was the one to welcome Scioscia into the Dodgers system, the Dodgers family. He was the one who believed Scioscia would be a major league catcher for the Dodgers before Scioscia even knew he would one day hoist the championship trophy with his Dodgers uniform soaked in champagne. Tommy believed this, and he made sure from their first meeting that Scioscia believed it, too.

Mike Scioscia was drafted by the Dodgers in the first round of the 1976 draft. However, he was planning on going to Clemson University to play baseball there, and to fulfill his mother's dream. About one month later, Scioscia, who was still 17 years old, was at home after waking up late in Morton, Pennsylvania, a Philadelphia suburb not too far from Norristown, where Tommy grew up. It was July 6, 1976, and the Dodgers were in town to play the Phillies.

The phone rang.

"Is Mike there?"

"Yeah, this is Mike."

"This is Tom Lasorda with the Dodgers. I want to take you out to our early practice with the Dodgers at Veterans Stadium. We want to work you out."

"Okay. Wait, how do you know where I live?"

"I know where you live. Are your mom and dad home?"

"No."

"Well, leave them a note and tell them you are going to go work out with me and the Dodgers."

Scioscia left the note, hopped in the car with Tommy and Tommy's brother Eddie, and started the journey that would change his life.

"You know, I was 17," said Scioscia. "I didn't know if it was a joke or not."

"When I got Mike in the car, I told him about what it meant to be a Dodger," said Tommy. "I told him that this would be his only opportunity to be a Dodger, and that he had to sign. I told him that our scout saw something in him and talked highly about him, and that we believed in him enough to draft him with our first pick, that I believed in him, and that he needed to believe it, too."

"We go down to Veterans Stadium, and he's throwing BP to me," said Scioscia. "He's throwing me curveballs and cutters, and I'm looking like I can't hit anything. After the workout I probably would have paid them to sign me! He gave me the whole full-court press about what it means to wear the uniform, and how much they thought of me to draft me so high."

In July of '76 Tommy was still the third-base coach. Before that he was a minor league manager, so he was used to dealing with young players battling to make it to the big leagues, battling the doubt that comes along with what is deemed successful in baseball: hitting .300. Before that Tommy was a scout for the Dodgers, so he was used to telling youngsters about the Dodgers, telling his story about how hard he battled to wear the Dodgers uniform, about what wearing the Dodgers uniform meant, not just to himself, but to guys named Pee Wee, Jackie, Duke, Sandy, and the like. Tommy was used to signing players who wanted to play for the Dodgers but had to get past their parents. He was a master at it, and when there was a tough case, Tommy's boss and mentor, Al Campanis, would challenge him.

"When Al would tell me that I couldn't do this or that, or that I couldn't sign a certain player, he knew that I would battle tirelessly until I accomplished the mission," said Tommy.

Scioscia proved to be a tough case for the Dodgers, but he wasn't for Tommy. They are both from Philly suburbs; they are both Italian. And Tommy was faced with Campanis' challenge, coupled with his belief in Scioscia as a player.

"I went home that night and told my mom and dad that I wanted to sign with the Dodgers," said Scioscia. "My mom started crying because she wanted me to go to school; she didn't like it. My dad was happy, but he couldn't show it because of my mom. Next day I was on a plane to Walla Walla, Washington, to play pro ball."

Tommy had welcomed another member into the Dodgers family. Although it was tough on Scioscia's family, Tommy made sure that they knew they were part of the Dodgers family, too.

"The next day Tommy wrote my mom a letter, when he knew that I was going to sign," said Scioscia. "It just said, 'I know it's an important decision. We are going to take care of Mike. We are going to give him every opportunity to reach his goal and his dreams, and we will take care of your son,' and he signed it."

Tommy believes in the power and purpose of family. His family is his strength, and besides the Lasordas, the Dodgers were his other family. He gave them every bit of his energy and enthusiasm, and in return the Dodgers gave him his life. He believed in the Dodgers' family structure, and it gave him peace. Tommy would in turn pass his joy of being a Dodger to anyone else in the family, including the Scioscias.

"That gave her a lot of peace," said Scioscia about the letter. "I was just 17 and going on the road, to get that from a major league manager...you know, that's what Tommy did. He had those special touches. He was very in touch with the humanity of this sport, but he is also the most competitive person I have been around in my entire life."

Years later, Tommy met Scioscia's mother in person and gave her the same Lasorda hug that her son would receive many times.

"Her happiest day was when I signed my letter of intent to go play for Clemson, and one of the saddest moments was when I told her I want to sign with the Dodgers," remembered Scioscia. "She passed away in 1983. She had cancer. I think when I made it to the major leagues she was happy I made it, but she still knew what I had given up. I think after we won the World Series in '81 she said, 'You know, this might work out for you.'"

So when Scioscia was rounding third base, touching home, and returning to the dugout on that fateful night at Shea Stadium, Tommy's humanity was on display. What is more human than the power of self-confidence? What is more human than the joy of sharing in success? What is more human than the love of a manager hugging his player like a father hugs his son? What is more human than the fun of tasting the fruits of victory, and knowing that all of your effort, all of your patience, and all of your belief helped someone you love do something miraculous? To have that type of effect on someone is what, for many people, makes life worth living, and for Tommy, what made managing his life's work.

You gotta believe.

"Tommy was the best I've ever been around at setting an environment," said Scioscia. "There were always expectations, but you always had the confidence that you could meet those expectations. It was just a way of life when you were with the Dodgers, whether you were at Dodgertown in spring training, or whether it was during the season and you were going to play a tough club like the Cardinals or the Mets on the road. There was an expectation for you to come and play the game the way it was supposed to be played, and you were expected to win. And those were never compromised."

Maybe that's why Tommy would say it—and say it again and again. He never let his players compromise, never let his expectations be compromised, would never let himself or his belief be compromised.

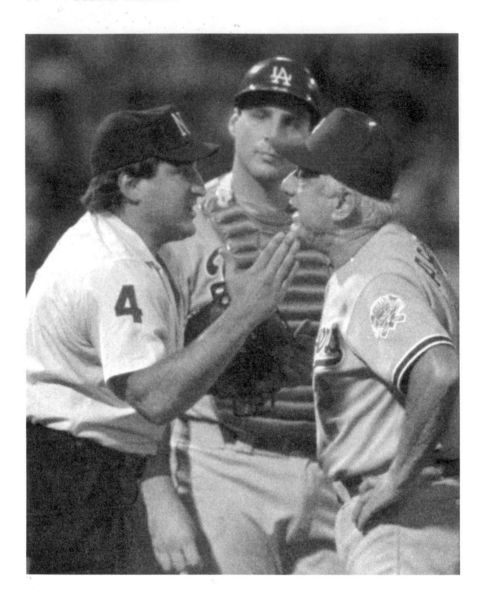

"When you were on his team you felt like you could do anything, and he had everybody play to their potential," said Scioscia. "Tommy was never intimidated by anything. We went in and played teams that in hindsight were so much better than us. Whether it was in a big series or a playoff, we felt like we were the best team. We weren't intimidated by anything, and it started with Tommy."

Scioscia played for Tommy for 13 years and wore many hats: catcher, field general, friend, champion, apprentice, and son. When they played, whether they won or lost, he learned. He learned baseball—the Dodger Way of playing baseball. He learned about dealing with personalities. He learned about setting expectations. He learned about winning. And he learned about the humanity of the game and of Tommy Lasorda.

• • •

Of course, Scioscia wasn't the only player to get a hug, nor was he the only player to hear Tommy preach self-confidence and belief, nor was he the only player to embody the message and reflect its power on the field.

Another player in particular got many hugs and lots of words of encouragement. He was a kid who came running into Tommy's life, an exciting kid, an athletic kid, an explosive kid, a winning kid who would grow into a ballplayer and into a star. He would become one of Tommy's favorite players, one of his favorite people.

"We were like father and son," said Tommy. "I started to love him the moment I met him."

Bobby Valentine was a local legend before an age when most people earn their driver's licenses.

"He was 13, 14 years old, something like that, and he went to Miami and won a dancing competition," said Tommy. "Coming out of high school people thought he was the next O.J. Simpson."

Indeed, most people from Valentine's hometown of Stamford, Connecticut, knew he was destined to be a star. At Rippowam High School he was a three-time all-state football player and a baseball star. He was recruited to play at the University of Nebraska for Bob Devaney's Big Red, Duke, Our Lady's Fighting Irish of Notre Dame, and the University of Southern California.

He was even recruited, personally, by Joe Paterno.

"Joe went to Bobby's house," said Tommy. "He figured he had this kid, no problem. All of a sudden Paterno heard some noise, and he looked out the window and saw a batting cage, and Bobby was taking batting practice before dinner. After that, Joe knew he had no shot."

In 1968 Tommy was still scouting for the Dodgers. Al Campanis, then scouting director, had convinced Tommy to move to Southern California a few years earlier. New to the area, USC was just about the only place Tommy knew. One day, he and Campanis were there watching a game. Valentine was there too, but as a football recruit. Campanis saw Valentine, and told Tommy to go talk to him.

"I can't do that, Al," Tommy told Campanis. "He's here with the football program."

"No sooner did I say that, the assistant coach recognized me and waved me down to the field. I went down there and he introduced me to all the recruits," Tommy says.

It just so happened that Tommy sat down next to Valentine, and they started to talk.

"I told Bobby who I was, and that the Dodgers were interested in him. Bobby asked me if I wanted to see him hit right there."

Maybe baseball was in his heart. Maybe the prospect of playing professional baseball was in his heart. Maybe Tommy was starting to get in there, too.

"That made me laugh," said Tommy. "He wanted to hit right away. I told him that he couldn't do that because he was there with the football players. But I told him that if we draft him that I wanted to be able to come in and sign him."

That was the start of a great day for Tommy and Valentine. It was the start of a lifelong relationship. Later that day Tommy saw Valentine again at a party hosted by USC baseball coach Rod Dedeaux. The party was at Dedeaux's house, and it was for his baseball recruits. Tim Foli was there. So were Bill Buckner and Lloyd Allen. Oh, and Casey Stengel was there, too.

"Bobby wanted to show me his swing at Dedeaux's party," said Tommy. From that first day, Tommy could see that Valentine had desire, and even though he hadn't seen him hit, he knew he had athletic ability. In the eyes of a scout, that's a lethal combination.

"I saw something special in Bobby," said Tommy. "He was an outstanding baseball player. We drafted him with our first pick. He was the type of player who would always rise to the occasion. After we signed him, I would always tell people that if I had to rely on one guy at the plate, it would be Valentine, because he would rise to the occasion and knock in that big run."

Valentine would enroll at USC, but he chose the Dodgers over Rod Dedeaux and his baseball program, over John McKay's football program, over Ara Parseghian's, and over Devaney's.

"I was there for about a month," said Valentine. "I think I only stayed for about two nights."

"It showed me a lot about who this kid was to choose baseball over all those great college football coaches," Tommy said. What it showed was desire and ability.

After being drafted by the Dodgers, Valentine would join Tommy in rookie ball in Ogden, Utah, where Tommy was managing. Valentine joined a stacked roster that included Steve Garvey, Bill Buckner, and Tom Paciorek, to name a few. There was a lot of competition on that roster for advancement in the Dodgers system, and for Tommy's attention. Although Valentine was a football star in high school and recruited heavily, Paciorek played college football at the University of Houston, and Garvey played at Michigan State.

"They would get on Bobby and tell him that if they played against him they would have cut him in half," remembered Tommy.

Never one to back down, Valentine would tell his teammates, "Yeah, but you would never catch me!"

Valentine had tremendous speed, and speed is something that cannot be taught. But Tommy was a natural teacher of the game. He would teach the fundamentals, but also how to become a winner and how to believe in oneself.

"He said it all the time," said Valentine. "He said it that whole year in rookie ball. After I had a bad night he was there to encourage me. He did it constantly. But he yelled at me a lot, too."

"I would tell my players that if they wanted to get their mail at Dodger Stadium, then they had to listen to me and do what I told them to do," said Tommy. "I was going to show them the way to the major leagues."

He certainly did. During his eight years as a minor league manager he sent 73 players to the major leagues. Some of those players were destined to get there. Some needed a bit of luck or an opportunity. Others needed to be pressed to work harder.

"Even with Valentine, a guy who was so gifted and really believed in himself, I would have to holler at him to work harder all the time," said Tommy.

The work paid off. Valentine won the Pioneer League MVP in '68. Although he only hit .281 that year, he beat out Garvey (.338), Buckner (.344), and Paciorek (.386).

"Bobby didn't hit as well as those other guys did, but he stole a lot of bags, made tremendous plays in the field, and when there was a big run on the line, Valentine would be the guy you wanted at the plate because he would knock that run in," said Tommy.

Valentine also excelled that winter playing for Tommy in the Dominican Republic, winning the MVP of the Caribbean Series that year.

Then, as fate would have it, Dodgers second baseman Jim Lefebvre succumbed to an injury. Campanis called Tommy and told him that there was a problem, that Lefebvre was hurt.

"You don't have any problems, Al," said Tommy. "I've got a better player for you right here—Billy Grabarkewitz."

Tommy had won the '68 Manager of the Year award for his work in Ogden that season, and was rewarded by being promoted to manage the Triple A team in Spokane, Washington. Campanis asked Tommy who should replace Grabarkewitz at second base on Tommy's roster.

"Al asked me if I wanted the guy from Double A, but I told him, 'No sir, I want Valentine.'"

"Valentine?" asked Campanis. "He's a center fielder! He's only played a couple months of professional baseball! He's only 19!"

"I don't care, Al," said Tommy. "I want Valentine."

"Okay, Tommy," said Campanis. "You can have Valentine, but they are going to run the both of you out of town."

"Well, if they do, at least we'll be together."

Campanis sent Valentine to Tommy in Spokane. Even if Campanis didn't believe it could happen, Tommy did, and he was going to make sure that Valentine believed it, too.

"I was in college, and when I got through with finals I was ticketed to go to Bakersfield, which was A ball," said Valentine. "My car was packed and the next morning I was going to drive to Bakersfield. There was going to be a 1:00 PM workout. I went to the Dodgers game that night, and when I was leaving my car was parked at the executive level. I decided to stop in the office and see if anyone was there. Turned out Mr. Campanis was in his office. I went around the corner and waved to him and he waved me in and told me to sit down, as he was talking on the phone. Turns out he was talking to Tommy, who was in Hawaii.

"As I'm sitting down, Al said, 'You gotta be kidding me. They'll run you both out of town!' I remember those words. But as I'm sitting there I don't know what he's talking about.

"'Well, he's right here,' Al said, and handed me the phone."

"When are your classes over?" Tommy asked.

"They ended today."

"Can you get to Spokane for our homestand next week?"

"I didn't even know where Spokane was," said Valentine. "I drove to Spokane and became the shortstop. I got to Spokane the day the team was flying back from Hawaii. I played the next day, and I played shortstop. I had never played a professional game at shortstop."

For most players, a jump from rookie ball to Triple A, from center field to shortstop, is impossible. But Tommy believed it was possible for a player like Valentine. They were together; their fates were linked. Tommy would not let Valentine fail. His will, his work ethic, his belief would make it possible, would make it work.

"I would take Bobby out every morning for extra BP and fielding," said Tommy. "We worked so much that Bobby would leave the clubhouse early so I couldn't tell him to show up for early work the next morning. Then I would call him on the phone to tell him, and he stopped answering the phone. I would have to go to his house, knock on the door, and remind him in person."

Despite all the work and effort, Valentine struggled. Despite the belief from his manager and his own self-confidence, he continued to make throwing errors from short and was only hitting in the .250s. Valentine, like many minor league players, was facing failure for the first time in his life. Baseball is a mental game as much as it is a physical one. Faced with constant failure, players are challenged to stay positive, make adjustments they never had to before, persevere, keep believing in themselves. In high school or college, a star stood alone. In the minor leagues, and with each advancement therein, the star plays against other stars, or plays against guys who were just better.

Valentine made 38 errors in 86 games.

"I was stinking the whole year," said Valentine. "It was a Sunday morning, and Tommy had to speak to a church group after Mass. Practice started and he wasn't at the ballpark yet. We were taking batting practice when he showed up. When he showed up, Dick McLaughlin, a player-coach, ran off the field into the dugout and talked to Tommy. I was taking ground balls. McLaughlin told him that there was a problem with the pitchers. In Tommy's unique fashion, I remember him walking in front of the hitter."

"Stop throwing," Tommy yelled. "Everyone in the clubhouse!"

"So we all went into this little clubhouse and sat in front of our lockers," continued Valentine. "We knew he was upset but we didn't know why. It turns out that the coach told Tommy that the pitchers didn't want to pitch if I was going to play shortstop.

"In my mind, this was fulfilling the prophecy of Al Campanis—we were both going to get run out of town. We had a player mutiny."

The players had stopped believing in Valentine, and maybe Valentine had stopped believing in himself, too.

Tommy hadn't.

"I hear that there are guys on this team, many of you pitchers, who don't want to play on this team while Bobby Valentine is the shortstop," said Tommy. He raised his voice. "Now I'm going to tell you what we're going to do. Not only is Bobby Valentine going to play shortstop, but when I go into my office, I want each and every one of you to get a pencil and paper and get this kid's autograph, because when he's playing in the big leagues, you'll all be carrying lunch buckets to work, and you're going to tell your kids and grandkids that you played with Bobby Valentine!"

He went back into his office and slammed the door shut. Tommy's speech left the clubhouse in silence.

"I'm sitting there with my head down, trying to crawl into my locker," Valentine said. "Next thing I know I see a set of spikes in front of me. I look up and sure enough there was a line of guys waiting to get my autograph.

"It was an amazing scene. From that time on, I was a different player. The next year I was the MVP at 20 years old. I led the league in seven categories. I was an all-star shortstop."

You gotta believe!

"I was wondering if I was going to be sent down the whole time," said Valentine. "Was it confidence-instilling? Definitely. After that meeting, I realized that not only wasn't I going to get sent down, but I was there forever."

"Success comes in can, not can't," said Tommy. "I wanted to hear my players say 'I will, I can, I must, I shall, I believe.'"

For Valentine, forever in Spokane didn't last long—he was called up to Dodger Stadium that September. He didn't get an at-bat, but he was there at the age of 19. Back in Triple A the next season, Valentine batted .340 with 29 stolen bases, 39 doubles, 16 triples, and 14 home runs, winning the MVP award yet again. He made the big league roster coming out of spring training in 1971 and batted .249 with one home run and 25 RBIs. In '72 he played in 119 games, splitting time between shortstop, second base, third base, and all three outfield positions. He improved his average to .274. Yet in the eyes of Al Campanis, Valentine was not destined to be a Dodger forever. He shipped him with Frank Robinson, Billy Grabarkewitz, Mike Strahler, and Bill Singer to the Angels.

In his first season with California, Valentine batted .302, but his forever in professional baseball was about to come to an end. On May 17, 1973, Valentine was playing center field in a game against Oakland. In the top of the second, Dick Green sent a shot flying over Valentine's head. The ball looked like it would go for a home run, but Valentine had a different idea. He ran and leaped toward the fence, hoping to rob Green and the A's. The ball just missed his glove, and as Valentine came back down to earth, his cleat got caught in the fence, snapping the bone in his leg.

Lying on the grass, shin protruding, writhing in pain, Valentine's forever was over. Valentine's bones didn't heal properly, so he had to deal with multiple surgeries and setbacks.

Tommy was in his corner forever though, because he loved him.

"He would come to our place, and I would go to see him," said Tommy. "We saw a lot of each other when he was in a cast."

"When I broke my leg," said Valentine, "I didn't think my career was over. I thought I would rehab it and be back."

Valentine was faced with yet another surgery, one that might possibly fix the problem, but would cost him the '74 season. He decided to play through it. Although he appeared in more than 100 games, he wasn't the same player and was relegated to backup duties.

Faced with the prospect of failure again, he turned back to Tommy.

"I wanted to bring him down because he didn't know what he should do," said Tommy of Valentine's decision to play that winter in the Dominican Republic. "So he came down to play for me so he could make a decision on his future as a player.

"He was on first base, and the batter sent a shot to the gap. Valentine ran around second and third, but about 15, 20 feet from home, he just collapsed.

"That's when I had to tell him that he should think about getting a job as a coach or manager. It was one of the hardest things I ever had to do. We were both crying, but I gave him a hug and told him that he had to believe that everything would be okay."

Valentine believed Tommy, but he also still believed he could continue his playing career. He would go on to play for the San Diego Padres, then was traded to the New York Mets, but was released in spring training in '79. Although the Seattle Mariners picked him up, he was never the same player. The former star who ran into Tommy's life and into his heart, who would always rise to the occasion, was forced to retire at the age of 29.

An injury can end a player's career in an instant. No matter how much confidence one has in oneself, one cannot defy the laws of physics. However, a player's career can be made by the sheer power of self-confidence, by a will

powered by belief. Such was the case with Scioscia and Valentine, as it was with numerous other Tommy disciples. Just ask Wes Parker.

During Tommy's stint as manager in Ogden, he was charged with shepherding players to the pros. As such, he had to convince young players to believe that they would become major-leaguers, that they would one day play at Dodger Stadium. The Dodgers, of course, usually fielded winning teams stacked with All-Star players. Even for the best high school or college stars, the prospect of supplanting a Dodger required an inordinate amount of belief. On one such occasion, Tommy had one of his own players believing so strongly that he almost scared himself to death.

Tommy went out to the mound to visit a struggling Bobby O'Brien, and told him to imagine the next hitter he faced would be the last batter he faced before going up to meet the Big Dodger in the Sky. Would he rather face the Lord after recording an out or giving up a hit?

"Before I got back to the dugout, he threw the ball and the guy got a base hit," Tommy said. "Two runs scored. I go to take him out, but I was wondering what happened, because I had him right where I wanted him. He said, 'Skip, you had me so afraid of dying that I couldn't concentrate on the batter.' Now that is motivation! If I could get them to believe they were going to die, I could get them to believe they could play better."

Tommy dared his players not only to believe it, but to do something about it, something beyond the countless hours of BP. During the '68 season, he called Valentine, Bill Buckner, Tom Paciorek, and Steve Garvey into his office. He told them to get a pen and paper—they were going to send letters to their counterparts in Los Angeles. For example, Buckner's letter to Wes Parker, the starting first baseman for the Dodgers, stated:

> Dear Wes,
>   You don't know me but my name is Bill Buckner. I play for Tommy Lasorda for the Ogden Dodgers, and he told me he is a friend of yours and that it was okay to write you this letter. Like I said, you don't know me, but I play first base here in Ogden, and I am going to take your job.
> Sincerely,
> Bill Buckner

Tommy had Valentine write a similar letter to Maury Wills. He had Garvey write one to Bill Sudakis. He wanted his players to know that self-confidence was the first step to success, and that they had to possess it at all times.

After all, you gotta believe.

• CHAPTER 2 •

HARD WORK

"I don't commend hard work. I expect it."

Winters in Norristown, Pennsylvania, are bitterly cold. An inland suburb of Philadelphia, there is no protection from the whipping wind or dumping snowstorms. Conditions were not much better inside the Lasorda home itself, where Tommy and his four brothers grew up. There was only one source of heat for the entire three-story house.

"In the dining room there was a little coal stove that heated the house," said Tommy. "By the time the heat rose to the third floor it was time to get up. The windows were so foggy I could write a letter on them. One little stove for all three floors."

Conditions were certainly worse in the stone quarry where his father, Sabatino, drove a truck for 12 hours a day. No heated seats, no Thorlo socks, and thin, steel-toed boots made for a chilling combination. Still, Sabatino drove the truck, working through the biting frost, through the freezing pain, to provide for his family. He was Tommy's hero and role model; Tommy learned mostly everything he knows, and has taught, about hard work from his father.

"I worshiped the ground he walked on," said Tommy. "When he would come home after a long day we would take his boots off for him, rub his feet until the feeling came back, and stick his feet in the oven to warm them up.

"He was a great father and a tremendous man. That's where I developed my work ethic, from him. He never missed a day of work. Worked six days a week because he had a responsibility to take care of his family. From the $70 a week he made he fed us, bought us clothes, put a roof over our head."

Although Tommy wanted to play baseball, he was expected to work when school was over. "My mother would wake me up the day after school ended and tell me to get a job," said Tommy. He worked hard shining shoes, shoveling snow, removing dead cats from beneath his neighbor's steps, and delivering potatoes around the neighborhood. "I worked all day long hauling 100-pound sacks," said Tommy. "We would only quit when the sun went down, or when we ran out of potatoes. And [my boss] would only give me one dollar!

"I also worked with a roofer, putting roofs on commercial buildings. I worked on the railroad, too. I was doing a man's job. We would report early in the morning with the humidity lingering in the air. We would push a handcart all the way out on the tracks to where we finished the night before. We would remove the old track, put down new track and hammer the spikes in on each side. Most guys were right-handed, and since I was a lefty, I was always working, hammering in the spikes. I only made 55 cents an hour working 10 hours a day on the railroads, but I was so proud to bring my money home to my mother."

Those days on the railroad proved long and depleting, testing the 16-year-old's work ethic, his will, and his tenacity.

"My father questioned whether I could handle it, but I told him I could," said Tommy. "I would come home from work, take a bath, come down and lay on the floor while my father told stories to the five of us. Mom would feed us, and I would get up, kiss them good night, and go to bed because I was so tired."

He even made money as a fighter. "My mother's brother, Uncle Tony, taught me to fight," said Tommy. "When we would go visit his friends who had kids my size or age, he would set up fights between me and them. If I kicked the guy's butt he would give me a quarter. The big fight was with Uncle Tony's brother-in-law. He was a Golden Gloves boxer, but he was a lightweight. Uncle Tony asked me if I could take him, and I told him I could take him any day of the week. So he set up the fight. We went down into the basement and put the gloves on. I just beat the heck out of him. For that he gave me half a dollar."

While Tommy worked hard each summer, he worked equally hard as a young baseball player. When he wasn't at school or at work, he would be at Elmwood Park playing with other kids. Sometimes that meant skipping out on working around the house. "We all had assignments to clean parts of the house," said Tommy. "I would take the bucket and scrub brush upstairs, but instead of scrubbing I would open the window, shimmy down the pipe on the side of the house, and run to the park to play." He would hit, field, throw, and pitch to anyone daring enough to dig into the batter's box. He too was daring, because he knew he wasn't supposed to be at the park and would face the consequences once he got home. "When I got home my father would be waiting for me with the belt in his hand," said Tommy. "I didn't care though. I just wanted to play baseball."

The combination of his work ethic and love of baseball drove him. He was given a chance to try out for the local Connie Mack All-Star team, which he made, and also played on the Norristown High School team. Although he didn't pitch much during high school he was still seen by scouts including Jocko Collins of the Phillies, who offered him a contract with a $100 signing bonus. "When Jocko came to the house I told my mother to fix him a big plate of pasta," said Tommy. "My parents didn't want me to sign because they wanted me to go to school. But all I wanted in life was to play baseball.

"My father looked at me and told me that this was my decision. He told me that if it didn't work out that I could never come back to him with hate and regret for not going to school." Sabatino signed the contract for his son because he wasn't legally old enough to sign for himself. "My father knew that all I wanted was to play baseball, even though he didn't really even know what baseball was. But he trusted in me, he believed in me." Maybe he did because he saw how hard his son worked on the roofs and railroads. Maybe he believed in him because he saw a lot of himself in young Tommy. Maybe he just saw and loved his son's enthusiasm. "I told Jocko that if he waited any longer that I would have paid him $100 to let me play!"

After signing, 17-year-old Tommy left the house for the first time to go to spring training. "I had never been more than 15 miles from home, and here I was getting on a train to go to spring training in Wilmington, Delaware." Because of World War II teams didn't train in Florida. Tommy had worked before in the cold weather, but not as a ballplayer. After camp broke he was assigned to the Concord Weavers of the North Carolina State League. At the end of the season, Tommy was drafted into the Army and reported to boot camp. After the service, he went back to the Phillies organization to play for a team in Schenectady, New York. The manager of that team was Lee Riley, father of future Lakers coach Pat Riley. "I used to bounce Pat on my knee," said Tommy.

During his stint with the Schenectady Blue Jays, Tommy faced the Amsterdam Rug Makers. It was a 15-inning game, and Tommy went the distance. He struck out 25 batters, recorded 12 walks, and ended up driving in the winning run in the bottom of the 15th. As fate would have it, a scout for the Dodgers was in the stands that night. At the end of the season, the Dodgers drafted Tommy, and so began his life as a Dodger. The next spring he reported to Vero Beach, Florida, for his first spring training with the team. While at Dodgertown in Vero Beach, Tommy learned a lot about pitching and made a few friends. One of them was his mentor, Al Campanis.

Tommy would become a disciple of Campanis, who himself was a disciple of the legendary Branch Rickey. Rickey could be described as a savant, a guru, a philosopher, and an expert; certainly all applied as he was best known for breaking Major League Baseball's color barrier by signing Jackie Robinson. He also drafted Roberto Clemente. He introduced the batting helmet and the first full-time spring training facility, made commonplace the use of the pitching machine and batting cage, and created baseball's minor league system. When Rickey spoke, everybody listened, especially players.

Tommy was a minor league pitcher but had a major league curveball. Eventually, Rickey heard about him and wanted to see what the talk was all about.

"I looked at the bulletin board for the next day's schedule," said Tommy. "I saw a note saying Tom Lasorda report to Branch Rickey at the pitching strings at 7:30 AM. I couldn't sleep all night. I mean, Branch Rickey wanted to meet with me! He knew more baseball than anybody, and he was going to work with me! Getting a meeting with Branch was like getting a meeting with the Pope."

As the sun rose over Dodgertown, a sleep-deprived Tommy rose and prepared to meet his fate. All of those windups, high leg kicks, and pitches; all of the wins and losses, all of the roof tiles, potato sacks, and railroad spikes; all of the confidence and even the doubts were about to be put on display for the great Branch Rickey.

"I reported to the string area the next day and it was just me, him, and a guy who took notes for him. I started throwing and he was talking to me, asking questions."

"Are your parents alive?" asked Rickey. *Yes, sir.*

"Is your mother okay?" *Yes, sir.*

"Does she drink?" *No, sir.*

"Does your father drink?" *Yes, sir.*

"Then he wanted me to start throwing curveballs," Tommy remembered, "so I did. Then he told me to put my hat on top of home plate."

"I'll bet you a Coca-Cola that you can't hit that hat two times out of 10," Rickey said.

Tommy threw 10 curveballs and never touched the hat. He apologized to Rickey for losing the bet.

"No, son, you won," Rickey replied.

"What do you mean?"

"Where were those 10 curveballs you threw?"

"They were all low."

"That's where you're supposed to throw them. You win."

That was the first of many lessons Tommy learned from Rickey. In fact, it was common practice in the Dodgers organization to attend lectures given by Rickey and the coaches who taught his system. "Every day there was a lecture in that big hall," said Tommy. "All 710 players were there, all the coaches and managers from the 26 farm teams, the scouts, everybody. One guy would talk about the infield, another guy would talk about the outfield, another guy would talk about bunting, another guy would talk about pitching. When he gave a lecture it was like the voice of God."

If Rickey was the voice of God and baseball was his gospel, Tommy was devout. "You were stunned just listening to him speak," said Tommy. "He loved the game so much and worked so hard. One day it was raining and it didn't look like we were going to play. He went out and rolled up his pant legs and brushed the water off the field so we could play."

Rickey once said, "Sweat is the greatest solvent there is for most players' problems. There is no cure, no soluble way to get rid of a bad technique as quickly as sweat." It was a lesson Tommy took particularly to heart, and he later made it his mission to prepare his players in the Rickey fashion: physically, mentally, and fundamentally.

He would teach them on the field during practices and games. He would teach them on the bus to and from stadiums. He would teach them over meals, in their hotel rooms or homes, in the clubhouse. To play for Tommy was more than a job or even a passion; it was a lifestyle. As Tommy would holler across the fields of the Pioneer, Pacific Coast, and National League, "The only path to success comes down the avenue of hard work!"

Speaking of his teams he said, "We were always together. We would eat together, play together, practice together, everywhere. When we weren't playing we were talking about the game. I was always teaching them something." While most kids go off to college to learn law or medicine, Tommy's players were enrolled at Lasorda University to learn baseball. "I told my players that if they enroll at Lasorda University, it won't cost them any money. The tuition is perspiration, determination, and inspiration. And when you graduate, you'll make more money than any professor at Harvard or Yale."

• • •

One of Tommy's students was a young man from Tacoma, Washington. Drafted in the third round of the 1968 draft, Ron Cey joined the Dodgers organization amid lofty expectations. When he signed with the team at age 20, he was already drawing comparisons to Ron Santo. Cey was first sent to Tri City, a Dodgers rookie ball affiliate managed by Ducky LeJohn. After batting .299, he went to Mesa, Arizona, for Instructional League play. That team was managed by Tommy, and that is where Cey enrolled in Lasorda University.

Cey's teammates in Tri Cities included Joe Ferguson, Doyle Alexander, and Bobby Buckner. In Ogden, Tommy had Bobby's brother, Bill. One Buckner told the other about Cey, so Tommy had heard all about the young prospect before he'd arrived in Mesa. He was Tommy's kind of player.

That Instructional League camp was run by Tommy with the help of Monty Basgall and John Kerry. Before the players hit the field, they got a taste of what was expected of them. "He was so outwardly passionate about things, it feels like he's addressing an auditorium even though there are only five people around. It's like, wait a minute, who's he shouting at?" remembered Cey.

"You are going to work harder than you ever have before!" Tommy would holler. "I don't commend hard work, I expect it. I'm running this camp, and while I never professed to be any smarter than anyone else, I will outwork them all, and so will you if you want to make it to Dodger Stadium!"

For Tommy, those demands were just the first step in preparing players. As any good teacher will tell you, actions must follow words, so work hard they did. "His comments about working from sunup to sundown were true. We worked all day long," said Cey.

"We would turn on the lights in Vero Beach after the games, that's how long we were on the field," Tommy said. "In the minors, I would work them before the games, and I would show up a few hours early before the other guys to get everything ready, as well as throwing extra BP, hitting extra grounders for guys who wanted to work on fielding. I did it all. I didn't have any coaches so it was just me teaching hitting, fielding, throwing, base running, pitching, whatever.

"They would ask me if they ever got any time off. Time off? Do you want to learn? Do you want to get to the big leagues? You can have all the time you want off, but where will you wind up? I'm trying to get you ready for the big leagues!"

Cey, however never wanted any time off. "If I took the Penguin out of the lineup he would want to fight me," said Tommy. A natural hard worker, Cey knew he'd have to work that much harder to achieve his goals. He hit .330 in the Instructional League and was promoted to Single A in Bakersfield. While there he hit .331 and earned a spot in Double A. Although he struggled to a .156 average, he rebounded and hit .331 again the following year. In 1971 he was assigned to Triple A in Spokane, where he was reunited with Tommy. He responded to the promotion by hitting .321 with 32 home runs and 123 RBIs in 137 games. Going into spring training in 1972, Cey thought he was the front runner to be the starting third baseman in Los Angeles. However, Al Campanis sent him back to the minors. The scouting report was that Cey needed to improve his fielding, and to work on his throws from third to first.

Faced with the all the competition that stood in his way, Cey continued to work hard for Tommy in the minors. More BP, more running, and, most importantly, more fielding. "Cey was an outstanding third baseman," said Tommy. "He never missed balls, but only because we worked on it for hours and hours."

"I am very grateful for the amount of time Tom spent with me, working with me, improving my skills, offensively, defensively," said Cey. "He spent countless hours hitting ground balls, fly balls, throwing BP. He'd be out there all day long. You basically have to kick him off the mound to get him out of there. But that's the kind of dedication and work ethic that rubbed off on all of us."

Cey played for Tommy for three seasons in the minor leagues, for four seasons in Los Angeles while Tommy was Walter Alston's third-base coach, and for six seasons while Tommy was manager of the Dodgers. He has numerous memories and anecdotes about their time together, but one of his favorite Tommy stories comes from his days in the minor leagues preparing for his career in Los Angeles.

"Tommy would hit me hundreds of ground balls every day," said Cey. "However, he moved up from home plate to halfway to third. He's hitting balls from 30 or 40 feet to me at third. He's hitting one-hoppers, line drives off my shins, bad hops, and every time I missed it I'd run a lap." For Cey, his path to success, his avenue of hard work, was littered with countless hours of grounders and bruised shins.

"He used to get so mad at me because of those ground balls I hit him," said Tommy. "I hit him scorchers hoping he would miss them so he would have to run, but only because I wanted him to prepare himself mentally and fundamentally on how to catch major league grounders at third. I told Al to bring him up many times. I thought he could help the Dodgers win the pennant."

"We all did things together," said Cey. "We went bowling together in Vero, and then we went to the Holiday Inn on the beach or to the smorgasbord. We were always together, we always hung out with each other, and we worked together. Spring training, Instructional League in Arizona— we just became a family. But Tommy was there throughout. He was there for me all the time. He fought for me, pushed for me in meetings, and we were mutually rewarded."

Cey would respond once again in Albuquerque in 1972. He hit .329 with 23 home runs and 103 RBIs. Finally, he got the call.

"We were playing at home to finish the season and Tommy called me and told me to meet him at a restaurant for lunch," Cey remembered. "Are you kidding me? What do you want me to go to lunch for? Seriously, if we were on the road I would understand, but we were at home so I wanted some free time. He said that Elten Schiller [general manager of the Albuquerque team] was coming with him and it would be nice for the three of us to go to lunch. I finally agreed to it. We go and he's telling stories and then he says, 'Oh, by the way, in the next couple of days you are going to go to the big leagues.' At that moment I raised my head again. 'Yeah, you're going to the big leagues. You're getting called up. You have to leave in three days.'

"I'm fortunate that he recognized my talents, that he took me under his wing, that he worked with me endlessly and stood up for me. I'll be forever grateful for that."

After hitting a combined .323 in five seasons of minor league baseball, Cey spent a total of 15 full seasons in the majors. He finished with a .261 batting average but amassed 316 home runs and 1,139 RBIs. Just as he drew comparisons to Ron Santo as a youth, he drew comparisons to Santo as a retiree. Santo played for 15 seasons, hit 342 home runs, drove in 1,331 runs, and was eventually enshrined in Cooperstown. Cey would have had more notoriety as one of baseball's great third basemen if he wasn't overshadowed by the best third baseman in the history of baseball, Mike Schmidt.

More impressively, he was part of an infield that played together for 10 seasons, a major league record: Steve Garvey at first, Davey Lopes at second, Bill Russell at short, and Cey at third. Indeed they were like a family, and Dodgers fans grew accustomed to the arrangement. Combined, the four players played thousands of games together, which was a mark of pride for their skipper. "After those guys left me in the minors, see how many games they played in the big leagues," said Tommy. "They never came back to the

minors! Count how many games Lopes played, how many games Garvey played, how many games Penguin played! They never would have played that many if they didn't work as hard as they did."

Yet Tommy never commended their hard work; he expected it. He expected to have all four of those infielders playing their respective positions to the best of their ability, or better. He expected to see Cey taking extra ground balls even as an established star. He expected the same from Russell. He expected to see Garvey, a player who had 200 hits year after year, to keep working on his swing during extra hours of batting practice.

From his experience as a player Tommy had learned an important lesson: all the hard work a player puts in isn't simply to prepare oneself mentally and physically; it also teaches a player to persevere. It is what helps a player push through nagging injuries, through annoying slumps, through the drowning humidity of July games in St. Louis and the unnerving cold of October games in New York. Those lessons helped Cey and his infield brothers not only stay and play together, but win together.

"I got hit in the head by a pitch in Game 5 of the 1981 World Series," said Cey. "Although I had a concussion I played in Game 6. I got hit, we had an off day, and then we had another day off because of weather. It was a bit of a struggle, and I actually came out of the game in the fifth or sixth inning because I was dizzy. I didn't feel like I wanted to jeopardize our situation. We had a healthy lead and ended up winning 9–2.

"In the moment all I wanted to do was make sure I was well enough to play. It was the last game that the infield played together. Lopes was gone the next year, and Sax came in. It was important all the way around to get that done."

When Tommy and Cey get together today, they laugh about all those hot grounders and the curse words Cey would bark while running those laps. Laughter is one of the joys of the camaraderie Tommy and his players had. So is love. "Tommy treated me like a son," said Cey. "But I was one of a number of guys like that."

• • •

Another one of those guys was a young man with a long Dodgers history. His story began before he reported to Tommy in Ogden in 1968. It began before he was drafted by the Dodgers earlier that summer. It began before his parents waited by the phone all day for Dodgers scout Guy Wellman to call with the news. It began before Wellman, or the regional scout, ever saw him hit his first home run playing at Michigan State, a grand slam that went over the wall and into the Red Cedar River.

Steve Garvey believed his career with the Dodgers was destiny. His grandfather, Joseph Patrick Garvey, was a Brooklyn beat cop patrolling the streets outside Ebbets Field while Duke Snider patrolled center field inside the hallowed ballpark. His father, Joe Garvey, drove a bus in Tampa, Florida, where Steve would grow up a Dodgers fan. On one special trip, a trip that allowed Steve to miss one day of school and ride the bus with his dad, the father and son were scheduled to pick up the world champion Brooklyn Dodgers from the airport and drive them to play the Yankees in a spring training game. The Kay O'Malley 1, a DC-7 with the Dodgers' name painted on the side complete with the flying ball logo, landed and taxied toward the bus on the tarmac. As the players walked off the plane and onto the bus, young Steve waited for his heroes. While he got a lot of head pats, Jackie Robinson, the legend, and Roy Campanella, the All-Star catcher, added words of advice.

"Looks like a pretty good player," said Robinson. Garvey's father nodded and agreed. Garvey smiled. "Is he a good student?" asked Robinson. Garvey's father nodded again, even though Garvey may have been the worst reader in his class. Then Campanella told Steve, "If you listen to what your coaches tell you and work hard, you have a chance. But you can be the best player out there and it won't make ay difference if you can't think, so work hard in school, too."

When Garvey reported to Tommy in Ogden, Campanella's words about hard work had been ingrained in the back of his mind. Little did he know that Tommy would take those words and yell them through a megaphone, all day, every day.

In college, Garvey had been a third baseman. However, during his freshman year he hurt his shoulder playing football. Since he had a short, compact swing, the injury didn't negatively affect his batting average. But while he remained a good fielder, his throw to first had suffered. That's where the hard work began.

"I wanted to work him real hard, but I just couldn't do much with his throwing because of his shoulder injury," said Tommy. "But I was determined to prepare him despite his deficiency."

"I first met Tommy when I reported to him in Ogden in 1968," said Garvey. "I flew from Tampa to St. Louis to Salt Lake and took a puddle-jumper to Ogden. I took a cab to the Ben Lomond Hotel, and there was Tommy with a few other guys. I go over to them and he says, 'Are you the Garv?' 'Yes, sir.' 'My name is Tommy Lasorda, son, and your life is about to change forever.'"

Although Garvey had endured the rigors of being a two-sport athlete at Michigan State, he was now a professional baseball player, and Tommy was going to make him work like one. "I worked hard playing football," said Garvey. "But I had never worked on baseball like I did with Tommy. When we first got there we had about 10 days of workouts before we started playing games. He worked us. We essentially had two-a-days."

"The earlier you get out there and work on your deficiencies," Tommy would say, "the sooner those deficiencies become a functioning level, and the sooner you are a major-leaguer."

Garvey's deficiency was throwing from third to first. However, Tommy was determined to prepare Garvey, and in his particular case he had to work most on the fundamentals of throwing. "We worked on that a lot," said Garvey. "My fielding was always there, and that's why I later won Gold Gloves at first base. I had the quickness and agility, I could dig it out of the dirt, I was fearless going up the line, but Tommy made sure that we worked hard on throwing. If I got on top of the ball, I had a tendency to airmail it.

"What we really worked on was my footwork. People don't realize that an errant throw comes from bad footwork, being out of position, and dropping your arm, so he always worked on footwork with me."

Garvey had success at the plate that first season in Ogden, hitting 20 home runs in only 216 at-bats. He finished the season with a .338 batting average. That performance earned him a promotion to Double A, where he hit .373, and a late September call-up to Los Angeles. In 1970 he was sent to Triple A in Spokane, where he was reunited with Tommy. He had another great season at the plate, hitting .319, and again was called up to Los Angeles. But in the field, he was still having problems making the throw to first. He made five errors in just 27 games. In '71, despite the continued work, he made 14 errors in 79 games. In '72, he made 28 errors in 85 games. At the end of that season, he was sent to the play for Tommy in the Dominican Republic during the winter.

While the hard work on Garvey's throwing continued in the Dominican, Tommy still made sure that Garvey and his teammates worked hard on their hitting. In fact, after games he would take a few of his core players back to his suite at the Jaragua Hotel in Santo Domingo. "I had a huge suite," said Tommy. "We would take all the pictures off of the walls, and I would throw tennis balls to them and they would hit them all over the suite. They would ricochet all over the walls. We would be doing that until 2:00 AM every night."

By this time Garvey was on the Dodgers roster, although he wasn't starting at third. He was in and out of the lineup and played some third base, but also played some games in left field and a couple in right. Garvey played for Tommy again in the Dominican during the winter of '73. In addition to working on his physical skills, Tommy was determined to improve his mental approach to the game.

"I was a gamer kind of guy," said Garvey. "I loved to play the game and never wanted to miss any. I played through injuries and all that stuff. To sit there and watch from the bench was extremely difficult. But for me it was motivational, to work harder to get back in the lineup, to get an opportunity and seize it, and stay there.

"I would talk to Tommy now and again, and he would always be real positive. He was always there in spirit, or be sending me a message. He was always willing to go beyond an in-person moment and try to continue to help."

Tommy's positivity was always part of preparing a player mentally. It helped Garvey as it did with the rest of the Lasorda University students. "Tommy was the perfect minor league manager for the organization at that time," said Garvey. "He was able to take us at a young age and really mold us. His positivity and work ethic rubbed off on all of us."

On June 23, 1973, the Dodgers were playing a doubleheader against the Reds. Between games, Garvey's hard work and positivity finally paid off. "Walter Alston comes to me and asks me if I had ever played any games at first," said Garvey. "'Well, sure,' I told him. I had played one game in Little League and some in Triple A, but I wasn't going to tell him I couldn't. I played that day, and that was the beginning. I had a couple of doubles and we won, and he put me back there the next day."

Garvey had started the transition to playing first base. He took to it rather easily, partly because of all the hard work Tommy had put him through. "As a right-handed first baseman, it is so much more difficult because you have to throw around the runners. But if you dropped down you can sail it around them," said Garvey. "That's what we worked on a lot in the Dominican and in the minors—changing the angle of my arm when I threw—so when I moved to first I was able to throw around runners."

Garvey had an acclaimed career playing first base for the Dodgers. After winning the spot permanently in '74, he won the NL MVP award and had the first of six 200-hit seasons. He was a 10-time All-Star. He won four Gold Gloves. He was the 1978 NLCS MVP, was part of the record-setting infield that also included Cey, and was a World Series champion in 1981.

Perhaps his most impressive feat was his Iron Man streak: Garvey set a National League record with 1,207 consecutive games played, from September 3, 1975, to July 29, 1983. The streak ended when he broke his thumb in a collision at home plate against the Atlanta Braves. It is the fourth-longest playing streak in Major League Baseball history. To be sure, it was in large part thanks to all the hard work he'd done with Tommy. "The toughest part of baseball is the mental side," said Garvey. "The mental part of it really takes a lot of control, a lot of discipline, a lot of compartmentalizing."

Garvey's streak required the ability to battle through a variety of injuries, including a hyperextended elbow, one he suffered after catching a high throw up the line and then slamming his elbow into the runner's helmet. He got 22 stitches in his chin after being hit by Bob Welch. A pulled hamstring, a bruised heel, migraines, the flu, and a 103-degree fever that would send most people to the hospital. An impacted toenail that hurt so bad doctors had to drill a hole in it to relieve the pressure.

Like Cey, Garvey has many stories about Tommy that he cherishes. One of his favorites comes from his dog days in Ogden, working hard and preparing in the Rickey fashion for a long career in the big leagues.

"We were down to the last day of the season in '68, and we were tied," Garvey said. "Our right fielder, Randy Smith, who was a pretty good athlete, went on a date after we won the next-to-last game. His date was a picnic at a local park. He gets stung by a bee on his big toe. The next day we come out to the ballpark early for the championship game. We walk in and there's Randy with a big red toe, and he's quickly dipping it in and out of a bucket of boiling hot water. Tommy comes in and asks him, 'What's the matter with you?'"

"I got stung by a bee."

"Stung by a bee? How in the world did that happen?"

"I went out yesterday to a picnic."

"You went to a picnic before the championship game? Are you crazy? You've got to be serious about this! This is your first chance for a championship, for a ring! All the hard work we put in and you go to a picnic?"

Tommy then turned his attention to the bucket of water.

"Why don't you just stick your foot in there?"

"It's hot, Skipper."

"So Tommy took his shoe and sock off and pushed Randy to the side," Garvey said. "He dunked his whole foot in the scalding hot water. 'This isn't hot! The rest of you guys get your butts out there!' We get outside and all of a sudden we hear Tommy scream, 'Ahhhhhhh!' We go back and peek in and he is lobster-red to the top of his calf. We were laughing and rolling over."

As Garvey said, Tommy would always lead by example, whether that meant staying late with the players to hit extra grounders or dunking his foot in a bucket of scalding water.

"We were losing 7–0 after the third inning," Garvey said. "'You better win this game,' Tommy would say. Then it was like 7–2, then 9–4, then 9–5. We ended up winning 12–11 and Smith hit the winning home run. After the game we are all celebrating with cheap beer and spraying it all around. Then we came to find out that the winning manager got a 35-inch color TV. We laughed as much about that as we did about Tommy's foot in the hot water."

Those fits of laughter were as common with Tommy and his players as were the buckets of sweat and all the sore muscles. It was part of why they love each other, part of why Tommy loves them like sons, and part of why he was so much more than just a manager.

"I had Tommy as my first manager all the way up to '82, 14 years maybe, we were together," Garvey said. "It's like being a parent. It's like growing from a kid, learning, going through difficult times and situations together. It was with us all of our lives."

• • •

Another player who Tommy worked endlessly was not even in the Dodgers system when their paths crossed. Burt Hooton was drafted by the Cubs in 1971. After pitching a few games in the big leagues straight out of college, he reported to Tacoma, the Triple A Cubs affiliate. That club was in the Pacific Coast League and competed against the Spokane Indians, a club managed by Tommy. Hooton was a star in college, and his transition to Triple A was an easy one. "I did really well in the Pacific Coast League, including against Tommy's team a couple of times," said Hooton. "I think he took notice of me right then and there, because I was striking out 15, 16, 17 guys a game in the PCL." Tommy always had an eye for talent, and a player with Hooton's was easy to spot. He finished that season with a 1.68 ERA, striking out 135 batters in 102 innings pitched. That success earned him a spot in the Cubs rotation for the 1972 season.

Although he was a hot talent, Hooton didn't progress the way he and the Cubs hoped he would. At the end of '72 he was 11–14 with a respectable

ERA of 2.80. The season after that he went 14–17 and his ERA rose to 3.68. His '74 season was worse yet: a 7–11 record and a 4.80 ERA. "I was out of shape, and there was a lot of inconsistency with the Cubs," said Hooton. "Three managers and four pitching coaches in three and a half years, and they tried to turn me into a different style pitcher."

Tommy had always liked Hooton though, and remembered him from his days pitching against his team in the PCL. He saw Hooton again at Dodger Stadium during BP and waved him over.

"I told Burt that I was going to be managing in the Dominican that winter and I wanted him to come down and pitch for me," said Tommy. "Believe it or not, he told me that he wouldn't pitch for me if I was the last manager on earth. I told him to get lost."

"When Tommy first approached me with the opportunity, I balked at it," said Hooton. "But after talking to my wife and a couple other guys who played for Tommy, I changed my mind."

Despite Hooton's rocky road, he didn't have a reputation as a lazy player. However, he was out of shape. While Tommy recognized that Hooton had great stuff, he also recognized that he needed to lose weight. "When he came down he brought his wife, Ginger," said Tommy. "I had never met her before. We all went out to eat, and when the dessert cart came around I told him, 'No, sir. No dessert for you.' She thought I was crazy."

"That first meal with Tommy was my last high-calorie meal," said Hooton. "After dinner we wanted to get a cab but Tommy made us all walk back to the hotel with him."

Hooton's physical preparation continued throughout winter ball. Tommy would have him run to the ballpark before games, and would make him run at the park after the games were over. And Tommy continued to lead by example; he would actually run with Hooton to the park.

"He convinced me that it would be worth my while to run and get in shape," said Hooton. "I don't know how well I pitched in the Dominican but I lost about 25 pounds." It was an important lesson for Hooton. Perhaps a more important lesson he learned was about how to approach baseball as a professional. "He pretty much taught me how to be a pro," said Hooton. "Coming out of college, everything is done for you. As a pro you have to do it for yourself, as far as people making you do stuff and get in shape and all that. In pro ball it's dumped in your lap and you have to do it for yourself. Being a pro is nothing more than taking care of your own business and keeping yourself ready to perform. Learning from your successes and mistakes and from others, and maturing as you go along. Tommy taught me that, to discipline myself."

Hooton was traded to the Dodgers in early May of 1975 for Geoff Zahn and Eddie Solomon. "When Al Campanis called me and asked me if I would make that trade, I told him I would carry those two guys on my back to Chicago for Hooton," said Tommy. His games against Hooton in the PCL and his time with him in the Dominican Republic had made Tommy a believer. Hooton would go on to play for the Dodgers from 1975 to 1984, the majority of those years for Tommy.

"Tommy was real good at making each one of his players feel special as a ballplayer and as a person," said Hooton. "He made them perform up to their capabilities. He turned my mind-set around. Tommy was always really good at keeping you positive and keeping you moving forward, not looking back. When you walked away from one of his talks, you felt like you could run through a brick wall. When you're out there on the mound, you feel like there's no one who can beat you."

Although he is most remembered for his knuckle curve and the no-hitter he threw as a rookie, he won 18 games in 1975 and 19 games in '76. In Game 2 of the '77 World Series, he pitched a 6–1 victory over the Yankees, allowing only five singles and retiring 14 of the last 15 batters he faced. He was also MVP of the 1981 NLCS.

Hooton had tough times, too. In the 1977 NLCS, he started Game 3 against the Phillies but was pulled after issuing three consecutive bases-loaded walks in the second inning. In the 1978 World Series, Hooton started Game 5. It was another brutal defeat; he was yanked after allowing four runs in the third inning. In the '81 Series, he started Game 2 but left during the seventh and took the 3–0 loss.

Through all of the successes and the failures, the hard work Hooton put in also made him mentally tougher. It was the source of his perseverance. "I was always a good competitor," said Hooton. "But Tommy was always there for you when times were going bad. He was always positive, and he was always good at getting you refocused on competing to the best of your ability. One of the things you've got to learn is that you still have to work when you're successful. The work's not over whether you're going bad or going good."

Tommy tells the story of an old man at Carnegie Hall that reflects how he felt about all the hard work that he did with his players.

"There's this guy giving this great performance at Carnegie Hall," Tommy said. "When he's through he gets a standing ovation from this tremendous performance he gave. Up in the balcony was his father with a tear in his eye. The man who motivated him, who made him practice, the man who pushed him, the man who wanted him to succeed. I told my players, 'When you guys get to Dodger Stadium and after you win a game, look up in the top deck, and there's old Tom with a tear in his eye knowing that he was part of your life.'"

The players he motivated, worked with, pushed, believed in, sacrificed for—the Ceys, the Garveys, and the Hootons—all graduated from Lasorda University only after learning and embodying the value of hard work. And with each success, old Tom had a tear in his eye.

CHAPTER 3

Competitiveness

"How bad do you want it?
What price are you willing to pay?"

Tommy Lasorda is a fighter. As a kid he had to fight his parents to play baseball. As a high school player he had to fight his coach to get on the mound. As a minor league pitcher he had to fight the other 600 players who would report to spring training with the Dodgers for a spot on the big league roster. As a major league pitcher he had to fight the manager to get the ball, and the general manager to stay on the roster. As a scout he had to fight the other scouts, and suspicious parents, to sign players. As a minor league coach he had to fight the other teams to show his players how to play and win, and to show the general manager of the Dodgers that his players should advance. As a major league coach he had to fight to become the manager of the Dodgers. It was one of the most coveted jobs in baseball. As manager, he had to fight to win. That's exactly what he did.

"People ask where I got that competitive spirit, and I tell them playing at Elmwood Park," said Tommy. "As a kid, we played nine innings. No manager, no coach, no umpire. We just counted the runs. We always wanted to win, because if you lost you would have to go wait on the swings till it was time to play again. I never wanted to leave the field. I wanted to beat you. I would throw at my own mother if she was crowding the plate."

That attitude carried him through 20 seasons as manager. To this day, it is still with him. "There isn't an 80-year-old alive that I couldn't take right now!"

Along the way there were a few fistfights, a few ideological fights, and many fights players had with themselves in times of trouble. At the core of this fighter was a deep and unwavering competitiveness.

Amongst all of these battles, he would ask two simple questions of himself, of his players, and of anyone who was trying to achieve a goal or realize a dream:

How bad do you want it? What price are you willing to pay?

"Only you can answer them," he would conclude. "When you wake up in the morning and look in the mirror to wash your face, brush your teeth, or comb your hair, when you look in that mirror there are two people you cannot fool. That's yourself and God! You have to ask yourself if you are making the most of your God-given talents. You must wake up every day and say to yourself that you will be better today than you were yesterday."

Tommy had to say this to himself many times throughout his life. He also taught this lesson, over and over, to his players. One of his greatest challenges came while he was scouting a local star named Rick Monday. Tommy had been to Santa Monica High School a few times to watch Monday play. The first visit was anticlimactic.

"When I saw him play he didn't swing the bat," said Tommy. "In his three at-bats he ran the count to 3-2. And in each at-bat he watched the third strike go by. He struck out three times looking.

"When I went back to the office, Al Campanis asked me what I thought about Monday. I told Al I didn't see him hit."

"What do you mean?" Campanis asked. "You went to the game yesterday."

"Yeah, but I never saw him hit."

"What are you talking about?"

"He went to bat three times and never swung, Al. He struck out looking each time."

Even though he didn't swing, Tommy saw something in Monday.

"I was very impressed with him," said Tommy. "You had to be impressed with him. He was so polite and proper, very intelligent and humble. He was the kind of kid that you wanted to see in a Dodgers uniform."

To sign Monday, Tommy had to compete with six other clubs, as well as with Rick's mother, who wanted her son to go to college. Before each encounter, Tommy would ask himself how badly he wanted to sign Monday. After each failed attempt, he would ask himself how much of a price he was willing to pay.

"I'll tell you how bad I wanted to sign Rick Monday," said Tommy. "I started out offering his mother $8,000. She didn't say yes or no, so I increased the offer. She never said a word about the money. I increased the offer again and again, and before I knew it she had me up to $20,000 and had never said a word about the money."

"Tommy," said Mrs. Monday, "you know how much I love the Dodgers."

"Yes, ma'am."

"I can promise you this," she said. "I want Rick to go to college for just two years. Just two years. After that, he's all yours. He won't sign with anyone else but the Dodgers." Tommy shook her hand and told her she had a deal.

After Monday graduated from Santa Monica High School, he got a letter from the Dodgers. It was an invitation to try out for a rookie team made up of local high school players. Monday accepted the invitation and Tommy coached that team. At this point in his career, coaching was new to Tommy. He wanted to make an impression on Campanis, just as the players wanted to make an impression on Tommy. He had to compete to show that he could coach, and get his players to compete to show they should be signed by the Dodgers.

"I showed up for the tryout and we broke into groups," said Monday. "I'm hearing this voice, and it's one of those voices that captures your attention. I finally look over and it's coming from this guy who's catching at the tryout camp. But the guy's left-handed—it's Tommy. I turn around a little bit later and he's pitching. I turn around a little bit later and he's working with the infielders. A few minutes later he's working with us outfielders. Then he's working with the base runners. Everywhere I go here's this guy, and this is just the first weekend.

"We come back for the second weekend and it's more intense and there are fewer guys. I finally make the Dodgers rookie team and we played I don't know how many games, but we played a weekend series down in San Diego against a U.S. Marine Corps All-Star team. We played in their stadium on base in San Diego."

For a bunch of high school players, even highly touted ones, playing against Marines can be intimidating. This was in the 1960s, when players slid into second with spikes high, when crowding the plate meant the next pitch would be at your ribs, when hitting a home run meant the next batter might get beaned. Who knew what a Marine might do to win a baseball game?

Tommy knew he had to light the competitive fire in his players' bellies. He had to show his youngsters how to compete.

"I felt like I had to light a fire under Rick," said Tommy. "But I did that with all my players. I wanted them to beat the opposition. I wanted to make sure they heard me and knew how bad I wanted to win, and that it was contagious."

How badly did the high school kids want to play? How badly did they want to impress Tommy? How badly did they want to be signed to a professional contract? How badly did they want to win? What price were they willing to pay?

Not only was Tommy competing as a coach, he was still a scout competing with other scouts. "I was warming my players up and all of a sudden I saw five or six scouts sit down to watch the game," said Tommy. "I wanted Rick really bad. I wanted him to be a Dodger. When I saw those scouts sit down as the game was starting, I wanted Rick to look bad! I didn't want the other scouts to like him!

"After the first batter walked on four pitches, I put the hit-and-run on. I figured that with the hit-and-run, Rick would have to swing at a bad pitch, make an out, and look bad."

"The runner takes off and the first pitch is at my nose," said Monday. "But since the hit-and-run was on, I swung."

Monday hit a home run. "Going around the bases Tommy would always have a celebration for you, and he would shake your hand and pat you on the rear end and would normally have some sort of inspirational thing to say to you," said Monday. "Well, I come to third base and Tommy is walking away from third base and he doesn't shake my hand."

One of the scouts in attendance was Bobby Winkles, the head coach at Arizona State. He sat with Mrs. Monday and offered her son a scholarship to play baseball in Tempe. Instead of signing with Tommy and the Dodgers, he went off to college. Tommy was content thanks to the deal he made with Mrs. Monday; after two years in college Rick would be a Dodger. Unfortunately for Tommy and the Dodgers, Major League Baseball instituted a draft in 1965, and Monday was the very first player selected— by the Kansas City Athletics.

Monday was later traded to the Cubs, and eventually to the Dodgers in 1977. He was back home, and, as though reunited by fate, Tommy was in his first year as manager. Monday would play for Tommy's Dodgers for eight seasons. While patrolling center field at Dodger Stadium and facing the best pitching the National League had to offer, Monday competed. He was part of the team that won the pennant in 1977, and again in '78. He was also part of the team that won the World Series in 1981. They competed too, against the Big Red Machine, who won the pennant in '76 by 10 games, and won the '75 pennant by 20.

Monday recalls that Tommy's competitive fire was a hallmark of his managerial style.

"In 1977, we picked up Boog Powell," said Monday. "I think it was sometime in June that Tommy called a meeting well before the game. Boog took the pitch counter with him to the meeting. Tommy had a meeting that lasted slightly over eight minutes, and Boog had the counter in his hand, and he would hit the counter after every expletive that Tommy would use. Any hyphenated word would count as two. We posted a sign that said Tommy had set a new world record for most expletives used in an eight-minute meeting.

And at the time we were 6.5 games in first place! Tommy was basically telling us that we were better than we were at the present time. You're 6.5 up, but you should be 9.5 up. It gave the entire club an awareness that we had a manager who demanded the best."

• • •

Although Tommy was happy the Dodgers acquired Rick Monday (along with Mike Garman) from the Cubs in '77, it came at a heavy price. Headed to Chicago were Jeff Albert, Ivan De Jesus, and a young man named Bill Buckner. One of Tommy's favorite players, Buckner epitomized competitiveness. Buckner was willing to pay any price.

Tommy scouted Buckner in 1968, when he was a high school player in Rancho Del Mar, California, a small town between Napa and Vallejo. Buckner played a doubleheader in which he had seven hits, but during one at-bat Buckner hit a grounder and didn't run to first. "He didn't run the ball out," said Tommy. "He was so mad that he just went back to the bench." For most scouts, not running out a grounder is a cardinal sin. But Tommy saw something in Buckner that day and fell in love with him.

The Dodgers didn't want to draft him, but Tommy wanted Buckner badly. "I told Al Campanis that I didn't care about the grounder, because if he played for me, or anyone else in the organization, that would just never happen," said Tommy. "I told Al that if he had to draft him number one, get him. This guy is going to be an outstanding player.

"After the game I said to Buckner, 'Can you fight?' If you sign and you play for me, we are going to have to get into a few battles, and I want someone who will battle real good.'"

Buckner was eventually selected in the '68 draft by the Dodgers with their second pick, behind Bobby Valentine. Tommy was being sent back to Ogden to manage in rookie ball. He had paid the price as a scout, and he was determined to pay the price there, too, to make his players believe, to work hard, to compete, and to win.

"I started to feel like I loved Tommy right away," said Buckner. "As a young player I couldn't have asked for anything better. To learn the love for the game, how to play, and appreciate the game, and play to win. We had a lot of fun."

But first, Buckner would have to learn how to compete at Tommy's level.

"The first day I reported, I showed up in Ogden and I was just in time to put my uniform on and play an intersquad game," said Buckner. "Tommy was pitching for both teams. He ended up pitching 18 innings. My first at-bat, first pitch, I hit one off the right field wall. Lasorda takes his glove off, throws it on the ground, and starts screaming at me. 'If you ever hit another ball like that off me, I'll cut my throat!' That was my first hour in professional baseball. I had no clue what was going on. I didn't know what to think."

Tommy made sure they were going to compete—in games and during practice. During one round of BP, Tommy challenged Buckner, along with Valentine, Steve Garvey, and Tom Paciorek, to a home run contest. "He bet us $50. We thought there was no way he could beat us," said Buckner. "But when he hit, he brought out brand-new balls, and when we hit, we hit with old, waterlogged balls."

It may have seemed like a joke, but Tommy was thinking about his players and their path to success. He was teaching them about how paying the price and being competitive would help them get better. Tommy would show them how competitive he was, and that was part of the price they had to pay. "I taught them how to be mean. I taught them how to want to win. That's how I taught them," he said.

Buckner excelled in Ogden. During the '68 season, his first in professional baseball, he racked up 88 hits in 64 games, batting .344 and slugging .492. In '69, after batting .350 in the Arizona Instructional League, he was promoted to Double A, where he hit .307. From there he was promoted to Triple A, where he hit .315, and later that summer he was called up to the big leagues. Although he only played in one game that season, he was a Dodger at age 19. In 1970 he started the season in Triple A with Tommy. He had another outstanding season, batting .335 and earning another call up to the big leagues. Before that call came, however, he would suffer a brutal injury.

"When I was playing for Tommy in Triple A, I broke my jaw. I had to have it wired shut for six weeks, but I kept playing," said Buckner.

"He and Valentine collided," said Tommy. "I had Buck playing left field so Garvey could play at first. When I called the office to tell them what happened, they asked me how long he would be out. Be out? He's going to play. And he played the next day! He had his jaw wired up, but never missed a game."

That's the kind of player Tommy wanted—a player who would not rest because of fatigue, who would not stop because of injury, who would even play with a broken jaw. That's the price Tommy wanted them to pay.

"One day, Buck's arguing with the umpire. He's trying to holler through the wires—zzz, zzz!" Tommy said. "It was the funniest thing I'd ever seen."

"I was crazy competitive, which you have to be if you want to be successful, unless you're really talented," said Buckner. "Tommy gave us that edge."

Buckner's fire was one to never be extinguished. After being traded to the Cubs in '77, he had something to prove. "When I got traded to the Cubs and we played the Dodgers for the first time, I wanted to beat them so badly," said Buckner. "I was wearing them out. One of their pitchers drilled me in the ribs. I knew he hit me on purpose, and I knew Tommy told him to do it. I'm running down to first and I look over at Tommy in the dugout. He's smiling at me and says, 'Hey, Billy Buck, I love you like a son. I would never do that to you,' but I knew."

Buckner knew as well as anyone how competitive Tommy is. He also knew that Tommy and his wife, Jo, loved him. When his jaw was broken, Jo would make health shakes for him to drink through a straw. They loved Buckner so much that he was a guest at their house many times for dinner, whether it was a shake or a steak.

But that didn't stop Tommy from doing whatever he had to do to win.

• • •

Of paramount importance to the managers and coaches at all levels of the Dodgers organization was to teach players the Dodger Way. Mastering the fundamentals of the game was critical, but so too was working on a player's attitude toward his teammates and the game. Coaches had to make sure the competitive spirit burned bright and the ego stayed dimmed. They had to make sure that the name on the front of the jersey was more important than the name on the back. Those were pillars of the Dodger Way and the foundation of Tommy's teachings.

Those virtues were on full display whenever the Dodgers took on one of their fiercest rivals, and none were more fierce than the Giants. Whether they were the New York Giants playing the Brooklyn Bridegrooms in 1890 or the San Francisco Giants playing the Los Angeles Dodgers in 1990, Dodgers were taught to hate the Giants from day one. It's a 19th-century rivalry that pitted a city against a borough and classes against the masses; white-collar Giants fans from Manhattan against blue collar immigrants from Brooklyn. Crossing the Brooklyn Bridge was a cross in identity and heritage. Who you cheered for told the world who you were.

The rivalry pitted the American Association against the National League until the Dodgers joined in 1890. It pitted Giants owner John McGraw against Dodgers owner Charles Ebbets in a personal feud that was manifested on the field in the Polo Grounds and Ebbets Field amongst the players, and in the streets amongst their respective fans.

It's a rivalry held in dramatic swings at the plate, in the standings, and in the history books. In 1951, the Dodgers had a 13.5-game lead on the Giants in August. The Giants charged through September, led by a young Willie Mays, to catch and pass the Dodgers, who rallied to win the final game of the season, forcing a tie and a three-game playoff for the pennant. The Giants took the first, the Dodgers the second, and in the ninth inning of the third game Bobby Thomson hit a home run, the infamous "Shot Heard 'Round the World." In 1959, the Giants had a three-game lead on the Dodgers into early September. The Dodgers swept the Giants in a three-game series later that month, eliminating the Giants en route to the 1959 World Series championship. In '65, the Giants went on a 14-game tear, giving them a 4.5-game lead, but the Dodgers answered with a 13-game streak of their own and won 15 of the last 16 to beat out their rivals. In 1962, the Dodgers and Giants were tied atop the National League West at the end of the regular season, forcing another three-game playoff. The Giants again took two out of three, with the deciding third game settled in the ninth when the Giants scored four runs to take the game, the series, and the pennant. In 2004, the

Dodgers and Giants were at it again. The Giants were trying to preserve a three-run lead in the bottom of the ninth at Dodger Stadium. The Dodgers tied it, then Steve Finley hit a dramatic grand slam, clinching the National League West title.

Tommy demanded competitiveness against any opponent, but especially against the Giants. At Candlestick Park, the visiting team's players would have to take a long walk down the line in right field to reach their dugout. Before each game on that long walk, Tommy would blow kisses to the fans in the stands, roiling them to no end. Mickey Hatcher once walked down the line with Tommy, but before doing so he donned his catcher's gear, just in case. Before the final game at Candlestick, the Giants asked Tommy to take that walk just one last time, even though he had since retired from managing. Of course, he agreed, and of course, the booing came again, louder than ever, as he blew them kisses. When he got to home plate a microphone was in place for Tommy to say a few words.

"You know, I finally have you people figured out," he said. "You don't hate me. You hate yourselves because you love me!"

Tommy and his Dodgers also formed a rivalry against the Yankees. As World Series opponents in 1977, '78, and again in '81, the two teams battled for the crown. Some of baseball's most memorable moments came from those series, including Reggie Jackson sticking his backside out to block a throw from second to first. Nicknames like Mr. October were borne from them. Baseball history was made in them, as Pedro Guerrero, Ron Cey, and Steve Yeager were named World Series co-MVPs in '81.

Before gaining their revenge in '81, the Dodgers lost the '77 Series in six games, and lost again in '78 despite getting out to a 2–0 series lead. For Tommy, these defeats were personal. Willing to pay any price to win, he carried the Ghost of World Series Past along with him like a BP pitcher lugs around bags of balls.

Tommy reveled in the rivalries and the passions they forged. After the '81 Series, Tommy and one of his four brothers happened to be in Tampa during the off-season. They pulled up to a red light, and Tommy noticed that the man driving the car next to his was wearing a Yankees cap.

"Take that hat off!" Tommy yelled. "That's the worst hat I've ever seen! It's brutal! You need a Dodgers hat!"

A few months later, during spring training in 1982, the Dodgers were back in Florida to play the Yankees. After getting off the bus, Tommy saw none other than George Steinbrenner running toward him. "Don't you ever talk to my driver like that again, Lasorda!" the owner yelled.

One player has unique insight into the Dodgers' rivalries with the Giants and Yankees, since he played for both of them. He also experienced first-hand how Tommy retained his humanity despite his hatred of losing. Dave Righetti played for the Yankees in 1979 and from 1981 to 1990. He signed as free agent with the Giants and played for them from 1991 to 1993. A left-hander from San Jose with a fastball that trailed away from right-handers and a slider that broke in on lefties, he posted an 82–79 career record with a 3.46 ERA and 1,112 strikeouts in 718 games. He also earned 252 career saves. After being released by the Giants, he caught on with the A's, the Blue Jays, and the White Sox before retiring and rejoining the Giants as pitching coach.

Although Righetti made his major league debut for the Yankees in 1979, he didn't blossom until 1981, when he won the American League Rookie of the Year award after going 8–4 with a 2.05 ERA. He was slated to start the third game of the World Series after the Yankees had won the previous two contests. "I was a rookie, so it was a big deal," said Righetti. "I was thinking about that lineup." Righetti was facing Davey Lopes, Bill Russell, Dusty Baker, Steve Garvey, Ron Cey, Pedro Guerrero, Rick Monday, and Steve Yeager. As he trotted out to the bullpen to warm up, Yankees teammate Graig Nettles came running out after him. Righetti had left more than 20 tickets for his family and friends to come see him pitch. Tom Nettles, Graig's cousin and a Giants broadcaster, saw Righetti's father, Leo, at will call, but Leo couldn't get into the stadium. As it turned out, Righetti forgot just one ticket, and in a selfless act Leo told the rest of his family to go on without him.

"I couldn't do anything about it because I was getting ready to start the game," said Righetti.

Tommy had played against Leo Righetti in the Sally League. The two knew each other from those days when Tommy was playing for the Greenville

Spinners and Righetti was playing for the Augusta Tigers, and had been friends ever since. "Somehow, Dad got a hold of Tommy, and somehow Tommy got him into the stadium."

Even though Righetti was about to compete against the Dodgers in a game Tommy was desperate to win, he was not going to let his friend miss a chance to see his son pitch in the Fall Classic. He wasn't going to let his competitive nature keep Righetti from pitching in front of his father.

"It was a hell of a game," said Righetti. "We lost 5–4 and it turned the tide of the Series and they won those three close games. Losing that Series was tough, and there was a lot of fallout in New York, but there was no shame in losing to that great Dodgers team, and our guys knew it. I was very disappointed, but felt no shame battling against that team."

Righetti allowed a three-run homer to Cey in the bottom of the first. Although the Yankees cut it to 3–2 in the second, Righetti wouldn't see the third inning. Despite the performance, he made an impression on Tommy that day. He was a free agent in 1987, and again in 1990; both times Tommy called him during the off-season to gauge his interest in becoming a Dodger.

Although the Dodgers and Yankees were enemies on the field, the two organizations shared a few things in common. Both teams had historic legacies. Both teams were committed to winning. Both had outspoken managers in Tommy and Billy Martin. There's a sign that every Yankee sees as he goes from the clubhouse to the dugout at Yankee Stadium that reads, IT'S GREAT TO BE A YANKEE.

"Yeah," replied Tommy. "Well, Branch Rickey indoctrinated us with a saying of our own: 'I'm proud to be a Dodger.'"

"The Dodgers in a sense are a lot like the Yankees are in the American League," said Righetti. "The Yankees are a polarizing team, and in a sense the Dodgers are, too. That part didn't bother me. I knew the Dodgers were always going to try to field a great team. I loved energetic managers and personalities. It didn't bother me being around Billy, and it wouldn't have bothered me to be around Tommy. I enjoyed it very much."

Leo Righetti passed away in 1998. He and Tommy both played sandlot baseball as kids. They were both sons of Italian immigrants. They both toiled in the minor leagues and never really got the shot in the big leagues that they thought they deserved. When Leo died, Tommy called Dave, the same man who had represented two organizations he hated. "I don't know how he found out. Maybe it was an Italian thing," said Righetti. "Tommy was one of the first three people in the baseball world to call me to express their condolences."

"I wanted him to know that his father was a good man," said Tommy. "He was a major-leaguer on and off the field, and I wanted him to know that. I also told him to thank God for all the time he had with him."

"I never forgot that," said Righetti. "He told me my dad was a hell of a guy and that he would be missed. He told me a couple stories and tried to make me laugh."

Certainly Righetti thanked his father for everything Leo had given him, including the competitiveness he showed while playing against Tommy's Dodgers. Rick Monday, Bill Buckner, and scores of other players feel the same way about Tommy. To play for Tommy was to emulate his drive to win. All you had to do was answer two simple questions: How bad do you want it? What price are you willing to pay?

• CHAPTER 4 •

DETERMINATION

"The difference between the impossible and the possible lies in a person's determination."

When Phillies scout Jocko Collins came to the Lasorda home and left with a signed contract, Tommy Lasorda's life and career were on their way. All the self-confidence he gained at Elmwood Park, all the hard work he put in on the mound at that field, and all the competition he faced as a member of the Connie Mack All-Star team had paid off.

"Growing up I was a Yankee fan. I used to go to bed and actually dream that I was pitching for the Yankees," said Tommy. "I looked in and Bill Dickey was giving me the signs. DiMaggio was in center, Gehrig was at first, and the Babe was in right. All of a sudden I would feel my mother shaking me and saying, 'Wake up, Tommy. It's time to go to school.' I did not want to leave that dream. The dream was so real!

"One day, many years later when I was pitching for the Dodgers, we were playing the Yankees at Yankee Stadium. I was in the bullpen and they called me in to pitch to Yogi Berra. As I took that long walk from the bullpen to the mound, I looked around and said to myself, 'I have been here many times, but in my dreams.'"

Despite the doubts that come with leaving home for the first time, the doubts that come as a kid playing against men, the doubts that come with

57

betting your future on a dream, Tommy was steadied by what his father told him as he left home for his first spring training. Sabatino hugged his son and told him something that Tommy never forgot and later preached.

"Remember that because God delays does not mean that God denies."

It was a pivotal moment in Tommy's life. That piece of wisdom served as the basis of Tommy's determination.

"Over the course of my life in baseball I have learned a lot about players and competition," said Tommy. "It isn't always the fastest man who wins the race or the strongest man who wins the fight. It is the one who wants it more than the other guy. All I wanted in life was to play baseball in the major leagues."

When he arrived in Wilmington, he was lost. "It was the first time I was away from home," said Tommy. "Here I was, just turned 17, and going to play professional baseball not knowing what's going to happen to me, where I was going to go, how I was going to do it. I just didn't know what was going to happen. I didn't know anything about anything. When I signed my first contract I thought I was going to pitch for the Phillies!"

After spring training Tommy was sent to play in Concord, North Carolina, the Phillies' Class D team. While his heart was full of desire and his belly was full of fire, his arm wasn't as full of as many wins as he hoped; he went 3–12 with a 4.09 ERA. In his first game, the shortstop booted a ball in the ninth that gave Tommy the loss. He was so fired up that he tried to fight his teammate in the clubhouse. The manager of the team, John "Pappy" Lehman, came out and broke it up. "Are you crazy?" Lehman asked his young pitcher. "Just because he made an error doesn't mean he was trying to lose the game." Lehman taught Tommy a lot about how to deal with players who make errors, and that nothing was more important than being a good teammate. "From then on, whenever a fielder made an error behind me I would try to encourage him," said Tommy. Lehman also had some words for Tommy that he didn't like. "He told me that I should start thinking about doing something else because I wouldn't make it in baseball," said Tommy. "I told him, 'Pappy, I'm going to make it. Somehow, some way, I'm going to make it.'"

After the 1945 season, Tommy was drafted into the Army. He spent the next two years serving in South Carolina, but also pitching for the team on base as well as for a local team. Following several ho-hum seasons in the Phillies minor league system, the Phillies had seen enough. Perhaps they shared Pappy's belief that Tommy should find something else to do with his life. Perhaps roster spots were tougher to come by now that servicemen were starting to return to the game. During the off-season he was drafted by the Dodgers in the minor league draft.

That spring Tommy reported to Vero Beach, Florida, for his first spring training with the Dodgers. When he arrived at Dodgertown, he immediately doubted his prospects. "There were more than 700 players there, and I didn't know where I would fit in. I figured I had no chance," said Tommy. That doubt carried Tommy into the office of minor league director Fresco Thompson. "I asked him to let me go somewhere else. He told me I was going to stay right there and I was going to play." Before the spring was over, Tommy had another request for Thompson. "I was going to play for the Pueblo club, but the night before we were going to leave Vero, I asked Fresco to put me on the Greenville team. I told him that my arm felt great in Greenville when I was stationed there. The weather was great for my arm. So he put me on that team."

The move changed Tommy's life forever.

He had a good year, recording a 2.93 ERA. More importantly, one night he saw a young woman in the stands and asked her friend if they would meet him after the game. As soon as the last out was made, Tommy showered and then met the ladies in the parking lot and introduced himself. He asked Joan Miller for her number, but her mother interceded. "I told her mother that Jo would make me a 20-game winner," Tommy recalls. He got the number. After numerous phone calls, she finally accepted Tommy's invitation. "On the 10th call I told Jo to just give me one date, and if she didn't like me after that I would leave her alone." The two went to lunch at a local kitchenette. Tommy was in love. "I looked at her and told her that she may think I was crazy, but that I was going to marry her." She laughed.

"Nobody thought it would work," said Tommy. "An Italian Catholic from the north and a Southern Baptist?" But Tommy was nothing if not determined.

The two married a year later and Tommy was promoted to Triple A in Montreal. "That was a big jump in that organization," said Tommy. "They had all those guys that were there that had been older players, guys who had played in the big leagues. I was the youngest guy on the team." While it felt good to have a taste of success, being just a short drive to Brooklyn and the major leagues was cruelly tantalizing. The stakes were getting higher.

In his first season in Montreal Tommy went 9–4 with a 3.70 ERA. Those were pretty good numbers, especially since they came from the least experienced arm on the team. He returned to Montreal the following year and improved, going 12–8 with a 3.49 ERA. Despite his progress, he was sent back to Montreal the next year; he responded by going 14–5 with a 3.66 ERA. He was working hard, improving, and believed he was getting closer to his dream of pitching in the major leagues. But the Dodgers returned him to Montreal in 1953, where he had his best year to date, going 17–8 with a 2.01 ERA.

By then he had pitched in Montreal for four seasons with no talk of being called up to the big leagues. Despite the success, the doubt started to creep back into his mind. "It was really hard on me," said Tommy. "Let's say you were a catcher on the St. Paul club and hit 40 home runs. Where do you go the next year? Back to St. Paul, because the guy in Brooklyn hit 40 home runs. Let's say you were a shortstop in Hollywood and you hit .350. Where do you think you went the next year? Back to Hollywood, because Pee Wee Reese hit .350 in Brooklyn. Who's going to beat Pee Wee Reese out?

"It actually made me want to quit. I thought it was no use, because I wasn't going to crack into that team. In those days, it was tough. There were only 16 major league teams and no free agency. I didn't know what to do. I was thinking about quitting and getting a job. I was thinking about living in Montreal, because they liked me there. I had a lot of things on my mind."

But the fire still burned in Tommy's belly. The dream still clouded his head and his heart. He was determined to pitch in the majors. "I kept believing," said Tommy. "I believed that if I couldn't play in Brooklyn, maybe I could play somewhere else. They ended up selling me to the St. Louis Browns, but the Browns couldn't afford me, so they had to send me back to the Dodgers."

Eventually, the doubt and adversity took their toll. All the determination in the world was no match for his disappointment. Luckily, Tommy's father was there to remind him that God doesn't deny. "He had come down to visit me in Richmond," said Tommy. "I told my father right there that I was ready to quit. 'Don't you ever say that again to me,' he said. 'Here you are in a nice room with air conditioning. It was so hot back home that I couldn't stand it, so I came here to visit you. We ordered our breakfast up here in the room. No, you're not going to quit, you are going to battle.' And that's what I did."

That determination was necessary, especially after Tommy got off to a tough start in '54. "I was 4–5 to start the season in Montreal, and I was really struggling," he said. "Don Drysdale, Wally Fiala, Johnny Bucha, and I were walking down the street in Buffalo and a pigeon just unloaded on my head. Those guys were laughing and laughing, and I told them 'Good, you'll see, this will change my luck.' I won 10 in a row and walked around looking for pigeons."

Finally, his chance came. "I was going to pitch a game for Montreal in Toronto," said Tommy. "The manager didn't say anything to me, but our coach, Dixie Howell, said, 'Tommy, Brooklyn called today and said that if you pitch a good game, you're going to Brooklyn.' I told him I was going to go pack my bags because I was going to Brooklyn. By golly, I beat Toronto 5–0 and got the call."

Tommy had been a minor league pitcher for eight seasons, and for the majority of them he played for Walter Alston, who managed in Montreal until he was given the job in Brooklyn in '54. Despite their history and shared success, Alston didn't give him a start; Tommy only pitched in four games out of the bullpen that year for the Dodgers. The following year was more of the same: he started the year in Montreal and was eventually called up to Brooklyn. Finally, he got his first start in the major leagues. On May 5, 1955, Don Newcombe was scheduled to start against the St. Louis Cardinals. However, Newcombe and Alston got in an argument, and Alston benched him. He came to Tommy and told him he was going to start.

Unbeknownst to both Tommy and Alston, Tommy's first start was also his last, at least for the Brooklyn Dodgers.

The first batter Tommy faced was Wally Moon. He walked him. Next up was Bill Virdon. Tommy leaned in and got the sign from Roy Campanella. He bounced a pitch that got by the catcher and Moon advanced to second. A few pitches later, Virdon walked. Up to the plate strode the one and only Stan Musial. Tommy leaned in again, and again let a pitch go that bounced before Campanella and sent Moon to third and Virdon to second. Despite two walks and two wild pitches in his first big league start, Tommy kept believing. He struck out Musial on a curve, the same curve Branch Rickey had told him to throw at his hat sitting on top of the plate, the same curve that whiffed 25 Rugmakers when he pitched for Schenectady, the same curve that caught Jocko Collins' eye in Norristown.

Next up was Rip Repulski. Tommy threw another wild pitch. As Moon raced toward home, Tommy raced to the plate to cover as Campanella retrieved the ball. Tommy blocked the plate, and Moon's spikes ripped Tommy's knee apart. "The cut was all the way open on the knee, all the way down to the bone," said Tommy. Curt Schilling's bloody sock would pale in comparison.

Despite the severity of the injury, Tommy was undaunted. "I'd be damned if I was going to leave that game," he said. He actually finished the inning, striking out Repulski and inducing Red Schoendienst to pop out. He hobbled back to the dugout. Blood was everywhere, and his teammates were queasy. Tommy wanted to keep pitching. The doctor said that if he went back out there he might never be able to walk the same way again. "I told them that if he wants to take me out he is going to have to do it on the mound," Tommy said. "He will not take me out on the bench."

But Alston had a game to manage and told Tommy he was through. The fire in his belly returned. Just a few moments earlier he had been competing against the Cardinals. Now he was competing against Alston and Russ Meyer and Don Newcombe, who were physically blocking him from returning to the field.

The doctor took care of Tommy's knee but the recovery kept him on the bench. He returned as determined to prove he belonged in the big leagues as ever. "When I came back, Alston asked me to throw BP, so I did it," said Tommy. "Then we went down to Pittsburgh and he asked me to throw BP again. Same day. He put me in the game that night after I had thrown two sessions of BP. Pee Wee Reese told me that I should never have gone in the game. But I couldn't tell Alston that I couldn't pitch. It was my shot to get back in there. I gave up a couple of runs from a two-run homer. I hadn't pitched in a while, so I didn't do well."

Tommy's '55 line was 0–0 with a 13.50 ERA. He had endured the injury and the subterfuge. He still believed he could pitch and win for the Dodgers. That was, until Buzzie Bavasi, then general manager for the Dodgers, called him into his office. "Tommy, I got bad news," said Bavasi. "I have to send someone out from this ballclub. If you were sitting in my seat, who would you send out?"

"Koufax."

"We can't send Koufax out. The rules provide that if you give a player more than a $4,000 bonus he has to remain on the major league roster for two years. Koufax stays and you must go."

And so the greatest left-handed pitcher in the history of baseball ended Tommy's playing career for the Dodgers. Tommy returned to Montreal, and after finishing that season he was purchased by the Kansas City Athletics and played there in '56. The Athletics traded him to the Yankees, then the Dodgers purchased him back in '57. However, he would never pitch in the big leagues again.

"I felt like I could have pitched there and didn't get the chance I deserved," said Tommy. That feeling taught Tommy a lesson he would teach to his players. "I don't know if determination is more important than talent and hard work. But without determination, your talent won't be enough."

As a manager, Tommy would go out of his way to give every player an opportunity, especially if he sensed a burning determination within them. During his 20 years managing the Dodgers, he had nine National League Rookies of the Year, easily a major league record. "You better believe I gave a player a chance if I could see his determination," said Tommy. "I didn't get that chance, even though I was determined. I wasn't going to let what happened to me affect those young players negatively just because I didn't get the chance. I was going to take the guys who could play, who had earned the spot through hard work and determination. I didn't care how old they were or how much experience they had."

• • •

One of those nine award-winning rookies was a player who had a lot in common with his skipper. They were both born in Norristown, both Italian. They were both doubted by scouts, coaches, managers, and the Dodgers organization. God delayed them both, but they both persevered. They both succeeded. They both turned the impossible into the possible.

Tommy John stood on the mound at Veterans Stadium facing Bake McBride of the Phillies in Game 4 of the 1977 National League Championship Series. He wound up, swept his front leg down the mound, and threw a breaking ball. As McBride swung and missed, John rushed toward the plate and catcher Steve Yeager rushed to the mound, meeting in the middle in a championship embrace. Their manager hugged every player he could wrap his arms around.

Back in the clubhouse, the celebration continued. The 1977 Dodgers were the champions of the National League. While all the players were sharing in the joy, a young boy was on hand to share in it as well. Just nine years old, Mike Piazza was having not only his first taste of professional baseball but of the fruits of victory, of the passion pumping out of the hearts of every Dodger in that clubhouse, and of the indelible passion of their manager.

Tommy first met Mike a year or two earlier. Tommy was *paisans* with Mike's father, Vince, and the two shared a true love of baseball. They also shared their Italian heritage, their Norristown roots, and the virtues of hard work and perseverance. "They were definitely cut form the same cloth," said Piazza. "Tommy's story and my father's story are one of many of Italian Americans coming over, their fathers leaving their home country, leaving everything behind with nothing, absolutely nothing, and becoming successful through hard work."

The two would share stories from their childhoods and families over bowls of pasta fagiole and linguine. They would share their experiences of going from nothing to something: Tommy's journey from Elmwood Park to Ebbets Field in Brooklyn and Vince's journey from collecting milk bottles in school to owning a car dealership. Whenever the Dodgers came to Philadelphia, the Piazza family saw less of their father, as he would be with Tommy throughout the entire series.

The two were so close that when the Dodgers won the '77 NLCS, Tommy had Vince and Mike come to the clubhouse for the victory celebration, which is usually reserved for players and their families. But the Piazzas were quickly becoming part of Tommy's family. Over the next few years, Piazza and his brothers would receive packages from Dodger Stadium from their new goombah: equipment, toys, and assorted Dodgers gear. In 1980, Tommy sent Mike a satin Dodgers jacket. Of course, he wore it to school and was harassed for it; they were in Phillies country, after all.

Over the years, Tommy's love for Vince's children grew as well. At a school assembly, in front of the entire student body, Tommy said that one day he would draft Piazza. He made Piazza his batboy when the Dodgers came to town, a practice that would continue until Mike was drafted. But Piazza wasn't relegated to collecting bats and helmets. Before one game Tommy had him take a few swings in the batting cage with Dodgers coach Manny Mota. Later that summer, Tommy invited Piazza to travel with the team to New York as the Dodgers played the Mets at Shea Stadium. He would take a few swings there, too. Back in Philadelphia at the Vet, he took a few more swings during batting practice. "I was determined to hit the ball into the seats," said Piazza. Eventually, he did.

As Piazza matured and his swing developed, Tommy and other Dodgers were taking notice. When Piazza was 16 years old, Tommy had him face Alejandro Pena in a simulated game. Piazza grabbed a bat and hammered one off the wall. "That was when Tommy started talking me up, telling everybody about this kid hitting a double off the ERA champ," said Piazza.

"I put expectations on myself to get drafted," said Piazza. "In my heart, I was positive that I was good enough, and felt certain, especially after what Tommy said at the assembly, that somebody would pick me up."

Piazza had access that few kids have. He had instruction from coaches, which even fewer kids have. Still, he didn't display that special quality that some scouts look for. "I got calls from scouts from the Giants and Blue Jays," said Piazza. "Jocko Collins came to see me play and I hit a fly ball to center, and then it rained. He never came to see me again. Tim Thompson told my dad that I should concentrate on getting my education."

Although he was doubted by some scouts, he had the backing of the Dodgers manager. "Mike had talent," said Tommy. "I saw something in him as a youngster that nobody else saw." Though Piazza wasn't drafted out of high school, he would persevere. He wouldn't let his dream of playing in the major leagues die, and neither would Tommy.

Tommy called his friend Ron Fraser, who was a college baseball coach at the University of Miami. "He was asking Fraser to take a chance on a slow kid from a small school in a northern state who didn't actually have a position or the academic standing to qualify," said Piazza. "Needless to say, Fraser didn't leap at the opportunity."

But Tommy was determined, and arranged for a tryout at Dodger Stadium, whereupon Piazza smashed the ball all over the field. Although his defense at first base wasn't the best, the scout from Miami was enamored with his bat—Piazza had his chance. Upon reporting to Fraser, he expected to become a freshman All-American. That was until he botched a chopper in the field during a scrimmage, until he faced a senior with a slider that carried him to be drafted. "I had never even seen a slider before," said Piazza. He earned a reputation as a "five o'clock hitter," someone who hit the ball well during batting practice but not during games. He didn't hustle, didn't perform, and subsequently rode the bench.

Instead of sending him back for another year riding the pine, Tommy called in another favor with another college coach. This time it was with Demie Mainieri, who coached for Miami-Dade North, a community college. That team proved more of a fit for Piazza, as he played and flourished. Before a game against Miami, Fraser and Piazza's father were talking about Mike returning to Miami. Instead of pursuing the opportunity, Vince mentioned he would prefer to have Mike enter the draft. Frankly, Fraser said, Mike wasn't ready for professional baseball.

Later that fall, Tommy arranged for Piazza to play one game with the Orioles in their Instructional League. The next spring, Tommy arranged for Piazza to work out with the Rangers, who were then managed by Bobby Valentine. At that point in his career he was only a first baseman, but Tommy suggested Piazza try catching. Piazza and his father agreed, so Tommy had Mike work with veteran catcher Joe Ferguson.

If anyone could convince Piazza to move behind the plate, it was Ferguson. He too had been an outfielder with dreams of making it to the big leagues, and he blanched when Tommy suggested he switch to catcher. But Tommy told him that Mickey Cochrane, Ernie Lombardi, and Gabby

Hartnett—all Hall of Fame catchers—had started their careers as outfielders. When Tommy told Al Campanis that Ferguson had agreed to the switch, Campanis pointed out that none of those players had ever been outfielders. "You know that and I know that, but Joe doesn't know that!" said Tommy.

Piazza went back to Miami-Dade and finished the year batting .364. With no prospects of returning to a four-year college and only a slim chance of being drafted, Tommy once again shepherded Piazza along. "Tommy kept me encouraged to chase that dream," said Piazza. "I knew if I could work hard and overcome the adversity and the frustrations I was experiencing, I could get to that higher spot, and Tommy was directly responsible for that because he gave me a taste of that as a kid."

Tommy made sure Piazza got another taste. On June 3, 1988, in the 62nd round, the Dodgers selected Piazza with the 1,390th pick in the draft. "They thought they were doing me a favor," Tommy said of the Dodgers front office. "But I was doing them a favor. When I scout players, I look for guys who are determined. I look for guys who take extra BP, who work on their deficiencies as much or more than their strengths, who won't take no for an answer, who battle at everything they do, who believed in themselves and rise to the challenge. What I saw in Piazza was a youngster with a lot of heart who knew he was going to make it because of his desire and will. He was going to show the doubters that he was there because he could play."

Unfortunately, Dodgers scouting director Bill Wade didn't share Tommy's enthusiasm. One month passed before he connected with Piazza. Piazza's father put him on a plane to Los Angeles, where Wade and few other scouts were on hand to watch Piazza work out. Tommy was there too, but he roamed the outfield grass and stayed out of the way.

Although Piazza hit about 20 balls into the stands, Wade was still reluctant to sign him. Tommy asked Wade if he would sign a catching prospect with that kind of power. When Wade said that he would, Tommy said, "Okay, he is now a catcher. Sign him."

The Dodgers' first-round pick, Bill Bene, received a signing bonus of more than $150,000. Piazza received $15,000.

"It was frustrating," said Piazza. "I am sure that Ben Wade was skeptical because he had never really seen me play, and I understood that, I was disappointed, but you have to look at yourself from an objective perspective. I knew it was just another obstacle I had to overcome."

Upon reporting to the Dodgers' Instructional League team, Piazza found the players split into two different squads. On his squad's first day off, he reported to the other team to get in extra BP and fielding practice. While the other catchers were busy eyeballing him and muttering insults, the instructor liked that Piazza was there to work. "A lot of my teammates were wondering what I was doing there, and at times I did, too," said Piazza. "I wasn't getting a lot of positive reinforcement in those days."

Still, Piazza persevered. His determination was reinforced by Tommy's, as his goombah refused to let him lose hope. After Instructional League play, Tommy sent Piazza to the Dominican Republic to continue his development. While Piazza had faced the adversity of doubting coaches and scouts, the Dominican would present a whole new set of challenges. He didn't know the language, didn't have any friends, and wasn't familiar with the food or the meager surroundings. "It was an eye-opener for me. I grew up in a middle-class suburban neighborhood, went to the University of Miami on a scholarship, thought I was going to be a freshman All-American," said Piazza. "But seeing extreme poverty, it's something you couldn't describe. They literally don't have shoes.

"I knew that at that point I my life I needed to play. I was too young and inexperienced to play in the traditional winter leagues. I was behind in catching. I needed to go there and play. I needed at-bats. At that point, I was willing to do anything. I would have crawled on my knees on broken glass to play. There were times when you wonder what you're doing there, but I knew I had to get through."

After the regular workouts, he was driven to catch more bullpen sessions for the professional Dominican teams. While other players in the Dodgers organization were enjoying their winters, their families, and their Christmases, Piazza had to find joy in what he was doing. "Being in the Dominican was hard," said Piazza. "But the pure love of the people, their enthusiasm, it was quite beautiful. They have faith, they enjoy life, they love family, and you can learn a lot from that. And I did."

Equipped with developing tools, a fresh perspective on life in professional baseball, and his beautifully powerful swing, Piazza reported for his first spring training as a member of the Dodgers organization. "It was heaven," said Piazza. "You could play as much baseball as you wanted. We would play a four-hour spring game, and then Tommy would roll out the cage and pitch to us as long as we wanted. We worked; that was Tommy's philosophy. Sunup to sundown.

"Tommy was a master at generating enthusiasm, especially among young players. From the beginning he made us feel like real Dodgers. Tommy would frequently put the greenest kids from the lowest levels in major league exhibition games. Me, Eric Karros, and Eric Young would be called up to the big field. Maybe we would hit, maybe we wouldn't, but we were there in the dugout next to the stars. That first year I made a trip with the team to West Palm [Beach] to play Atlanta in a split-squad game. It was amazing. I was actually catching in a big-league game and it was just my first spring training. Dale Murphy was hitting and I'm behind the plate. I was thinking, *How in the world did I get here?*

"Tommy was revolutionary. As a kid, to have a big-league manager play you in a big-league game, it's powerful. That's something Tommy did a lot, but now it's common. I can't deny that Tommy looked after me in those days, baseball-wise. Indisputably he was the steward of my entry into pro ball and my conversion to catcher."

"I believed in him," said Tommy. "And I wanted him to believe in himself. I believed he had the talent, but they didn't believe that he had the talent. They believed that he was only there because of me, but I didn't want them to think that. I got him there because he had talent."

While playing in that big-league exhibition game was a thrill for the young Piazza, it was still just a start. After spring training he reported to rookie ball in Salem, Oregon. While there his manager got tired of watching him chase passed balls to the backstop and split his playing time with another catcher, Hector Ortiz. Although he only batted .268 that season, he hit eight home runs in 57 games and was named an All-Star.

Back at Dodgertown for his second spring training, Piazza played on the Single A team managed by Joe Alvarez, a Cuban native. Early in the season Piazza got sick, and Alvarez told him he would be splitting time with Pete Gonzalez. Later in the season, Alvarez pulled Piazza from a game when Piazza swung instead of bunting as directed, even though the count was 0-2. Then Alvarez pulled him from the game and yelled at him in front of his teammates. Piazza took off his uniform and went home. "I really felt like I was at the end of the line, with the Dodgers at least," said Piazza. "I'd been sick, benched, embarrassed in front of my team."

"I told Michael to go back the next day and apologize. They fined him $200, which I didn't think was fair. The manager chewed him out in front of his team and embarrassed him by saying that he had to run to the big-league manager for help," said Tommy.

Piazza was invited back to the team and apologized to his teammates. The whole episode with Alvarez made Piazza develop a chip on his shoulder. Just as John Lehman and Walter Alston had doubted Tommy when he played, Piazza was doubted by his manager, too. "My career turned around at that point," said Piazza.

The episode also took a toll on Tommy. "It was tough on me because they were doing it to spite me. They were taking their anger at me out on him by not playing him," said Tommy. "It upset me because I knew he was there because of me, but that he could play."

Piazza finished the year hitting just .250, but his power was developing. The following year at Single A in Bakersfield, he hit .277 and crushed 29 bombs. That stat line earned him a spot on a Winter League team, Mexicali. He homered three times in the next spring's big-league camp, one of which was a grand slam. He started the year in Double A, and after hitting .377 in 31 games he was promoted to Triple A, where he hit .341.

Piazza beat out Carlos Hernandez and started the 1993 season as the Dodgers catcher. He finished the season hitting .318 with 35 home runs and 112 RBIs. He was voted an All-Star and won the Rookie of the Year award.

He also won the Silver Slugger Award, which goes to the best offensive player at each position. "What made me proudest was catching 141 games as a rookie and throwing out 58 runners trying to steal," said Piazza. "It was the most in the major leagues and in Dodgers history."

Piazza would hit 177 home runs over parts of seven seasons with the Dodgers. He made the All-Star team five times. Perhaps one of his favorite home runs came on June 23, 1996, against the Astros. The score was tied in the in the bottom of ninth, and Piazza hit a solo shot to win the game. That game was Tommy's last as manager of the Dodgers, as he suffered a heart attack that night and retired shortly thereafter.

"I wanted to reward Tommy's confidence in me," said Piazza. "I definitely wanted to prove not only to myself, but to my dad and Tommy, that I could play, and convince Tommy that he was right, and that his efforts and energies toward me were fruitful. Tommy stuck his neck out for me, he put a lot of energy and invested his time, his pitching, his love, so yeah, I definitely wanted to pay him back."

Piazza was traded by the Dodgers in 1998 to the Florida Marlins, and then played for the Mets. He finished his career with 427 round-trippers. "Show me a guy with desire and I'll show you a winner," said Tommy. "A guy who will never quit when faced with problems. It's the guy who doesn't have that desire and determination who quits."

Piazza never quit; his determination was palpable. There were many guys like Bill Bene, who were drafted ahead of him; guys like Eric Ganino, D.J. Floyd, and Bill Wengert, who heckled and fought him in the minors; guys like Hector Ortiz and Carlos Hernandez, who he beat out for playing time. He beat the odds thanks to his determination, because of those learned behaviors he acquired from his father and Tommy, because his manager, his goombah, loved him.

"He was so dedicated," said Piazza. "He cared. He cared about the players as a whole, their families, their kids. He always understood that a player was not a one-dimensional being, that there are many layers to the person. He always understood that and knew that contented cows give better milk. He wanted the players to be happy.

"Tommy for me is like family. I love Tommy and always will, I cherish him. He has done so much for me and I will always appreciate it. I think he's a national treasure, and the game of baseball owes him a huge debt of gratitude for all he's done for the game."

• • •

Tommy was determined to see Mike Piazza succeed. He went to great personal and professional lengths to do so, and even transformed him from a first baseman into a catcher. Tommy made a similar move with another player, a change that transformed the man's life and career. That player was Charlie Hough.

Drafted in the eighth round of the 1966 draft, Hough was a solid high school player from Hialeah, Florida. Hough was drafted as a third baseman.

"I was pretty good, but I didn't have the real physical skill that the big-leaguers had playing third or first," said Hough. When he reported to Tommy in Ogden in 1966, he and his new teammates went through a week or so of workouts before the games started. That is when Tommy saw which tools Hough had, and which he needed. "Our scout told me that he could play first, third, or pitch," said Tommy. "He could hit, he could swing the bat, and he had good hands, he could throw and catch well, but when I saw him run, geez." That's when Hough found a permanent home on the mound.

"As a pitcher, I was just okay," said Hough. "I had a very mediocre fastball, a curve and slider, and a lousy change. Believe it or not, I had really good control." What he also had, as Tommy would discover and develop, was determination. During that season, Hough's mediocre fastball was on display—and on a tee—for the hitters of the Pioneer League. He went 5–7 with a 4.76 ERA, hardly the stuff of a future major-leaguer. But Tommy gave Hough a good scouting report because he saw something in him, and also because he knew the importance of patience. "Some guys learn right away," Tommy said. "Other guys it takes them a little while, and other guys it takes them a long time. Patience is the greatest quality you can have as a coach."

"I was 18 years old, tying to impress people as a young Dodger, and I've got this maniac manager," said Hough. "Then as I played a little bit I saw there was something special about Tommy's determination to let you get good. I played for 29 seasons, and something that always stuck with me about Tommy was what he said again and again: do you want to pay the price to be good?"

Hough finished his Double A season well. He went 16–5 with a 3.09 ERA. Despite his success, Hough's odds were about to go from long to incredible. Over the next couple of seasons he developed shoulder problems. Luckily, Tommy was in his corner, just as he had been with Valentine and Cey and Garvey and Piazza. He was determined to see Hough succeed.

"He had such a great attitude about the game. He really and truly loved baseball," said Tommy of Hough. "I just couldn't have him released."

Tommy taught his players how to persevere, a lesson not lost on Hough. "He made you believe that if you were prepared to compete that you could, but if you weren't prepared and walked out there with doubt, you're not going to survive. That simple," said Hough. In order for Hough to survive, Tommy knew he'd have to take drastic action. Tommy told him to learn a new pitch. "Make it one you can master," said Tommy.

"One of the minor league pitching coaches was Goldie Holt," said Hough. "He showed me how to grip a knuckleball. I played catch. I threw one pretty good after about 10 minutes, and I went to Tommy and told him that from now on I was throwing a knuckleball, which Tommy liked because he wanted to give me the opportunity to succeed. I never threw a knuckleball in my life, and I'm a knuckleball pitcher after 10 minutes. He went for it. He was as much into it as I was. Tommy's the guy who just pushed me into it. He gave me a chance to pitch. When I first started throwing it in the Instructional League, I was awful. I was absolutely awful. I could strike out the side and give up four runs. When I threw it right it was pretty good, but most of the time I didn't throw it right. It was a walk, hit batter, home run, strikeout, strikeout, walk, hit batter—it was ugly."

The knuckleball proved a perfect metaphor for Hough's career. The point of the pitch is to minimize spin, causing an unpredictable and erratic trajectory. When thrown properly it is hard to hit, and nearly impossible to do so squarely for power. Hough had started his career as erratic and unpredictable. Ironically, the knuckleball, with all its darting and diving and dipping, made Hough one of Tommy's most reliable pitchers. "I went to spring training in 1970 not knowing whether I had a job, whether I had a chance," said Hough. "Tommy kept me on the Triple A club in Spokane, Washington, in 1970. I got off to a great start, and he used me every day, it seemed like. I was pitching a ton. He gave me chance to learn even though my bad days throwing a knuckleball were pretty ugly. Tommy being as tough as he was, he was the kind of guy who could take the harassment of fans and maybe the bosses who were saying, 'What are you doing with this guy?'" Hough was determined to learn the pitch. Tommy was determined to see him succeed.

As all of Tommy's players did, Hough worked hard in the minors. He was hanging his hopes on a pitch that was purposely impossible to keep still. He was betting his career on impossible odds. "I think everybody goes through a moment of *Wow, can I do this? Can I really do this in the big leagues? Can I go out there and pitch against Willie Stargell?*" said Hough. "The most important thing I had was the knowledge that I could because I worked hard for this. Tommy instilled that belief in us from day one."

"I called Charlie the Hope Diamond," said Tommy. "When I went home at night I would lock him away in my safe because he was so valuable." Hough went on to do something very rare in baseball. He logged 400 starts as well as 400 relief appearances. He persevered, he wouldn't quit, he wouldn't let better pitchers beat him out of a roster spot. Tommy had made him into a competitor and a winner. God delays, but doesn't deny.

Of course, Hough wasn't always like that. His favorite Tommy story, and the lesson it taught him, came from his earliest days in Ogden. "Just a few days after I reported he was giving a speech at a chamber of commerce luncheon, and all the players were there," said Hough. "We were all new to the organization, new to professional baseball, and new to Tommy. There were 30 or 40 guys at the luncheon, and Tommy was the featured speaker. He had no notes or anything written down, but he introduced all the players by name, where they were from, what they did, what position they played, the school they went to, what round they were drafted in, and it was amazing. He knew everybody in the matter of a couple days. He introduced the team as the 1966 Pioneer League champions. We hadn't played a game yet. We thought he was crazy.

"The best thing I can say is that he cared. My kids that are grown up still call him Uncle Tom. My granddaughter calls him Uncle Tom."

The Ogden Dodgers indeed won the Pioneer League championship in '66, just as Tommy had predicted and dared his players to dream about. "Dreams become reality," Tommy said. "The impossible can be possible."

CHAPTER 5

WINNING

"How sweet it is, the fruits of victory!"

In 1988, the National League Championship Series was tied at three games apiece. The Mighty Mets and Tommy's Dodgers were facing off at Dodger Stadium for the pennant, for a chance to play the Oakland A's in the Fall Classic. Despite 56,000 in the stands and a city of believers behind them, doubt was hanging in the air like a lazy curve floating over the plate. The Mets had stolen victory in Game 1 in the bottom of the ninth after trailing 2–0 all night. The Mets had also stolen Game 6, in Los Angeles.

Game 7 would be Orel Hershiser's fourth appearance in seven games. Despite breaking an unbreakable record by pitching 59 consecutive scoreless innings during the regular season, despite leading the league with 23 wins, 267 innings pitched, eight shutouts, and 15 complete games, he was 0–0 with one save in the NLCS. However, he was the Dodgers' ace, their All-Star, their go-to guy, their Lefty Grove. He was the Bulldog. Who else would you want on the mound for the most important game of the season?

Armed with a sinking fastball that dove on either side of the plate, a cutter, a curve that he threw at three different speeds and angles, and a change-up, Hershiser would kick his leg high, flick his left foot behind his right knee, bend his back, and use his long stride toward the plate to deliver dismantling pitches to the hitters he faced. His motion was ingrained in the minds of every boy who dreamed of pitching for the Dodgers. Also ingrained in their minds was his stare. Steely, focused eyes burning a hole through the slit between his glove covering the bottom of his face and his Dodgers cap on top, burning a hole from the rubber to Mike Scioscia's glove, burning a hole through the approach of every hitter he faced.

One of the keys to his success was his pitch selection to each particular hitter. "I threw my sinker at the player and had it come back over the corner of the plate," said Hershiser. "They told me that ball would get hit, and I would say it's not going to get hit." Another key to his success was his location. "You'll hear pitchers say, 'I had great stuff and got bombed,' but you never hear them say, 'I had great location and got bombed.'"

With one out in the top of the first, Wally Backman singled and Keith Hernandez walked. Hershiser got himself out of trouble, getting out Darryl Strawberry on a fielder's choice and forcing Kevin McReynolds to line out. With the Dodgers at bat, Steve Sax led off by singling to center and moving to third on Mickey Hatcher's double to left. Kirk Gibson drove in Sax to score with a sacrifice fly to center.

The Mets only got one hit in the top of the second, but the Dodgers exploded in the bottom half of the inning. Scioscia singled to right. Jeff Hamilton singled to left. Alfredo Griffin tried to move the runners over with a sacrifice bunt, but he beat it out for a base hit. Up to the plate came Hershiser with the bases loaded and no outs. He hit a grounder to third, a one-hopper, but Gregg Jefferies booted it and allowed Scioscia to score. With the bases still loaded, Sax singled, driving in Hamilton and Griffin. The Dodgers were up 4–0, and Ron Darling was pulled for Dwight Gooden, the Mets' own ace. Hatcher grounded out, moving Hershiser to third and Sax to second. The Mets walked Gibson with first base open. Mike Marshall grounded to second but the throw was off, an error, scoring Hershiser. With the bases still loaded, John Shelby drove in the fifth run of the inning with a sacrifice fly to left.

As the inning ended and the Dodgers prepared to take the field for the top of the third, Tommy hollered to Hershiser as he left the dugout. "Don't let up! Go hard! Don't save anything!"

Gooden retired the next six Dodgers batters and didn't allow another run all night. Despite a six-run lead, Hershiser was as focused as he would have been in a scoreless tie. He allowed a single to Lenny Dykstra in the third, but only one more hitter reached base for the next three innings. In the seventh, Jefferies hit a double to right and advanced to third on a wild pitch, but Hershiser would get the next to two batters to pop up. "We could start to taste it," said Hershiser.

Dykstra batted with one out in the eighth inning, and Hershiser hit him. Next up was Backman, who walked. "The last thing I wanted to do was come out. I wanted to finish this one. I wanted to shut out the Mets," Hershiser said. He got Hernandez and Strawberry to ground out to end the inning, and took the 6–0 lead into the top of the ninth.

Throughout his career Hershiser would often sing hymns to himself to keep his mind clear and focused. "The moment can get so big, and be so consuming, and be so important, that it gets out of perspective and it actually makes you dysfunctional," said Hershiser. "The nerves can make you too tight, too strong, the excitement can be too distracting, so the singing was to calm me down and give me perspective.

"I also used visual cues, like keeping my head down. When I got on the grass around the field, I allowed myself to think about the situation of the game. When I was on the dirt of the mound, I would think about what pitch it would take to get a good result. When I was on the rubber, I thought about only that next pitch. So it went from strategy to smaller strategy to execution. Then my eyes were straight down on the rubber, and the next thing I saw was the dirt, then the grass before home plate, then the dirt of home plate, then home plate, then the catcher's fingers.

"I didn't look out and see the whole world and then zone back in. I started from a very fine focus and kept it fine right to the target. My eyes would bring in so much information—from the vendors to the San Diego Chicken to Tommy yelling from the dugout to all the things that happen in a big-league park—so instead of taking all of that in I looked down. I never saw it."

McReynolds flied out to left, and Jefferies grounded out to short. Lee Mazzilli reached first after being hit by a fastball. Next up was Howard

Johnson. Hershiser ran the count to 0-2. "We worked Johnson all series with the curve," said Hershiser. "So we went with a fastball." Strike three, game over, National League champions.

Back in the clubhouse, Tommy's love could be heard from end to end. From Pasadena to Long Beach, from his corner of the Dodgers dugout in Los Angeles to the old mound at Elmwood Park in Norristown, Tommy's love was being expressed for everyone who helped him get to the 1988 World Series.

"We kept hearing about the Mets, how they led the league in homers, ERA, extra-base hits, and all that. There's no doubt they were the best all-around team in the National League. It was hard to imagine that we even belonged on the same field as them, especially after they won 10 of 11 during the regular season. But once again it proves that it isn't the fastest man who wins the race or the strongest man who wins the fight. It's the one who wants it a little bit more!

"How sweet it is, the fruits of victory!"

• • •

Hershiser was named the NLCS MVP in 1988. He would later be named the World Series MVP, and win the Cy Young Award. He was an All-Star, and of course broke the scoreless innings record. However, Hershiser didn't always enjoy the fruits of victory; he was not always the ace, the Bulldog. "When Hershiser reported to me, his reputation wasn't that good," said Tommy. "They said he didn't have it inside, that he didn't have heart."

Drafted in the 17th round of the 1979 draft, there were many other players in the organization in whom the Dodgers put greater stock. The scouting report on him said he that he had a weak fastball, poor mechanics on his curve, and little control. It went on to say that he was easily rattled and had questionable makeup.

"I always called myself a suspect, not a prospect," said Hershiser. "I always suspected I could be good but nobody ever said I *would* be good." Still, he worked his way up through the minor leagues. In Single A, he started four games and appeared in 11 in relief, ending the season 4–0 with a 2.09 ERA. He spent the next two seasons in Double A, and led the league in saves.

During spring training, he had his first serious conversation with Tommy. "I was pitching in an intrasquad game and struck out nine batters in a row," said Hershiser. "Tommy pulled Dusty Baker off the bench because he wanted to see me pitch to a big-league hitter. I struck Dusty out—10 batters in a row. Two days later we are sitting in the stands watching another game and Tommy comes over to sit with me. He gave me a motivational speech, saying if I didn't make it to the big leagues he will have an investigation as to why not. That was the opening line, and it went on for six, seven minutes, but that was the first time that Tommy motivated me and told me I could be a big-leaguer. He probably gave that speech to 100 minor-leaguers, but it meant a lot to me. It still took me another two years, but I made it."

In 1982, he was promoted to Triple A and went 9–6 with a 3.71 ERA in 47 games. His star was on the rise; he was almost included in a trade to the Rangers, but the deal fell through. He won the Mulvey Award in 1983, given to the top Dodgers rookie in spring training. He was expected to make the club, but was sent back to Albuquerque for the '83 season. Going 10–8 with a 4.09 ERA, he was called up to the Dodgers in September. In eight appearances he recorded a 3.38 ERA. Coming out of camp in '84, he was a member of the Dodgers.

"I started the year going 2–2 with a 6.20 ERA," said Hershiser. "I was trying to hang on for dear life in my first full season in the big leagues. I couldn't maintain any consistency or get anything going. I might get a guy or two out, but then I'd get too fine, too careful, and walk somebody. I'd get even more careful, and before you knew it someone had doubled up the alley. I'd be yanked, aired out for not doing what I was being paid to do, and then I'd sit, wondering what was happening to my brief career."

The most frustrating word that one can attach to a young player is potential. Everyone has potential, but can it be developed, can it be used to help the team win? As Tommy has said many times, "Talent that is used develops. Talent that isn't used wastes away." He was determined to make sure Hershiser did not squander his.

"It was the 'sermon on the mound,' as Tommy called it," Hershiser recalls. "Ron Perranoski, our pitching coach, told me that Tommy wanted to see me in his office. I was intimidated by Tommy. He was loud and brash, but he was a manager any player would want behind him. He could be an encourager and a motivator, but I didn't know where I stood. I feared I was on the bubble."

"Hershiser, you're giving these hitters too much credit," Tommy told him. "You're telling yourself that if I throw the ball there, they are going to hit it, instead of telling yourself that I'm *gonna* throw it there and they *ain't* gonna hit it! You've got a negative approach to pitching! You don't believe in yourself! You're scared to pitch in the big leagues! Who do you think these hitters are, Babe Ruth? Ruth's dead. You've got good stuff. If you didn't, I wouldn't have brought you up. Quit being so careful. Go after the hitter. Get ahead in the count. Don't be so fine with him!

"If I could get a heart surgeon in here, I'd have him open my chest and take out my heart, open your chest and take out your heart, and then I'd have him give you my heart! You'd be in the Hall of Fame! If I had your stuff, I'd be in the Hall of Fame! I've seen guys come and go, son, and you've got it! But you've got go out there and do it on the mound! Take charge! Make them hit your best stuff! Be aggressive! Be a bulldog out there! That's going to be your new name—Bulldog. When Dale Murphy hears, 'Now pitching for the Dodgers, number 55, Orel Hershiser,' man, he can't wait to get up there! But if he hears, 'Now pitching for the Dodgers, number 55, Bulldog Hershiser,' he's going to be scared to death!

"Starting today, I want you to believe you are the best pitcher in baseball. I want you to look at the hitter and say, 'There's no way you can hit me!' You gotta believe you are superior to the hitter and that you can get anybody out who walks up there. Quit giving the hitters so much credit! You're better than these guys."

"He was right," said Hershiser. "At first the nickname for me was a negative, because I wasn't a bulldog. But if you read between the lines he was telling me I'm a big-leaguer. He's telling me I can succeed here. He's not telling me my fastball isn't good enough or my breaking ball isn't good enough. He's not saying I couldn't throw strikes. He's saying here's the formula: you're going to be really tough, and when you're not I'm going to remind you to be. Being tough in his eyes was throwing strikes and getting ahead, getting the ball down, and never backing down, keep attacking, believing I was going to throw the ball there and they weren't going to hit it."

Two nights after the sermon, the Dodgers were in San Francisco. They needed a reliever, but the arms in the bullpen were sore. Three or four nights earlier, Hershiser might not have volunteered for duty. But on this night, despite his fatigue, Bulldog answered the call. "I jogged to the mound thinking about what Tommy had told me a couple nights earlier," he said. "He believed in me, and now he needed me to step up."

"Let's go, Bulldog! You can do it! You're my man, Bulldog!" hollered Tommy from the dugout.

On top of the cutter and sinker and curve, Hershiser was now armed with a new attitude. His approach had changed. "I challenged hitters, kept the ball low, and got ahead in the count to every batter," said Hershiser. He gave up one run in three innings. "I believed I deserved to be there, competing with big-leaguers, because I was a big-leaguer."

In late May, an injury to Jerry Reuss gave Hershiser a start. Facing the Cubs he went the distance, pitching a complete game and only giving up one run. One month later he joined the Dodgers rotation for good. His start against Chicago began the longest consecutive scoreless inning streak in the National League that year, at 33⅔ innings. He pitched four shutouts in July alone, and was named pitcher of the month. He was tied for the league lead in shutouts for the year, and finished third in ERA, sixth in complete games, and eighth in strikeouts.

• • •

The Bulldog's story is one of self-confidence. That's what Hershiser lacked, and that's what Tommy gave him. Hershiser was a winner, and he combined the self-confidence he gained from Tommy with the other qualities of a winner: hard work, competitiveness, and determination. Tommy had a hand in teaching him the importance of all of those.

"I think that Tommy portrayed hard work himself. The hours he put in, the intensity in which he put into the long hours," said Hershiser. "That intensity, that work ethic, it made me work that much harder behind closed doors when people weren't watching, because you knew that he was working when people weren't watching.

"Was he on? Yes, he was on. Was he on for the camera? By far. Was he on in the dugout? By far. But was he also on at midnight in his hotel room when he was talking to you about the game. He was also on at 2:00 in the afternoon at the ballpark when no one else was there, when he walked to the park from lunch and you could see the sweat coming off him in his street clothes, but he wasn't going to give up and get in a cab because he wanted to walk off his lunch. His life portrayed hard work. He never stopped. He never had an off day.

"He loved to teach, was always teaching, wherever we were. He used to critique and correct me on how to twirl my spaghetti. I said, 'Skipper, I'm twirling it this way as a right-hander, which as a right-hander I would twirl it right to left, counter-clockwise, because that's the way my sinker goes and I'm training my sinker.' Then as I became successful he would brag to people about the way I twirl my spaghetti. 'Look, I taught him how to twirl his spaghetti! It helps his sinker.' He took credit for it."

"One day Kenny Landreaux came to me and told me he was trying," said Tommy. "Try? Try? I can get a truck driver to try! If I brought a truck driver in here and told him he would make the type of money you're making if he tried, he would be out there from sunup to sundown trying!"

"I don't win with triers, I win with doers!"

Hershiser was a doer. He was known for compiling his own scouting reports on hitters on a computer, well before it was mainstream to do so. He was also known for using video well before it was popular. He was also committed to taking care of his body. "When I think of working behind closed doors, continuously working, I think about making sure I was on time for treatment to make sure my body was in shape," said Hershiser. "That's what allowed me to come in and pitch in relief. Also, having a manager that was that type of pitcher when he was pitching. I think if I had a conservative manager I wouldn't have been able to do any of that. But I had a manager who thought that the game today was the most important thing on earth and didn't care about tomorrow."

In Game 3 of the 1988 NLCS, Dodgers closer Jay Howell was ejected for having pine tar in his glove. The weather that afternoon was brutal. Cold and wet, pitchers and hitters alike had a hard time gripping their tools. In the bottom of the eighth, Howell ran the count on McReynolds to 3-2. Before the payoff pitch, Mets manager Davey Johnson came running out of the dugout. He talked to the home plate umpire, Joe West, and the two approached the mound. West asked to see Howell's glove and discovered the pine tar. Instead of McReynolds being awarded a base, Howell was ejected. His glove was given to National League president Bart Giamatti for inspection, and Howell was suspended for three games.

"The whole incident was totally uncalled for," said Tommy. "Pine tar does absolutely nothing to the flight of the ball. It is strictly used to get a better grip, just like a rosin bag." As always, Tommy had his players' backs. "I told Bart that I knew a chemist, and the chemist told me that pine tar is a liquid form of rosin. He reduced the suspension from three games to two. The truth is I never knew any chemist. I just wanted the world to know that my pitcher was not a cheater. If he had sandpaper in his glove and had scuffed the ball, I would have understood, but not pine tar."

In any case, Howell was out for Game 4 in New York. Tommy only had seven pitchers available because Tim Belcher, who was scheduled to start the next game, was back at the hotel resting. Plus, Hershiser had just thrown 110 pitches the night before. But Tommy was determined to win. "I held a meeting before the game," said Tommy. "I told my players that we were going to win with or without Jay Howell. The fate of our ballclub did not depend on one man." As the players were leaving the clubhouse, Hershiser walked over to Tommy and said, "I'll be your Jay Howell tonight."

The game went into extra innings, and in the top of the 12th, Kirk Gibson strode to the plate with two outs. As he approached the batter's box, Hershiser approached Perranoski. "I told him I was ready to go down to the bullpen," said Hershiser. "He thought I was kidding, but Tim Leary was warming up in the pen, and I told Perry that Timmy was our last right-handed pitcher. I would be ready if they needed me."

"I used to tell my players that there are three types of people, just like there are three types of players," said Tommy. "The first is the one who makes it happen, the second is the one who watches it happen, and the third is the one who wonders what just happened."

"Tommy wants you to be the one who makes it happen," said Hershiser. "He understands and teaches guys to embrace the big moment. He doesn't back down from it. When you embrace the moment, and you have his intensity, his determination, his passion for winning, you have the whole package."

Hershiser went into the clubhouse to put on his cleats; he was going to make it happen. A few of his teammates were huddled in the corner, and when they saw him getting ready, they asked what he was up to. "If Gibson hits one out, they might need me," he said.

Hobbled by injury, Gibson had endured a tough NLCS. He was just 1-for-16, and he was at the plate facing Mets reliever Roger McDowell, who had only given up one game-winning home run all season. Gibson smashed one to the center-right gap, and as the ball sailed over the wall, Hershiser strode toward the bullpen. When he got to the bullpen coach Mark Cresse was as shocked to see him as the Dodgers were to see Gibson's blast.

In the bottom of the 12th, Leary got into trouble. He gave up two singles, got an out, and was set to face the heart of the order. "If we lose this game we are down 3–1," said Tommy. "The night before, Jesse Orosco had a bad game, but he was our only lefty in the pen. I told Perranoski that if I was going to manage this game right, I had to bring him in to face Keith Hernandez, who was a lefty." Perranoski reminded Tommy that Orosco was their last relief pitcher, to which Tommy replied, "Go get him."

Orosco proceeded to walk Hernandez, which loaded the bases with only one out and the Dodgers protecting a one-run lead in the wee hours of the morning. Next up was Strawberry. He took a massive swing at the first pitch that sucked the air out of the stadium. If he had connected the ball would have landed on a runway at LaGuardia, a few miles away from the ballpark. He then threw three straight balls. "Before he was going to throw another pitch," Tommy said, "I was going to tell him exactly what I thought about him, so I ran out to the mound. I said some choice things to him that he had never heard before. Before the next pitch, I made seven promises to God in about a minute. I asked Perranoski if he thought the Lord would make it possible for Strawberry to strike out or pop up, because if he did I was going to bring in the Bulldog." Before Perranoski could even answer, Orosco got Strawberry to hit a short pop fly to second for the second out.

"Go get him, Ronnie," said Tommy. "I'm putting the whole ball of wax on the Bulldog!" As Hershiser took that long jog from the bullpen to the mound, the thoughts raced through his mind. "I had asked for the opportunity," said Hershiser. "But now it was real. I was thinking about pestering Tommy and Ronnie about relieving, about getting dressed, seeing Gibby's home run, warming up, being the last pitcher on the roster, and now it was my turn to perform. We needed this game, and it was the bottom of the 12th with the bases loaded and two outs. I had no days' rest and was about to face one of the best hitters in the game. I was afraid, but there was no looking back."

Tommy probably wasn't afraid, but he was well aware of the situation. "All I could think about was if Bulldog walked a guy, threw a wild pitch, or if the game gets tied, that I wouldn't have anyone else," said Tommy. "I peeked out of the dugout again and looked up and asked the Big Dodger in the Sky that if He could see it clear to letting this guy make an out that I would never ask Him for anything ever again!"

As McReynolds dug into the box, Hershiser dug in on the mound. He looked in for the sign with the same steely glare that hitters had seen all year. McReynolds fouled off the first pitch. The next pitch was a ball. Then Hershiser threw a fastball in, with a bit of movement on it, and McReynolds took a swing and made contact, sending the ball to John Shelby in center. "I felt like I was pulling for a thoroughbred coming around the third turn," said Tommy. "I kept yelling, 'Come on, John! Come on, John!' Thankfully he made the catch."

"We won 5–4," said Hershiser. "It was the most emotional win of my career, because of all the adversity."

As that last out was made and the Dodgers were celebrating their survival, Tommy sat in the dugout looking like a prize fighter in his corner of the ring, drenched in a mixture of sweat, exhaustion, and relief. "After the game Perranoski came over to me and asked me what I would have done if Bulldog didn't get the out," said Tommy. "I told him that my four brothers were in the stands, and that if they tied it I would have had them blow out the lights!"

While the qualities that allowed Hershiser to rise to the occasion again and again were always somewhere inside him, Tommy forced him to bring them out, to use his talents to the best of his ability, to change his approach and attitude. "Tommy changed my life," said Hershiser. "He wanted more than what you had, and he believed it was his job to pull it out of you. He wasn't going to convince you, he wasn't going to cajole you; he was going to pull it out of you even if he had to yank it out of you. That was his style.

"Looking back on my career, I can recognize all the things he did for me as a person and really appreciate it. I stood next to him three times last season during the national anthem and kissed him on the forehead each time. He's my baseball dad."

• • •

While Hershiser was the Bulldog of the '88 Dodgers, Kirk Gibson was the leader, and as such was always attuned to the rhythms of the team. When asked about Hershiser's performance in relief, he said that it proved that Hershiser put the team before himself, and that his only motivation was winning. While Hershiser did something miraculous in 1988, so too did Gibson. While Hershiser's life and career would be changed forever because of Tommy's teachings, so too were Gibson's.

Gibson's home run in Game 1 of the 1988 World Series has gone down in baseball lore. It is a story that has been told by fathers to their sons, by coaches to their players, by pastors to their congregations, by teachers to their students, by anyone trying to motivate someone to persevere through adversity, by anyone trying to get someone else to believe in themselves, by anyone trying to convince someone else that the impossible can happen, that the long odds can be beaten, that the house doesn't always win.

It's a story that makes you believe. Anyone can be the Kirk Gibson of an impossible situation; anyone can be a hero if he or she wants it badly enough. Anyone can be a winner, if you believe.

Gibson had been a star wide receiver for Michigan State University, and only played college baseball to improve his NFL draft leverage. After being selected by the Detroit Tigers and reporting to his first spring training, he realized that translating college success into major league stardom would be a huge challenge. He had never even used a wooden bat. Still, the Detroit scouts liked him. They thought his talent and grit would overcome his lack of experience. After seeing him play, Detroit manager Sparky Anderson compared him to Mickey Mantle.

Gibson combined his talent and football mentality and made it to the big leagues in just two years. Even though he was a big-leaguer coming out of spring training in 1980, he was still learning the game from Anderson. "I was a young kid and he taught me how to play the game," said Gibson. "With Sparky, the first thing you do is learn how to be a professional baseball player: the schedule, spring training, travel, and then the mechanics of it, and the fundamentals and the philosophies of your manager. And if you weren't going to do it Sparky's way, you weren't going to be around."

In January 1988, an arbitrator ruled that the owners were in collusion and made Gibson a free agent, and with that the Dodgers offered him a contract. After signing and reporting to the Dodgers for spring training, he met Tommy and soon saw the differences between the Tigers and Dodgers, the differences between Anderson and Tommy.

"Sparky was a very serious, mechanical, this is what we're going to do, no nonsense, let's get to work kind of guy," said Gibson. "Tommy was much more outspoken, vibrant, humorous, and vocal. He took me to the next level in my game. We had a meeting before practice and Mark Cresse would go over the schedule. There were equipment trunks in there and there would be clowns jumping out of the trunks, and Tommy was telling jokes, and it was a very different environment for me. It was one that was very uncomfortable because I was coming from someplace different.

"After the meeting I went out to the field to stretch and run. I got lathered up with sweat and I took my hat off and wiped my head and saw all this black stuff all over my arm. Everybody was laughing at me. Someone had put eyeblack inside my hat. I came running off the field and Tommy was walking on the field and I said, 'You go find the guy who did that!' He had no idea what I was talking about."

Gibson was already in a bad mood, because earlier in the practice some of his teammates had taken a lackadaisical approach to fielding bunts. Finding out that Jesse Orosco was the one behind the eyeblack prank, and then watching everyone laugh about it, didn't help matters.

The next morning, Tommy called Gibson into his bungalow at Dodgertown. "He went on this long story about trying to obviously get me through the moment," said Gibson. "He realized where I came from and where I was and the intention was all fun but I was a no-nonsense guy. He talked for 15 or 20 minutes and I never said a word."

Tommy then arranged for Gibson to speak in front of the team. "I stood up in front of them and said, 'Hey, this is what's bothering me,'" Gibson recalled. "'We are practicing bunt plays and guys are picking them up and throwing them into right field, everybody's laughing. It's not funny. You finished in fourth place the last two years, the Cardinals are running around you like you're Little Leaguers, and you guys don't know me but I'm very serious about this. What are we here for? We're here to be world champions. I've been a world champ. You don't become world champions by just stumbling into it. That game yesterday was like the seventh game of the World Series to me even though it was the first game."

With that, and with quite a few expletives, Gibson made them realize how important winning was to him. He also made them a promise, one that he would fulfill that October as he dug into the batter's box at Dodger Stadium before 55,983 fans and one All-Star closer. "I will be your best teammate. I promise you I will," said Gibson.

"I saw a lot of me in him. I saw a player who would do anything to beat you, who wanted to win," said Tommy. "He believed he was there to win. I would tell my players that if one half of the team got on one end of the rope

and the other half got on the other end, we could pull all day long but we would be pulling against ourselves. But if we all got on one end of the rope, we could pull the rest of the league with us."

After that meeting, Tommy was a believer in Gibson. Tommy wanted him to be an extension of the manager, to be the team leader. But before he could count on that, he needed to build the trust between the two. Early in the season, Tommy invited Gibson out for a drink. The two sat together and talked baseball and about themselves. They talked about Gibson's wife, his newborn child, and his parents. "We became close," said Gibson. "He took the time out to know me and we spent the time together. He's amazing with names. I remember my brother-in-law Mike came in one time, and then one day out of nowhere, Tommy said, 'Hey, how's Mike doing?' He's a master at that. You understand that he does care about you. We became friends and I began to trust him, then I began to trust his words and understood him. I understood the hugs and all the jokes."

Just as Gibson embraced the work ethic that Tommy taught, he fully embraced and embodied his manager's competitiveness. He was an intimidator in the cage, in the batter's box, and on the base paths. In a June game against the Reds, he led off the top of the ninth against John Franco, who hadn't blown a save all year. He hit a line drive to left-center and was determined to leg out a double, even though the ball didn't get past the center fielder. After an ugly slide and a cloud of dirt, Gibson was safe at second. Two batters later, Shelby drove him in to tie the score. The Dodgers won the game.

In another game against Cincinnati, Gibson singled in the bottom of the ninth, trailing 3–2. With two outs, Shelby hit a grounder to third that the third baseman had to dive for. He made a bad throw to first, and Gibson had never stopped running. He scored from first on sore legs. The Dodgers won 5–3.

In a September game against the Braves, while Hershiser was in the middle of his streak, Ron Gant hit a shot headed for the wall. Gibson raced back to the track and crashed into the wall to make the catch. In the ninth inning he walked, then scored all the way from first on a Mike Marshall double. The Dodgers won 1–0.

Gibson hated to lose. He was so determined to be a good teammate, to be there in the clutch, to deliver on his spring training promise, to live up to Tommy's expectations, that he played through numerous injuries. Chronic hamstring soreness and strained buttocks were only worsened during a game in September against the Mets. He singled and stole second, and felt a burning in the back of his leg. In the field, he felt a knot in his leg and had to stand on his left foot.

As the Dodgers prepared to play the Mets for a chance to go to the Fall Classic, Gibson was truly hurting. Playing through the nagging injuries had taken a toll. He had played in six of the final 14 games of the season despite the pain. When asked about his availability, he said, "I will be in the lineup." When asked the same question, Tommy said, "If he's breathing, he's in there."

He was in there. He was 0-for-6 with two walks in the first two games. The conditions for Game 3 were brutal. A Michigan native, Gibson said it was the coldest game he'd ever played in. Despite the weather conditions and the condition of his body, he made a diving catch and bumped his knee on the ground. In Game 4, in the midst of a 1-for-16 slump, he hit that solo bomb off Roger McDowell in the 12th to give the Dodgers the lead. He hit another home run in Game 5. Later, with the score 6–4, he stole second and felt a pop in his leg. After the game the injury report was an aggravated right hamstring. The Dodgers won 7–4. He was back in the lineup for Game 6 but went 0-for-4. The Dodgers lost 5–1.

Even with his slumping bat and sore legs, Gibson was back in the lineup for Game 7. The Dodgers were up 4–0 in the bottom of the second when Gibson was intentionally walked. Marshall hit a grounder that looked like a double-play ball. Running hard on his bad legs, Gibson slid into second and pulled Kevin Elster off the bag. His gutsy slide allowed a run to score and gave the Dodgers a 5–0 lead. He had also pulled a ligament in his knee. He stayed in the game but only lasted three more innings.

The Dodgers won that game and the National League pennant. Instead of celebrating with his teammates, Gibson was reflective. "All I was thinking was, *What am I going to do to get myself ready to play in a few days?*" he recalls.

The Dodgers and the A's had two days of rest before the World Series started. During that respite, Gibson received shots, treatments, rubdowns, and stayed off his legs as much as he could. The medical care, combined with his determination and a few prayers, weren't enough to heal his ailments.

He wasn't on the field for the pregame introductions, as he didn't want to be a distraction to his teammates. He knew he wasn't going to play and even called his wife and told her to go home to tend to their newborn. But the pain in his legs wasn't as bad as the pain of being out of the lineup. "It crushed me," said Gibson.

In the bottom of the third inning, the cameras caught him talking to Jeff Hamilton in the dugout. Vin Scully said, "His knee was injected with lidocaine and cortisone. His condition is day-to-day. Maybe he can play later in the series, but not today."

The Dodgers trailed 4–3 in the eighth. Gibson was sitting on the trainer's table with ice on both legs. He heard Scully say, "Is Gibson in the Dodgers dugout? The answer would appear to be no." Gibson hated hearing that. "I realized we had Dave Anderson left and myself," he recalls. "It was the moment I knew my teammates really expected me there."

He gingerly climbed off the table and told a clubhouse attendant to get his uniform. He made his way to the batting cage in the tunnel of Dodger Stadium that connects the clubhouse to the dugout. His knees were numb from the shots and the ice. Taking wincing swings, he hit balls off a tee, then gave Dodgers clubby Mitch Poole a message to give to Lasorda: "Go tell Tommy I can hit."

Tommy inserted his aching slugger into the lineup to pinch hit for Dave Anderson as the crowd rose to its feet. Dennis Eckersley, the All-Star closer for the A's, thought he was ready for his crippled opponent. After working the count to 3-2, Eckersley found out that Gibson was ready for him as he swung at a backdoor slider.

Nobody in Dodger Stadium expected to see his swing, a swing of pure upper-body strength, connect with the pitch. Nobody expected to see the ball sail toward the right field bleachers. Nobody expected that game-winning home run, a blast that propelled the Dodgers to a World Series championship. As Gibson rounded the bases, Vin Scully famously said, "In a season that has been so improbable, the impossible has happened!" Later, Tommy said, "I have seen many home runs of great significance, but none as paralyzing as Gibby's."

Gibson had delivered on his spring training promise. Throughout the season he was the embodiment of what it takes to win. "When it all comes together, you understand that we are operating as a 'we' not as an 'I' and you are so much more powerful," he said. "I was hurt and out of the game, and as I watched the game unfold I decided I was going to do it. I was compelled to do it. I wanted to do it for our team. I wanted to do it for Tommy."

That one swing cemented Gibson's legacy as a winner, a culmination of the lessons Tommy had taught. "He was such a great motivator. It was just how he brought us all together," said Gibson. "When I see him today, it's like '88 was yesterday. He is ageless." So is that home run. So is the trust between them.

As Hershiser knelt to the ground in thanks after winning Game 7, perhaps he was remembering the sermon on the mound Tommy gave him. And as Gibson hobbled around third base on his way to an ecstatic mob of teammates waiting for him at the plate, perhaps he was thinking about the conversation he had with Tommy when the two went for a drink earlier in the season. No matter what they were thinking, in the end, we think of them as winners.

CHAPTER 6

FAMILY

"The foundation for life is love and respect."

It was early November 2007. While the weather was overcast at Dodger Stadium, the sun was shining on the Dodgers family. Joe Torre, the legendary manager who guided the Yankees to four World Series championships, was being introduced as manager of the Dodgers. A New York native, Torre spent his childhood rooting for the New York Giants, and thus rooting against both the team with which he found glory and the team he was about to lead. Still, he respected the Dodgers for what they had been in Brooklyn, and for what they did in Los Angeles.

In his remarks at the podium he said, "This is one of a handful of organizations you automatically say yes to. The Dodgers were always special and I certainly expect the Dodgers will always be special. I get choked up. Look at Tommy over there. He used to hug all his players and we laughed at him. Now we all do it."

That statement of fact was also one of reverence. It was an indication of how Tommy helped change the game of baseball. It was an indication of how his style of managing had an effect on the competition. Torre was fired by the Mets, the Braves, and the Cardinals before finding success with the Yankees. Surely part of what he learned through his failures, part of what he learned that helped him finally succeed, was that managing is about relating to your players, about treating them like people.

That approach was a hallmark of Tommy's managerial style. It is part of why he is in the Hall of Fame, part of why his teams won World Series championships, part of why he helped transform careers, part of why his players and teams did the impossible on the field, part of why he sent so many minor league players to the big leagues, and part of why so many of his players love him like a father. He is godfather to 18 children, and numerous children of former players call him Uncle Tommy to this day.

"If I wanted respect, I would have to give respect," said Tommy. "I felt that if I gave respect they would give it back."

The love and respect Tommy gave his players, and received in return, was something he developed along his way from Norristown to Cooperstown. In the Lasorda household, love and respect were always on display; displaying good manners was a sign of respect. "If our table was full and a guest showed up, I would have to get up from the table to give them my seat," said Tommy. "If I wore my hat in the house, my father would knock it off my head."

Most of Tommy's lessons came from his parents, but one in particular came from the back of a Carnation can. "I was sitting at the table one day and what possessed me to read the back of the can I'll never know, but on the back it said CONTENTED COWS GIVE BETTER MILK," said Tommy. "I never forgot that. That's how I treated my players."

Tommy showed love and respect to his players in many ways. He would dream with them about playing in the big leagues. He would work with them toward realizing those dreams. He attended their weddings, birthday parties, and the christenings and bar mitzvahs of their children. He would console their worried parents. He would stand up to the organization for them. He would joke with them. He would encourage them. He would motivate them. He would believe in them. He would give them the Lasorda hug. He would treat them as family.

The Dodgers organization also put a priority on family. As a young player, Tommy wanted to marry his beloved Jo but couldn't afford it. "I had saved up $700 playing in Panama," said Tommy. "But in those days we were five or six guys to a room and someone stole my money. I wanted to get married though, so I went to Mr. Rickey and told him my problem." Rickey directed Tommy to Buzzie Bavasi, who was the general manager of the Montreal team. Just like that, Tommy had the money he needed.

"When my first check came I didn't see any money deducted. I told Buzzie that he needed to take the money out of my check so I could pay the loan back. He told me not to worry about it, that we would settle it. At the end of the season, he called me in and told me to sign this letter. It said DEAR MR. RICKEY, THANK YOU FOR THE LOAN OF $500. I WAS HAPPY I COULD PAY IT BACK TO YOU. But Buzzie never took the $500."

When Tommy became manager of the Dodgers, treating his players and coaches like family was a practice he was determined to institute on the big league level. He did so because he believed in its effect. It was a practice he started while coaching in the minors, and it was manifested in part by taking his guys out to eat.

"When I would come down in the mornings, there would be seven or eight of them waiting for me and we'd go get breakfast," said Tommy. "We would go to the Chuck-A-Rama buffet in Ogden. The manager cried when he saw us coming. It was all you can eat for $1.50. We cleaned the place out. We crushed it. We would be at the table eating, but I would be teaching, going over the game situations, ways to improve each player.

"I knew every player's wife's name, every player's kids' names. Why? Because when you do that you feel even closer. You know them better because you know their family. Al [Campanis] told me that I wasn't supposed to go out and eat with my players. I said, 'Al, let me ask you a question. If I speak at the Rotary Club and there are four of my players there, do I sit with them?' He said, 'Sure, but the manager never asked me to sit or eat with them.' And I said, 'Well, maybe he didn't want you to eat with him!'"

Another manifestation of Tommy's family-oriented managerial style was the Lasorda hug. If a manager eating with his players was considered unusual, hugging them was considered completely over the line. But Tommy loved his players; he respected their effort, he shared in their desire, and he basked in their glory. "It just came natural," said Tommy. "I was so engrossed in the game that when something good happened, I would just give them a hug. I would hug them when times were going bad, too, because that's when they needed it more than ever."

Dodgers fans have seen hugs in person at Dodger Stadium, on TV, in highlight reels and celebratory parades around the streets of Los Angeles. Hershiser got one after his performance in Game 4 of the 1988 NLCS. Gibson got one after his home run in the '88 World Series. Over the years, so did Cey and Garvey, Scioscia and Valentine, Buckner and Monday, and Hough and Piazza. Tommy loved his players and was never afraid to show it, a trait he developed as a child. "My brothers and I were thick as thieves," said Tommy. "We didn't have any money growing up, but we had a house full of love."

It also came from his upbringing in the Dodgers organization as a young player. "I was playing in Montreal, and Jo was about to give birth to our first child. I couldn't be there because we were on the road," said Tommy. "I never wanted that to happen to any of my players. They were away from home so much that when they came home, they wanted to do things with their kids but they couldn't because they were playing. I told them to bring them to the clubhouse, let them see what a major league clubhouse was like, major league players. If they wanted to go out on the field and work with them that was fine, too."

Tim Wallach joined the Dodgers in 1993 after playing for the Montreal Expos for 13 seasons. He quickly became one of Tommy's favorites. "I admired Wallach [while] playing against him. I had a lot of respect for him," said Tommy. "I saw the way he conducted himself on the field, played the game. When we got him it was a privilege and honor to be his manager."

Tommy and Wallach had a lot in common. They both lived in Orange County. They both played in Montreal and have since been inducted into the Canadian Baseball Hall of Fame. They both managed in Albuquerque. They share the same middle name, Charles. They were both passed over by scouts. They both love the game of baseball. And they are both family men. A Southern California native, Wallach grew up watching Tommy's Dodgers play. Before joining them, he knew Tommy only as the competition, but when he put on the Dodgers jersey he came to know him in a new light.

"I played for eight managers over my career," said Wallach. "Tommy was one of a kind. The biggest thing Tommy taught me is how to relate to your players. He was the best motivator I played for. At times it was tough motivation, but it was always to make you better. He knew what it took to be at your best every day. He knew that to get the most out of the players, they need to know that he loved them. When I came up, relating to players was probably the last quality managers thought about having. It was all about running a game. When you were a young guy coming up they didn't spend as much time with you getting to know you. Basically, if you could help them, you made the team and you played. That was the way the majority of the managers were. Now, I think a majority of the managers are more like Tommy. You pretty much have to be in this day and age."

Wallach had great career in baseball. In 17 years he amassed 2,085 hits, 260 home runs, and drove in 1,125 runs. One of his fondest memories came as a Dodger: on September 22, 1995, Wallach collected his 2,000th career hit. It also made a great birthday present for Tommy, who turned 68 that day. In the bottom of the fifth inning, Wallach stepped to the plate against Bryce Florie of the Padres. In front on 43,627 fans at Dodger Stadium, Wallach lined the first pitch between third and short. When Wallach reached first the crowd gave him a standing ovation, and in return he tipped his helmet in appreciation twice.

"Besides making the playoffs in 1995 and '96, that was definitely the highlight of my career with the Dodgers," said Wallach.

Fewer than 300 players in the history of baseball have reached the 2,000-hit mark. When Wallach returned to the dugout after scoring later in the inning, he got a Lasorda hug from his skipper. After the game, he got a couple more.

"I used to scout Wallach when he played for Cal State Fullerton," said Tommy. "I was impressed with him then and I hoped we could draft him. He went to Montreal and had an outstanding career, but to be his manager when he collected his 2,000th hit, I was so proud."

But what struck Wallach most about his time playing for Tommy was his manager's emphasis on family. "One of the amazing things was he remembered everyone's name," Wallach says. "Kids, wives, relatives. He would remember my father-in-law's name. He was amazing at that. I still look back to my first year in Los Angeles, 1993. My three boys at the time were seven, four, and I had a one-year-old. My youngest son, Chad, was always a pretty good eater. He was always a big kid. Tommy always had a spread in his office after the game. He always allowed the kids to come down after the game, and he always wanted them in the clubhouse with him. He just loved the kids. He would always have Chad on his knee, feeding him ribs. He would come out of there with barbeque sauce and whatever else was in the room all over his face. I was there for four years with Tommy, and he helped him grow probably faster than he should have."

While Chad Wallach was busy crushing ribs, Wallach's other sons were busy crushing baseballs in batting practice. As the Wallach boys grew and improved, Tommy was there teaching them. As they played in high school, he was there scouting them. As they graduated, he was there to give them a hug and to help them realize their dreams. Matt Wallach was picked by the Dodgers in the 22nd round of the 2007 draft as a catcher. The Dodgers selected Brett Wallach as a pitcher in the third round of the 2009 draft out of Orange Coast College. Chad Wallach, the rib eater, was also drafted by the Dodgers but decided to go to college. He was selected by the Miami Marlins in the fifth round of the 2013 draft.

While the Wallach boys loved their Uncle Tommy, so too did the Shelby boys. John Shelby joined the Dodgers in 1987, and in doing so, his wife, Trina, and their six children joined the Dodgers, too. John T. III, Jeremy, Justin, JaVon, and Jaren could fill an infield with their sister, Tiara, on the mound. Before joining the Dodgers, Shelby played for the Baltimore Orioles. In the 1983 World Series he went 4-for-9 and drove in the game-winning run in Game 4 as the Orioles went on to beat the Phillies for the championship. His manager was the great Earl Weaver, another Hall of Fame skipper.

"Earl was a very, very good manager," said Shelby. "He knew how to use his players well. But he wasn't one that did a lot of joking. That was the difference when I got to the Dodgers. Tommy was a lot more personable. He was fun to be around. He laughed and joked. It was different. It took a little while to get used to because you never saw a manager walking around joking, interacting the way he did. But I liked that. I really liked that. I enjoyed it. I think a lot of the players enjoyed it, too.

"Being traded to the Dodgers was the best experience of my life. Baltimore was a great organization but the Dodgers were first class. Once I got traded over to the Dodgers it was like family. Mr. O'Malley and his family cared about the organization, they cared about family. Coming over with Tommy, he just took all the kids like they were his own children. Spoiled my kids, spoiled my wife—we just felt like it was the best organization I ever played for."

Shelby started in center for the Dodgers in 1988 and hit .263 with 10 home runs. He was a key component to their World Series roster and made clutch plays throughout the postseason. "I didn't really know what type of season we would have, but there were some good players on the team and there was a lot of excitement at spring training," he said. "It started with whoever put the black stuff in Kirk Gibson's hat. Goodness gracious! So much stuff went on that it wasn't like we were winning every game. We may have been a little over .500, but we were having fun. It was a team that was together. It really stood out because Gibby was a leader and everybody enjoyed playing. We had a lot of things that added a lot of flavor to the ballclub. Just one of those seasons that you didn't want to see end."

Shelby's favorite memory of his time with Tommy and the Dodgers is telling. "I'll never forget when my oldest son was little," said Shelby. "With the Orioles, you couldn't bring your kids to the locker room. All of a sudden I get to the Dodgers and Tommy is asking about my little boy. I told him I wasn't used to bringing him to the ballpark, and he said, 'Everybody brings their sons to the ballpark and then the moms come and get them.' I told him I didn't feel comfortable with that, and he looked at me and said, 'He better be here tomorrow,' and he turned and walked away. John T. was at the park the next day."

Shelby was able to fulfill a dream that just about every father has: playing catch with his son in a major league ballpark. "Justin may have been around seven. He was standing in the outfield and put his glove up as I hit him pop flies. My two youngest boys had caught I don't know how many balls, and my son Justin had never caught a fly ball. All of a sudden he's standing in the outfield like the movie *The Sandlot*, a fly ball comes, he puts his glove up, catches it, and all of a sudden he's looking inside his glove and looking around and he's jumping up and down. My boy made his first catch at Dodger Stadium!

"Those are memories, had it not been for the way that Tommy and the Dodgers did things, that I would have never had. That's what the Dodgers were: committed to family."

After Shelby retired from playing he had the opportunity to coach. From Butte, Montana, in the Pioneer League to rookie ball to an Independent League team, Shelby was gaining experience. Eventually Tommy found a spot for him on the Dodgers staff. "One thing he said that I'll never forget," Shelby said. "'If I ever get a chance to get you back up in the major leagues, you can believe I'm going to bring you.'"

Shelby has since been coaching at some level of the game since 1998. Wherever his career has taken him he has taken some of Tommy with him. "One of the things I really enjoyed was the way he interacted with his players," said Shelby. "He got a chance to know them. He had fun with them, and that's one of the things I wanted to do. When I came up you didn't really interact with the coaches. It was more they're the coach, you're the player, and you do your job and be a ballplayer. But with him and the Dodgers organization, it was like a family. I just never had a manager who talked to you and asked about your family, about your sons. It wasn't just my son; it was everybody's sons. That was the difference."

• • •

One of Shelby's teammates on the '87 Dodgers was Glenn Hoffman. Like Shelby, he had been acquired by the Dodgers in a trade and would become one of Tommy's favorites. Like Shelby, Hoffman went into coaching after his playing days were over, and even managed the Dodgers. And like Shelby, he came to the Dodgers with an infield's-worth of kids who loved baseball, kids who would grow up loving their Uncle Tom. Hoffman and his wife, Cheryl, brought Sarah, Stacy, Sabrina, and twins Drake and Dylan to the Dodgers family.

"Tommy was like a father to me," said Hoffman. "I was so blessed to play for him, to be around him in my early years of coaching, and for him to give me the opportunity to manage and be my GM."

After retiring and taking some time away from the game, Hoffman rejoined the Dodgers organization as a minor league coach in 1991. During the '98 season, manager Bill Russell was fired and Hoffman was given the job on an interim basis. "I was happy for Glenn," said Tommy, who was serving as the interim GM at the time. "I had just left him when he was the Triple A manager. I told him not to get down because he would be a big league manager one day. Two days later he got the job."

"It was exciting and nerve-wracking," said Hoffman. "I am real appreciative of what people go through being a manager, and what he did, and how he was the glue to the Dodgers. He managed people by making them feel welcome."

Tommy had started a tradition of walking around Dodgertown after dinner with the minor league coaches. "He would take us out to eat at Bobby's on the Beach or at the dining room at Dodgertown, which was outstanding," said Hoffman. "We would go back and walk the streets of Dodgertown and talk baseball, walk and talk, walk and talk, until he was tired and ready to go back to his bungalow. They would be long walks because he loves to talk about the game. He taught me to be positive, to have enthusiasm while you coach, because if you love this game you have to show it to your players. Show the players you care for them, because when they know you care for them their hearts are connected to you. He has the biggest heart."

Once, Tommy was to be honored at an event at the Waldorf Astoria in New York. Due to a problem with his plane, he found himself stranded in Phoenix and asked Hoffman for a ride. Hoffman and his family were on their way to dinner at a Boston Market restaurant, so Tommy tagged along. "He's got his suit on and he's sitting there with my five kids," Hoffman said. "At the time my twins were probably about two years old, and he wanted to sit right between them. The kids were throwing food but he was having a great time. He kept joking by saying, 'I could be in New York getting honored but instead I'm with the Hoffman family getting food thrown at me!'"

"One of his sons picked up the ketchup with his left hand and threw it at me," said Tommy. "I thought we might have found our next star pitcher."

"We were at winter workouts at Dodger Stadium and I brought my two boys to the workout," said Hoffman. "Tommy got a hold of them and was having them run around and slide headfirst into the bases, and the boys were just loving it. Little did he know the boys were going into the hospital the next day to have surgeries for their hernias. During the entire workout he kept after my boys, asking them how they felt, and each time they would say fine or good. He would holler at them, 'I want to hear you say you feel great! Next time I ask you how you feel, all I want to hear is great!' He had my boys saying 'great' all day long. They next day we are at the Children's Hospital and both boys were on gurneys being wheeled around. I asked them how they felt, and they both said, 'Dad, we feel great.'

"The impression he makes on kids, and anyone whose life he's touched, it's just unbelievable. The day that you are around him, you are blessed. As a player or a person, it's amazing that when you are around him he just gives you the confidence and the belief, and I just can't thank him enough for what he's done for me and my family."

• • •

The list of players who felt and witnessed Tommy's commitment to family is a long one. It includes those who only had a cup of coffee in the big leagues, perennial All-Stars, and all manner of players in between.

Kenny Howell was drafted in the third round of the 1982 draft out of Tuskegee University. A towering 6'3", Howell was a hard-throwing right-hander with a sharp slider and a good split-fingered fastball. He reported to his first spring training in 1983, where he met Tommy. "I was there to be an extra guy," said Howell. "I would make trips but wouldn't pitch, but finally

I got into a couple games and he brought me on every trip. That's how I got to know Tommy, and how I got to the big leagues so fast."

Howell only played minor league ball for about 18 months, but that was long enough to become schooled in the Dodger Way. "Competitiveness is one of the major points of being a Dodger," said Howell. "You have to believe that you are better than anyone else on the field, and we were always taught that. We established what class meant to an organization. Everywhere we played teams hated us, because the O'Malleys treated us so good, and Tommy made sure everything we did was first class. Tommy taught us how to go out there and defend ourselves, and how to defend playing for an organization like that. I understood what it meant to be a Dodger through Tommy and Al Campanis. Those guys were like our fathers. They weren't just managers or coaches, they were like parents for us. I learned from Tommy, especially as a young player, that you are going to spend more time with those 24 other guys than you will with your family. You better get to know them, get to know how to be with them. I think that was the biggest thing I had to learn, understanding that I had a family away from home that I had to be around all the time. Tommy kept us all together and made sure that we understood what the brotherhood was about, and what being a teammate was about."

Tommy also understood how important a strong support system was to any young player. That's why he'd go out of his way to nurture it at every turn.

"I had just been called up," Howell said. "I was in the bullpen and Tommy had me get up and throw. He knew I wasn't going to get into the game, but he had me get up to throw so my parents could see me on TV. That was cool. He knew I wasn't going to pitch, but did that for me and my parents anyway. Vin Scully said my name and who I was, and my parents saw it. Tommy wanted to make sure I felt like I was part of the team. I wasn't sure when I would ever get in a game, but it felt good that he did that for me. The TV showed me warming up and had my name on the screen. My parents called me and were so excited. Tommy understood when young players came up how important it was to get them feeling like part of the team, feeling like a big-leaguer, as quickly as possible."

"In spring training I used to get a minor leaguer or two and invite them to my table to eat with me," said Tommy. "I would bring the phone over to the table and let them call their parents. Half of the parents didn't believe I was sitting right there next to their sons."

"I was happy to do that for Kenny, because I thought the world of him. Kenny was a die-hard. He gave every ounce of energy he had, but more importantly, he was a great guy. You could tell how he was brought up. You could tell by watching the way he acted and the way he conducted himself. You saw Kenny and you had to love him, because no way would he ever give you any problems on or off the field. He had great ability. I used him in clutch situations. I had no fear in sending him out in any situation in the game, early, late, middle-man, whatever. You knew he would give it all he had, and he had a lot to give."

Tommy played a role in another baseball family, a family that grew up in Northern California hating the Dodgers but would come to love Dodger Blue after two boys played in the organization. Tommy gave confidence to one of the sons and comfort to both when they needed it most.

Steve Sax was drafted by the Dodgers in the ninth round of the 1978 draft. His brother, Dave, was signed as a free agent by the Dodgers later that year. The Sax brothers hailed from West Sacramento, California, and were Giants fans as kids. In fact, Steve once told his father that he wouldn't play for the Dodgers if they paid him $1 million to do so. His youthful hubris proved wrong, as he was part of the 1981 and '88 World Series champions. He was one of Tommy's nine Rookie of the Year award recipients, his coming in 1982 after limited playing time at the end of '81 and into the postseason. An above-average hitter with a lifetime batting average of .281, Steve stole 40 or more bases six times and finished his career with 444 steals. Dave didn't have the career that Steve did, but he did play in the big leagues.

The Sax brothers' father, John, was a truck driver and a farmer. His fatherly advice was delivered in a booming voice, whether he was behind the backstop during Little League games or at the family dinner table. "My dad commanded respect," said Steve. "We would never argue with him or disrespect him. It was his way or the highway. My dad brought us up to be tough, work hard, and to take a lot of pride in whatever we did. That's how he lived his life. But at the same time he loved us very much. He was always there for us because he loved being with his family. He put my mother on a pedestal every single day."

When the brothers joined the Dodgers, John Sax couldn't have been prouder. "My mother told me that seeing his sons play major league baseball was one of the proudest moments of his life," said Steve. Although John was German and Tommy was Italian, they shared many characteristics. When Steve joined the Dodgers and met Tommy he felt right at home; it was as if he was hearing his father yelling from behind the fences of the fields in Sacramento, rather than Tommy yelling from the dugouts at Dodgertown in Vero Beach.

"My dad was a little more reserved than Tommy was, but they both commanded respect, they both had the same goals, both worked hard, they had the same values," said Steve. "Tommy was like a father figure to me."

"I liked his enthusiasm and I like that he played hard," said Tommy. "I also liked that he was part Italian. Half a loaf is better than none!" He liked him even more after Steve's stellar '82 season: he hit .282, stole 49 bases, and was named to the National League All-Star team, which was managed by Tommy.

"Steve was a breath of fresh air," said Tommy. "He played baseball like my wife shops—all day long. The only problem with Saxy was that his intelligence never reached the level of his play. We were in San Francisco and I was behind the cage during BP. I had been harping on Saxy all season about using the entire field, hitting the ball to all three parts of the field. He came to me and said, 'Skipper, instead of hitting the ball to left field, I am going to start hitting to all fields. Eighty percent of the time I'll hit the ball up the middle. Twenty percent of the time I'll hit it to left, and the other 20 percent I'll hit it to right.'"

As endearing as that was, it also gave Tommy a few more grey hairs. Sax gave Tommy few more while he was on base. "We only had four signs: take, bunt, hit-and-run, and steal," said Tommy. "If you are on first base you don't have to worry about the take sign or the bunt sign, so you are down to two. If the steal was on and you weren't sure, you could look at the first-base coach, and if he winked at you then you knew the steal was on. With Steve Sax, you never knew what was going to happen. I once gave the steal sign to Joey Amalfitano, who was the third-base coach. He gave it to Sax on first base, but Sax doesn't go. I give the sign again, but again he doesn't go. I give the sign for a third time, but he doesn't go. Manny Mota was our first-base coach. I asked him if he winked at Sax. 'Yeah, I winked,' Manny said. 'But he winked back!'"

Despite his great success as a player, Sax might be best known for his 1983 season, during which he committed 30 errors—most of them on errant throws from second to first. The affliction came to be known as the Steve Sax Syndrome. Physically he was fine; during practice Dodgers coaches would blindfold him, and he was still able to make the throw perfectly. It was only during games that he would sail the ball into the stands. "There were a lot of season ticket holders who wanted their seats moved from behind first base," said Tommy. Despite his struggles, Tommy would still give him the Lasorda hug; he continued to believe in him. "Not only did he not send me down, he didn't even take me out of the lineup," said Sax. "He never took me out for a defensive replacement. Later on, he told me that he felt that it would have destroyed my confidence. What I learned from him is the way to treat people. Give them the confidence to go out and play, treat them like a man, with respect, and it'll come right back to you."

Tommy was determined to help Sax keep his confidence, to help cure the syndrome. The Dodgers were on the road and Tommy took Sax for a father-son chat around the warning track.

"How many people can hit .300 in the big leagues?" Tommy asked.

"Not many."

"How many people can steal 40 bases in the big leagues?" Tommy asked.

"Not many."

"How many people can make the throw from second to first? Millions!" Tommy hollered.

The advice doesn't seem too profound, but it worked. It was the same advice Sax received from his father. "He told me that what I was going through was horrible, but that one day I would wake up and it would all be over," Sax said. "He told me that he went through the same thing when he played. I thought, *Wow, my invincible father went through this? If the toughest guy in the world could go through this, maybe I'm not so bad.* He told me that there was nothing wrong with me, it was just my confidence. I took that advice, and that was the last thing he ever told me."

Two days later, Sax's father suffered his fifth heart attack and died at the age of 47. "It was one of the most heart-wrenching things you can think of," said Sax. But just as he would hug his players when they slumped on the field, Tommy would be there for the Sax brothers during their time of need.

"Tommy was the guy who told me I lost my father," said Sax. "I remember that day coming from Atlanta to Cincinnati. It was a quarter to 6:00 in the morning and I got a call from Tommy. He told me to come to his room. I thought I was traded because I was going through the throwing problem. It was in the midst of the worst year of my life. I hit the elevator button and I see my brother on the elevator. He was on the team, too. We looked at each other and said, 'It's Dad.' We went to the room and Tommy was there, crying. He said, 'This is the hardest thing I have to do as a manager, but I have to tell you boys that you lost your dad.' He gave us hugs and told us that we should thank God for all the time we had with him. Tommy would tell me how much he loved me, but my dad was different. My dad never said it to my siblings and me, but he showed it in many different ways. There was a lot of love in our house, but I can't remember my father ever saying it to me, or me saying it to him. I finally did at his funeral. A couple years later I was talking to my mother, and she told me that he never had a throwing problem. He had just said that to help me get over mine."

While Tommy had a lot in common with John Sax, he also had something in common with Steve; both men idolized their fathers. As Sabatino laid on his deathbed, the man who motivated Tommy, who taught Tommy everything he knew about life, Tommy had to wait for his turn in the rotation to pitch before he could drive home to Norristown to kiss his father on his forehead and say good-bye. Tommy played in an era when the team came before family. It hurt him tremendously when he had to miss the birth of his daughter, Laura. Tommy was scheduled to pitch in Montreal. His wife, Jo, had gone home to Greenville to be with her family while Tommy and the Royals were in the latter part of the season battling for the pennant. "It was just expected of us to play," said Tommy. "I would never have been allowed to leave the team without pitching."

Tommy won that game and hopped on the next plane. When he arrived, his brother-in-law, Lee Miller, picked him up. Before leaving the airport, Tommy stopped to help a blind man with his bags. Before arriving at the hospital, he and Lee stopped for a hot dog. He was more nervous about being a father than he was about pitching a game with the pennant on the line. "He probably would have wanted to wait to meet Laura when she could say hello," said Jo.

Years later, it hurt him when Laura would cry when he and the team went on the road. It hurt him when she would cry on the phone and ask her daddy to come home. "I wanted to pack my bags right then and there," he said. Laura was the apple of his eye. He would hold her as a baby, swinging her in his arms, father and daughter dancing around the living room of their apartment as Tommy would sing to her.

> You're the end of the rainbow, my pot of gold.
> You're Daddy's little girl, to have and hold.
> A precious gem is what you are; you're Mommy's bright and
>   shining star.
> You're the spirit of Christmas, the star on our tree.
> You're the Easter Bunny to Mommy and me.
> You're sugar, you're spice, and you're everything nice.
> And you're Daddy's little girl

It was their special song, a song that Tommy would sing to her throughout her life, including at her wedding. After all, Tommy never had any trouble showing people how much he loved them. As Sabatino said many times, "*La famiglia è la patria del cuore*" ("Your family is the homeland of your heart").

CHAPTER 7

LAUGHTER

"Laughter is the food for the soul. If you can laugh you can forget any problems you may have."

The manager might have the toughest job in baseball. He is tasked with taking 25 players from different backgrounds, with different skills and deficiencies, with big egos and bigger doubts, and getting them to play as one team with one goal. He is tasked with winning, even though the players control the outcome of the games. He must also contend with counseling struggling players, consoling slumping players, nurturing young players, and aiding older players. All the while he is second-guessed at every step of the way—by fans, by the front office, and in many cases by his own players. He is also only one bad game away from the rumors of replacement, one bad series away from the scorn of the media, one bad season away from packing up his office.

"If I listened to the fans it wouldn't be long before I was in the stands with them," said Tommy. "Bobby Darwin pitched for me in Triple A Spokane. Even though he was a pitcher, he could hit, too. I didn't think he could pitch in the big leagues so I decided to give him a shot in the outfield. There was a leather-lunged fan sitting behind the dugout screaming at me: 'Hey, Lasorda, you dummy, how can you play a pitcher in the outfield?' Bobby hit a fastball for a three-run homer. As he comes around third base,

I gave him a big pat on the back. I turned around to look for this fan. The same fan stands up and says, 'Hey, Lasorda, you dummy, why hasn't that guy been playing the outfield all season!'"

In a game often defined by failure, Tommy looked for opportunities to laugh at every turn. "If people can laugh, they can't have problems at the same time," said Tommy. In 1977, Tommy's first year as manager, the team started the season by winning 22 of its first 26 games. By September 17, the club enjoyed a healthy 11½-game lead in the division and had lowered their magic number to three games. To add to the thrill, the Dodgers were giving away jackets to all fans in attendance that night.

"When I became manager all the stars used to come visit me in the clubhouse," said Tommy. "Gregory Peck, Burt Reynolds, Frank Sinatra. I used to get my friends to be my batboy for the game. I had Tony Danza suit up, Mike Fratello, Mel Levine, a U.S. congressman. I even got Don Rickles to dress up."

While Rickles has performed before many crowds, he had never performed before 52,527 people. Wearing number 40, Rickles patrolled the dugout that September night. With the game well in hand in the ninth and Elias Sosa on the mound, Tommy decided it was time for a little laughter. "I told Don to go out to the mound and ask for the ball," said Tommy. When he arrived, Sosa had no idea who Rickles was and refused to give him the ball. Eventually, home-plate umpire John McSherry trotted out to the mound to see what was going on. Instead of blowing up upon seeing Rickles, McSherry asked the comedian for tickets to a show in Las Vegas.

Several weeks later, the Dodgers began the NLCS against the Phillies. Philadelphia dealt Tommy's team a gut punch in the series opener, winning 7–5 in Los Angeles. Part of his job as manager was to set the tone in the clubhouse and to keep his players focused, motivated, and upbeat. "I walked in the clubhouse and I was as bitter and mad as you could be, but I didn't show that to my players," said Tommy. "I put a smile on my face, because if I was depressed and dejected my team would have the same attitude. I would put on a new face, and it would be an enthusiastic face, a confident face, a happy face, because that's how I wanted my players to be. I wanted my players to be relaxed and happy."

And what better way than to invite Rickles back? Before Game 2 he and Sinatra paid a visit to Tommy and the Dodgers. Although Tommy didn't ask him to dress in a uniform, he did ask Rickles to address the clubhouse during the pregame meeting. "He worked the clubhouse like a Vegas show," recalls Tommy. "He went from player to player, getting all over the guys." Whatever he said to the Dodgers, it worked. Although the Phillies scored first, Dusty Baker hit a grand slam in the bottom of the fourth and the Dodgers won 7–1. They went on to win the series. In that case, laughter may indeed have been the best medicine.

• • •

Before the 1977 season, Tommy wrote each of his players a letter telling them what he expected of them personally, and what he expected of the team. Seventeen of the 25 players on that roster had played for Tommy in the minor leagues; he knew who they were and what they were capable of.

One of those players was the great Steve Yeager. "Steve was the best defensive catcher I had seen," said Tommy. "He could throw anybody out. He used to holler from the plate to the runner on first, 'Come on, run. I dare you!' He could throw bullets back there." Lou Brock, the great base-stealer for the Cardinals, once said Yeager was the best-throwing catcher in the game. One day, the Dodgers were playing on national television and Yeager threw down to second as a runner was trying to steal the base. The network's radar gun timed Yeager's throw at 98 miles per hour.

In his letter to Yeager, Tommy expected his backstop to be tough, to block the plate, to throw out anyone who dared to run. He also expected him to be a field general, to take command of the pitching staff, and to be a leader. Yeager took those expectations to heart. In a tie game against the Pirates in Pittsburgh, Dave Parker, who stood 6'5" and weighed 230 pounds, was rounding third after a base hit from Al Oliver. Although the throw had Parker beat, he lowered his shoulder and punished Yeager for his plate-blocking bravado. As destructive as the play was, the collision didn't force Yeager to the disabled list. Tommy told reporters after the game that Yeager had a better chance against a pickup truck. When the media interviews were over, Tommy found Yeager on the trainer's table and tried to make him forget his pain.

"When I was managing in the minors, one of my players told me he had a sore foot and wanted to sit in the whirlpool. I told him to put his foot in the toilet and flush it! That's our whirlpool," said Tommy. "I might have said something like that to Yeager."

"That plate collision and the rigors of being a catcher, it's a long season," said Yeager. "But the laughter helped to keep you motivated and take your mind off your troubles. The laughter we had, the relationships we all had with each other, you wanted to play, you wanted to go out there the next day. I don't think we ever had a boring clubhouse."

In that season's World Series against the Yankees, Tommy elected to start left-hander Doug Rau. Reggie Jackson led off the second inning with a double. Lou Piniella singled and Jackson scored. Chris Chambliss followed with a double, scoring Piniella. Tommy had seen enough. Yeager joined Tommy on the mound, where Rau told the manager that he felt good. But the skipper had made up his mind. "I'll make the decision here, Dougy," said Tommy. "Keep your mouth shut!" Tommy unleashed a torrent of expletives to underline his opinion. "Tommy was yelling and screaming," Yeager said. "It wasn't very funny, although he did have a mic on because we were on national television!"

"But Tommy was a motivator," continued Yeager. "Whether it was yelling and screaming or poking fun at somebody and having a few laughs, that's what he did. He did it the best. Through all the stories—and God knows there's a lot of them—there's one particular story that comes to mind. Jerry Reuss is pitching, and Tommy comes out of the dugout. I'm heading to the mound when he tells me to stay back there, so I stayed behind the plate and watched Tommy go to the top of the bump. He and Reuss are arguing, and then he called me out.

"'Is this a democratic society?' Tommy asked me.

"'Yes, it is.'

"'He wants to stay in and I want to take him out, so you are the deciding vote.'

"'You should have taken him out last inning!' I said.

"Of course, Jerry didn't like that, but Tommy was laughing. Tommy was going to take him out regardless of what I said. But to see the expression on Reuss' face, and to see Tommy go out there and make a thing of it, was a reminder of how sometimes you gotta bring a little laughter into the game of baseball, and you gotta have some fun with some people.

"A lot of times, Tommy would come out to the mound and ask the umpire what he thought about making a pitching change. Sometimes he'd have an argument with the umpire just to give the guy warming up more time to get loose. Tommy is a smart cookie."

Tommy was also smart enough to "invite" Yeager, along with Burt Hooton and Charlie Hough, to his house for some extra work. But this time there was no extra BP, no bouncing balls off walls. This work was done with hammers and nails.

"I remember enclosing his backyard patio," said Yeager. "The cops came at 1:00 in the morning to shut us down because we were still hammering nails. And that was *after* a game!"

• • •

One of Steve Yeager's teammates on the late-'70s Dodgers was Rick Rhoden. Drafted in the first round of the 1971 draft, he reported to the Dodgers that summer and played in the Florida State League, and later for their Instructional League team. The next spring Rhoden met Tommy in Triple A. Rhoden was a fastball pitcher and had outstanding control for his age. "He knew what he was doing on the mound," said Tommy. "He knew how to pitch."

"I had some success and knew I was on a good team," said Rhoden. "But Tommy made you feel like you could do anything. Tommy was a real good judge of talent, of people. He knew what made each guy tick, and he would know how to get the best out of each guy. I'll never forget this: he used to take me out with a few other kids to hear him speak so we could hear what he was saying—and so we could get a free dinner. Whenever I was with him and he would introduce his guests to the audience, he would always say that I was going to be a star. I thought he knew something I didn't!'"

Rhoden played for Tommy in the Dominican Republic as a member of the Tigres del Licey, where their adventures at restaurants continued. "Sometimes Tommy went to eat with the owner of the team," Rhoden said. "Their favorite was Vesuvio, an Italian place right on the ocean. We would go there too and sit at a different table. Tommy would always try to get the owner to pick up our tab, but we never knew if the meal was free or not. We would order a pizza to start while we were waiting for the sign from Tommy. If he tugged his ear, the owner was buying dinner. If he wiped his forehead, he didn't know yet, and if he rubbed his chin, we were paying. If we got the chin we would order light, but if we got the ear we would order lobster diablo, langoustine parmesan, and all the good stuff."

Tommy was as competitive as they come, but he believed that sometimes laughing on the field resulted in a winning ballclub. "We had a pitcher named Pedro Borbon," Rhoden recalled. "We were playing at home, which was a huge ballpark. Borbon was getting rocked. Tommy went to the mound to make a pitching change, and instead of giving Tommy the ball, Borbon turned around and fired the ball well over the center-field fence. We could all hear from the dugout as Tommy yelled, 'If you threw like that in the game, I wouldn't be taking you out!'

"Another time Yeager was catching. It was a playoff game, and a foul tip hit him in the crotch. He was rolling around on the ground crying in pain. Tommy ran out there and stood over him and said, 'You can cry all you want but you ain't coming out of this game. You are going to catch!'"

Despite all their laughter and camaraderie, Rhoden's favorite story about Tommy is more telling. "Tommy met my brother one time, and three or four years later when I got to the big leagues he came to a game with me," Rhoden said. "Tommy walked up to us and remembered his name. I can guarantee that Walter Alston didn't know anybody's name. It was more like a family deal. That's how he was with everybody.

"When I was with the Pirates, I got a phone call at 6:00 AM on a Sunday morning. It was Joe Lonnett, one of our coaches, and all he says is, 'Your brother got killed in a car wreck.' That's it. My dad had called them, and that's how they told me. I couldn't leave because I was pitching that day. The next morning I tell the traveling secretary to get me a flight to Florida to see my folks. I'm there till Thursday, when I fly back. I pitch on Friday, didn't miss a start. I turned around and flew back to Florida for the funeral. I flew back to Pittsburgh for my next start. I pitched, flew to North Carolina where my brother lived to help straighten out his affairs, flew back to Pittsburgh, and made my next start. I pitched the day he died and made my next two starts. When I got my check, they took out the airfare."

It was a far cry from the fun and loving atmosphere Tommy fostered with the Dodgers. Rhoden pitched for the Pittsburgh Pirates, the New York Yankees, and the Houston Astros, and throughout his time in the big leagues he carried with him the lessons he learned as a Dodger. When he would play against Tommy, it would be like old times.

"Once when they came to Pittsburgh, I introduced him to a guy who ran a restaurant in Pittsburgh, Rico's," said Rhoden. "Next thing I know, Tommy is taking seven or eight guys there to eat, signing balls and pictures, and then Rico's is catering to Tommy's office before the games. One day I snuck into Tommy's office and ate his veal, spaghetti, and cheesecake. I would go out to the dugout before the game started and he would look over and drop a few F-bombs my way. It was so much fun to get him going."

Rhoden is now a professional golfer, but every spring he spends a few weeks during spring training with the Dodgers as an instructor. While there he is reunited with Tommy and former teammates such as Charlie Hough and Steve Yeager. "Every time we get together we tell these stories," said Rhoden. "Now that I'm a coach, I can really appreciate how great Tommy was with players. He was a master at relating to his guys, getting to know them, and figuring out how to motivate them. In order to be a good coach, the player has to know that you're a good guy and that they can trust you. You can't build that trust without finding a way to relate to them."

• • •

Rick Rhoden loved to laugh, but he wasn't an instigator by nature. By contrast, Mickey Hatcher was well known as a clubhouse comic, in addition to being one of the Dodgers' most valuable players. Hatcher was the leader of the Stuntmen, a group of bench players on the 1988 Dodgers who loved to lighten the mood in the dugout but were all business when they hit the field. Tommy once said of Hatcher, "He is one of my most valuable foot soldiers. I need him on my team. There are players who say, 'Man, I have to leave for the ballpark in 15 minutes.' Then there are players who say, 'Man, I get to go to the ballpark in 15 minutes.' Those are the guys I want on my teams, and that's the kind of guy Mickey Hatcher was. He loved the game and loved being with the guys."

Hatcher was drafted by the Dodgers in the fifth round of the 1977 draft. He made his major league debut in 1979, and stayed with the club until being traded to the Twins in 1981. He came back to the Dodgers in 1987 and retired with them in 1990. During his first stint with the team, he was productive on the field, but perhaps even more so in building the camaraderie it takes to be a winning team.

One of his Dodgers teammates was Joe Beckwith. A right-handed pitcher from Auburn University, Beckwith was a Southerner through and through. "I'm sitting in the hotel lobby and Joe comes over," said Tommy. "A few of his buddies were there visiting him. He asked if I could come over and visit with them, tell them some stories and jokes. One of the guys raised Yorkshire pigs for a living. A week later I get a huge box and something in there is moving around. I open it up in my office and it's a Yorkshire pig. He sent me a live pig!"

Beckwith, Hatcher, and a few other players thought it was time for Tommy and the pig to get better acquainted. "The guys locked Tommy in his office with the pig," said Hatcher. "We didn't know if the squealing was coming from Tommy or the pig! When we opened the door, I had to catch the pig so Tommy could get off his desk. He was standing on it."

"The game starts and I'm in the dugout and I get a call in the third or fourth inning," Tommy said. "'There's a pig walking around the eighth floor of the stadium.' Those guys snuck into my office, took the pig, put him on the elevator, and closed the door!"

Even after Hatcher was traded to the Twins, the pranks between him and Tommy didn't stop. "I had a pair of beautiful blue slacks," said Tommy. "I wasn't sure if I should wear them for just a bus ride, but I felt so good when I wore them that I decided to. I loved them."

"The Dodgers were already on the field and I went into the locker room," Hatcher recalls. "I said hi to [Dodgers visiting clubhouse manager] Jerry Turner and walked into Tommy's office. There were Tommy's pants hanging in the locker. I just happened to be by the trainer's room, so I grabbed a pair of scissors and made designer shorts out of them. During the game, Mark Cresse saw what I did. The first time I came up to the plate, Tommy is waving to me and Cresse puts his arm around Tommy and whispers in his ear. Tommy looks up at the flagpole and there are his cutup pants flying high. I think Orel Hershiser was pitching. All of a sudden you could hear it through the whole stadium: 'If you don't hit him in the head and kill him, you'll never make this team!' I've never seen him so mad in his entire life. Those pants meant a lot to him, so I knew payback was going to be special. He sent someone out to the parking lot to flatten the tires. He never found my car though." Tommy would later order Cresse to hang Hatcher's pants from a flagpole, too.

While Hatcher loved to have fun, he also loved to play hard and tried to inspire and motivate his teammates to do the same. He instituted the Bust Your Butt Award, which was given to a Dodger who lived up to the award's name. The "award" was a picture of Hatcher mooning the camera. Hatcher was merely trying to emulate his manager's approach, to always maintain a positive attitude.

"Tommy was an amazing individual, especially for my career," said Hatcher. "He was one of the best motivators, just a very positive individual to be around. I think just like every player that had a chance to be around him, Tommy found a way to get the best out of him. Whether he had to challenge us or do whatever he needed to do, he found a way to get the best out of the players.

"He challenged me. He cornered me a few times. He called me in his office and gave lectures and stuff. He was always like that. If he felt like you were getting down on yourself, or you're quitting on yourself, he was a guy who would sit down with you, but he wouldn't baby you. He would tell you that it's time to grow up and be a man and get out there and compete and play this game hard. Don't ever feel sorry for yourself, and give it everything you've got. If you're going to be one of those quitters, you're not going to play for him. He was very straightforward with whatever he did."

The Twins released Hatcher at the start of spring training in 1987; he was a utility man whose numbers were slipping. He begged his agent to call the Dodgers but was told that the team had no interest in him. He persisted, and as soon as the agent called, the Dodgers offered him contract. Just as Tommy had taught him, he hadn't gotten down on himself. He never quit. He made the 1987 Dodgers.

Hatcher embraced Tommy's belief in positivity in his own unique way. During the '88 season, Hatcher would wear a batting helmet with a propeller affixed to the front. Once he lent the helmet to Tommy, and the Dodgers rallied to come from behind and win. A season before he persuaded a priest to sprinkle holy water on the Dodgers' bats after an Easter service. Although Hatcher didn't get an at-bat in that game, the Dodgers won 9–1.

When the Dodgers opened the '88 World Series, Hatcher had only one home run all season. When he came up to bat in the bottom of the first in Game 1, he launched a home run off Dave Stewart. Hatcher, playing for the injured Kirk Gibson, was so elated that he sprinted around the bases in a fit of the enthusiasm that Tommy loved to see in his players. He made it home in less than 20 seconds.

In Game 5, Hatcher again hit a home run in the first, another two-run shot. And again he sprinted around the bases in fit of enthusiasm. The Dodgers went on to win that game and the World Series. Hatcher was supposed to be awarded with the World Series MVP, but at the last minute it was given to Hershiser instead.

Hatcher had an amazing season in '88, and his career has gone down in Dodgers history as much for his play as for his clubhouse antics. And Tommy, for one, never stopped trying to keep the laughter alive. "The hardest thing I had to face in my career with the Dodgers was the day they released me," said Hatcher. "I felt that I still had another year or so to play. When I left the game it was tough because I loved the Dodgers so much. But Tommy and Peter O'Malley wouldn't let me leave the game after all. They talked me into going down to Triple A as a player-coach. I think it was a lifesaver. I really enjoyed it, and now in all the years I've been a coach, I learned a lot from Tommy and took it with me wherever I went.

"His players were his family. He was like a father to everybody who had an opportunity to play for him."

• • •

Just before Mickey Hatcher left the Dodgers, Lenny Harris arrived. Traded from Cincinnati with Kal Daniels in July of '89, the utility infielder hit .308 in 54 games. He also made an immediate impression on his skipper.

"How could you not love Lenny?" asked Tommy. "The scouting report on him was he was a good contact hitter, played hard, loved the game, and when he put the uniform on he'd never disappoint you. That scouting report turned out to be as good as any."

To the Dodgers front office, Harris was just a throw-in; Daniels was the coveted player. But Harris was used to facing adversity. Growing up in Liberty City, Florida, ambulances screaming past his window was a nightly occurrence, and crime often enveloped the community. Harris' father worked at a local fruit market; his mother was a maid at a hotel. His parents could field a baseball team of their own, as Lenny was one of nine children in the family.

Harris was the youngest of his siblings, but by the time he was a Dodger he had become the leader of his family. His mother had died six years earlier, and over those six years his siblings visited their father less and less. While Harris was battling for a roster spot, he was also battling on behalf of his siblings. Help with the rent was a monthly request. Help buying food was a weekly request. Harris was quoted as saying he was his family's last hope.

Baseball was his reprieve. As he reported to spring training the season following the trade, he felt at home with his new club and his new manager. They were at home with him too, so much so that Tommy decided to play a joke on Harris.

"Tommy called me into his office," Harris recalled. "I sat down at his desk and he told me that I was being sent down to Triple A Albuquerque. He told me that it was the hardest thing a manager had to do, and I think tears were coming down his face. I said, 'Aw man, I'm not going to Albuquerque! I'm going home.'

"'You better get your butt to Albuquerque like I said or I'll fine you for insubordination!'

"I got in my car and started to drive home to Miami. I was halfway down the turnpike before Darryl Strawberry and Eric Davis called and told me it was an April Fool's joke.

"He would try to fine me for insubordination every day. If you said something to him that he didn't like, he would chew you out and try to fine you. We thought it was the funniest thing. I love him so much. I never loved another person like I loved Tommy. He was real special to me, not just as a manager, but also as a person. He's always been there for me."

Harris saw time at third base, second base, shortstop, and in the outfield. At the plate that season he hit .304. Despite his success, he was platooning at third with Mike Sharperson because Jeff Hamilton, the starter, was down with an injury. Harris would play against right-handed pitchers while Sharperson would play against lefties.

"I wanted Lenny and Sharpy to be good teammates. I wanted them to understand what it was all about, which was we were all working toward one goal as a team," said Tommy. "I had to bring them into my office, and I told them that if they listened to me and did what I told them to do, they would both make a million dollars."

"Me and Sharperson were fighting for the same job," said Harris. "He said, I know how you guys want to play so much but you guys have to stop arguing with each other. Just do what I tell you. He gave us the opportunity to split the job at third base and he didn't lie—we made a lot of money. Every time he would go to dinner he would call me and Sharperson. 'Hurry up and meet me downstairs in five minutes and don't be late or I'll fine you for insubordination! We are going to eat!' I don't think I spent one dime going to dinner with him. After all those spaghetti dinners, I told him that I should be Italian. We laughed and he named me Lennyo!

"To play for Tommy was remarkable. He was one guy who, if he couldn't get you ready to play a game, nobody could. He would walk up and down the locker room telling you what you need to do to prepare to play and compete. He used to say that we had to be like Ali-Frazier, that we had to go out there and kick their ass. Whatever it took is what he did. It's a little different in the game today, but he was big-time motivation."

Harris left his jersey hanging in the Dodgers clubhouse after the 1993 season. He was granted free agency and re-signed with the Reds. He had an outstanding career that spanned 18 years, and he still holds the major league record for most career pinch hits (212). After retiring as a player he began coaching. He rejoined the Dodgers in 2009 as a minor league hitting coach and stayed with the organization for several seasons.

During spring training in 2012, Harris was going through his regular routine: a morning jog and workout, breakfast in the dining room at Camelback Ranch, and then out to the mound to throw early BP for the minor league hitters with whom he was working. As Matt Wallach was halfway through his time in the cage, Harris doubled over clutching his chest. His elbow started to tingle and he was rushed to the hospital by a Dodgers trainer. Harris had suffered a heart attack, and doctors performed a triple bypass.

"When I woke up I looked up and Tommy's face was right there looking over me," said Harris. "I said, 'Oh, lord, I thought I died and went to heaven! Wow, you're here with me too? When did you die?' He started laughing and said, 'Lenny, we're going to go eat real good when you get out of here, because you just got a tune-up. You got brand-new plugs inside of you!' He made me laugh so hard my chest hurt. He had me in tears."

Tommy also received as good as he gave. "One day I threw batting practice and all day and I thought I'd take a nap before the game," said Tommy. "While I was sleeping, they changed the clock in my office. When I woke up it said 8:15. 'Oh my god, the game has been going on for over an hour!' I ran out there and doggone it the game hadn't started yet.

"One time in spring training they locked me in my room. They tied a rope from the door handle. I picked up the phone to call for help but they had taken the voice box out of the phone so I couldn't talk into it. It was almost time for the team to leave. I used to tell my guys that if the bus is about to leave and you're not on it, then bye-bye. I figured they were going to go without me. I was getting ready to throw the chair through the window. I was screaming. Ralph Avila was walking by and he cut the rope and let me out.

"Another time, when I was just a minor league manager, I was asleep, and you never locked the doors at Dodgertown. All of a sudden I see someone coming through my door. It was the night watchman and Walter O'Malley. I'm lying in bed and he says, 'Where are my wheels?' *Is this guy crazy?* I thought. The guy looks under my bed and his golf cart wheels are right there. The guys took the wheels off his cart and hid them under my bed."

During spring training you would never see Tommy without seeing his golf cart. All the other carts were nondescript, but Tommy's had his name painted across the front in Dodgers script. "Glenn Hoffman sunk my gold cart in the lake at Dodgertown," said Tommy. "One time my golf cart was missing, I look around, and I see it in a field far away. When I went over to get it, it was turned over on its top. Another Glenn Hoffman move. He was funny. He pulled a lot of tricks."

In an atmosphere where laughter was encouraged, the players used to get on each other, too. "We always used to joke around with Cey because he had big front teeth," said Tommy. "We said it was the first mistake God ever made. He put a horse's teeth in Penguin's mouth and there's some horse in Hollywood walking around with the Penguin's teeth. Well, the guys put a bale of hay in Cey's locker. He wasn't too happy about that."

The Prince of Pranks, Jay Johnstone, pulled more than his fair share. Some of his more notorious feats include putting a melted brownie in Garvey's glove; going into the stands during a game in full uniform to get a Dodger Dog; putting pine tar in Al Campanis' shoes; and roping off a section behind first base after the shortstop made four throwing errors the night before. He was also the person responsible for locking Tommy in his room.

Johnstone, along with Jerry Reuss and Kenny Brett, once removed all of the pictures from the wall of Tommy's office. Gone were photos of Sinatra, Rickles, President Reagan, and a host of celebrities; in their place hung pictures of Johnstone, Reuss, and Brett. "They told me they belonged on my walls because they got hits and struck guys out for me," said Tommy. "Not the celebrities."

"We had a lot of laughs in those days," said Tommy. "I felt like all the laughter helped our teams win. You have to be relaxed. When it was game time, that's when the fun stops."

But the fun never stopped with Tommy and his longtime friend, Joe Garagiola, one of the game's greatest jokers. Blessed with a comic wit and a caring heart, Garagiola shares a lot in common with Tommy. They both come from Italian immigrant families—although Tommy's parents spoke broken English while Garagiola's spoke none. They are both Catholic, they have both been inducted into the National Baseball Hall of Fame and the Italian American Sports Hall of Fame, and they both love to help people.

"There was this priest, Father Tom," said Garagiola. "He was great. He was funny, loved to tell jokes, and was always positive. I went there during Lent and he delivered a great homily. I told Lasorda about him and told him he had to come to Mass and hear this priest. He agreed. I picked him up, and riding out there I told him not to try to convert him to being a Dodger fan. He liked the Giants."

"I said it might take me a little bit to convert him," said Tommy. "We go there and he's shocked to see me. Afterward we are outside waiting for him, and he's greeting everybody. I told him it was a great service and he said thanks, and that he couldn't believe it was me. I was touched by his service and decided to send him a letter. He read the letter during Mass, like it was a letter from the Corinthians."

"I couldn't believe it," said Garagiola. "I told my wife, Audrie, 'I don't mind Matthew, Mark, Luke, and John. They're pretty good. I've been hearing them since grade school, but I don't know about listening to a sermon by Lasorda.'"

"I wrote Father Tom another letter," said Tommy. "But this time I sent him a Dodgers jacket, too."

"We go back to Mass," said Garagiola. "Father Tom comes in from the back of the church and is dressed in his vestments, but he has on a Dodgers jacket! He reaches the altar and takes the jacket off. He folds it like it's one of his priestly vestments. Who could get a Catholic priest to walk down the center aisle wearing a Dodgers jacket? I've seen a miracle."

Asked about Tommy's impact on the game, Garagiola replied, "Baseball is a serious game, but you can have fun and enjoy it. I don't think there's a rotten bone in his body. Tommy always has time for you. He makes you feel like you're his best friend and he is so glad to see you. I did a commercial in Los Angeles for Chrysler. Lo and behold I look up and who's watching me? Lasorda. We had lunch, and I told him I would be there again the next day, and he was there, too."

Jim Murray, the greatest baseball writer ever, once said, "The game without its cutups is just another balance sheet." To many, Murray's words about baseball are gospel. Over the course of a month and a half of spring training, six months of a regular season, and into the postseason, baseball's balance sheet is a long one. Luckily for Tommy, he and the cutups on his teams put the Dodgers balance sheet in the black every year.

• CHAPTER 8 •

PATRIOTISM

"Baseball is America's game!"

Tommy stood on the shores of Ellis Island in 2006, flanked by his four brothers, with Lady Liberty and his father's spirit shining behind him. He was on hand to accept the Statue of Liberty Ellis Island Foundation's Family Heritage Award. Amidst the other honorees, press, dignitaries, and tourists, he made his remarks.

"I thank God every night that my father did not miss that boat," said Tommy, referring to Sabatino's arrival in the United States in 1920. "However, if he *had* missed it, you would all be addressing me today as Pope Thomas XXVI."

The crowd laughed, but the Lasorda brothers wiped the tears from their eyes. Emigrating from Tollo, Italy, a small town in the province of Chieti in the Abruzzo region, Sabatino came to America to seek a better life for himself. "I think he had about $25 on him when he left Italy," said Tommy. "I can only imagine the courage it took to leave everything he knew and loved with only the shirt on his back."

Sabatino served in the Italian army in World War I, but he was also a farmer. Tollo is known for its vineyards and olive groves, with a gentle sea breeze from the Adriatic circulating throughout the hills of the town. "He loved to work with his hands," said Tommy. "All Abruzzese do." After clearing Ellis Island he made his way to Pennsylvania and into Norristown, an Italian immigrant enclave. He got a job working on the railroads, then a meatpacking company, and on to Bethlehem Steel, driving the truck in the quarry. He met Carmella Cavuto. Sabatino and Carmella's fathers were both from Tollo, and when he visited their home in Norristown, he saw her and was in love. The two were soon married, and life for Sabatino was on its way.

"The most important thing in life for my father was his family," said Tommy. "When we would eat together he would tell us stories about himself, about his life in Italy, and he was always using those stories to teach us a lesson." Tommy is the second of five boys. The Lasorda brothers were notorious in Norristown for working hard and eating a lot. "We ate like mules," said Tommy. "One day he was telling us about his home in Tollo. He made his home sound like a castle, and I often wondered why he would leave if it was such a wonderful place."

For as wonderful as it may have seemed, for all the wisdom Sabatino gained there, for all the love he had there, he traded the gentle Abruzzo breeze for the shining City upon a Hill. "My father loved Italy," said Tommy. "But he loved this country, too. He used to tell my brothers and I that we were lucky to live in the greatest country in the world. He would say that we had to do all we can to keep it the best. He said that we may have to fight for this country, that we may have to give up our lives for this country. Can you imagine a father saying that to his sons?"

Tommy and his brothers would all serve their country in the military. All of the Lasorda brothers loved America. Wherever Tommy went, he took his patriotism with him. As a young player he would frequently play during the winter in Panama, Puerto Rico, Venezuela, Colombia, and Cuba. American tourists loved vacationing in Cuba, and American players loved playing in Cuba, including Tommy. He pitched for Marianao and Almendares, on which he was teammates with the great Willie Mays.

"The Cuban people were wonderful. They loved baseball," said Tommy. "Jo and I were walking down the street in Havana and a kid had a puppy. I traded him a baseball for his dog. The fans would sing and dance in the stands. We loved Cuba. George Raft was running the Capri Hotel. Every

Sunday we would go to the hotel, and George would have a table for us to see the show. He would feed us dinner, and then he would dance with our wives. He was a great dancer, and a movie star."

Cuba had always been a wild place. During one game Tommy pitched, he got into an argument with Amado Maestri, the umpire behind the plate. "Tom Gorman, who was an American umpiring in Cuba, had told me to be careful because the umpire behind the plate was packing. I threw three curves that I thought were strikes but he called as balls," said Tommy. 'You're the worst umpire I've ever seen! How can you call those balls! You should be ashamed of yourself!' He unbuttoned his coat and right there tucked in his waist was the biggest pistol I had ever seen. '*Maestri*, you're the best umpire I've ever seen!'"

Amazingly, Tommy was twice in the country when the government changed hands. While playing for Marianao, he saw Fulgencio Batista overthrow Carlos Prio in 1952 and Fidel Castro overthrow Batista in 1959. "On New Year's Eve 1958, Jo and I were with Art Fowler and his wife and Bob Allison and his wife," said Tommy. "We were leaving a party at about 3:00 AM when three large planes flew low overhead. I wondered who would be flying that late at night. I found out later that it was Batista and his cabinet fleeing the country."

Tommy and his wife were confined to their home in Club Nautico, an exclusive resort on the beach. "When Castro overtook the city, we thought he was going to come get this guy who owned Club Nautico," said Tommy. "He was a member of Batista's cabinet, and we thought they were going to destroy the place. We got word they were coming, so we confiscated whatever weapons people had in their homes. We patrolled all night. They came to the gate and we were ready for them, but they changed their minds and left.

"The city was shut down. Castro sent a police car to pick me up. Howie Haak, a scout for the Pirates, came with me. We got in the car and we got to the hotel, and they took us up to the penthouse. Fidel was there waiting for me. He wanted to talk baseball. We spent an hour and a half talking about the game."

Despite the civil strife, Cubans loved baseball. The grandstands of the Gran Estadio de La Habana were packed with 10,000 fans enjoying Hatuey beer, chicharrones, and *cigarros*, ready for some action. "The first game back after the strike I was going to pitch," said Tommy. "There were *barbudos* everywhere with guns over their shoulders. One of them was warming me up! I waited until the catcher came out and the *barbudo* went back to the dugout.

"It was a sad situation for the country. When Castro came in, the people were celebrating because they thought he would be good for the country, and so did I. We had a general manager, Monchy de Arcos, and he told me that Castro was not a good man, that he was a communist. I thought when he took over that he would be a savior for the country. I found out I was wrong. I wanted to get out of there, but we continued playing baseball after the strike was over. It was a gorgeous country, until Castro took over."

Castro dismantled the existing baseball league and rebuilt Cuban baseball into a powerhouse that would dominate international tournaments over the years. Cuba won the Pan Am Games 12 times; America's single victory came in 1967. Baseball was only an exhibition/demonstration sport in the Olympics until 1992; between '92 and 2008, Cuba won the gold three times and the silver twice. America's only Olympic gold came in the 2000 Games in Sydney, Australia. That team was managed by Tommy.

After retiring from the Dodgers in 1996, Tommy made known his interest in managing the next Olympic team. While there were many worthy candidates, no one else had a plaque hanging in Cooperstown or two World Series rings. No one else had 1,599 major league wins in their record. No one had developed as many minor-leaguers into big-league stars as Tommy had.

Being out of the dugout for a few years had Tommy missing his life's work. He missed the camaraderie, the game strategy, the competition, and the glorious spoils of victory. When asked why he wanted to return to managing for the Olympics, he said, "I wanted to beat the Cubans." As he told Jo, "There's going to be a quiz 25 years from now asking which manager won a World Series and a gold medal for his country. That manager will be me!"

"You don't even know the players," she countered.

BUSINESS REPLY MAIL

FIRST-CLASS MAIL   PERMIT NO. 128   BENNINGTON VT

POSTAGE WILL BE PAID BY ADDRESSEE

HEMMINGS CLASSIC CAR
PO BOX 196
BENNINGTON VT 05201-9940

NO POSTAGE
NECESSARY
IF MAILED
IN THE
UNITED STATES

Hemmings
CLASSIC CAR

$32.95!

GET *HEMMINGS* CLASSIC CAR
FOR THIS VERY LOW PRICE

SUBSCRIBE AND SAVE!

☐ Send me two years (24 issues) of *Hemmings Classic Car* for only $32.95

☐ I prefer one year (12 issues) of *Hemmings Classic Car* for only $18.95

☐ Payment Enclosed ☐ Bill Me Later

Name _____

Address _____

City _____ State ____ Zip ____

E-mail _____

Sign me up for my free eDaily newsletter from Hemmings Motor News: ☐ YES ☐ NO
Hemmings will not sell or share your e-mail address. Hemmings Motor News may contact me via e-mail regarding special Hemmings promotions: ☐ YES ☐ NO
Please allow 4-6 weeks for delivery. Please add appropriate sales tax. Canadian add $12.00 per year; foreign add $14.00 per year. U.S. funds only.

CSBLSEP19

"I don't care, just as long as they are alive."

"Everybody was saying we couldn't beat the Cubans," Tommy said. "Everyone said that they had won every existing tournament and that they couldn't be beaten. I asked if they had ever lost a game before, which they had. Well, they are going to lose again."

On May 5, 2000, at a press conference in Los Angeles, Tommy was given the opportunity to do just that for his country. At the press conference, he said, "It is a privilege and an honor to represent the greatest country in the world at the Olympic Games. I have managed World Series champions and other great teams, but this means more, because this time I'll do so on behalf of my country."

Tommy wasn't the only professional that would be representing America in the Olympics. In past years, international tournaments were reserved for amateurs only, a rule that was also a source of Cuba's success. However, for the 2000 Games, the rules had been changed and professionals would now be allowed to participate.

Before players could be contacted to gauge their interest in playing in the Olympics, the general managers of each team were asked for permission. As Olympic baseball was played in September, they coincided with major league rosters expanding from 25 to 40. As a result, most minor league stars and blue-chip prospects were unavailable to Tommy. Of the 24 players on the final roster, only one of them had played in the big leagues at that time. "I only knew one player," said Tommy. "Pat Borders, our catcher, had played for Toronto for many years, and he was the only guy I knew."

When they assembled for the first time as a team for their only workout before leaving for Sydney, Tommy addressed them. "I don't know who you are or where you came from," he said. "I don't know if you're married or single, if you're good, mediocre, or bad. But I'm going to tell you something right now. When this thing is all over, the whole world is going to know who you are. You want to know why? Because you are going to bring the gold medal in baseball back where it belongs, in the United States of America! You do not represent your family, you do not represent your hometown, you do not represent your school or the organization that signed you. You now represent the United States of America, and the only thing you are going to do over there is win! You want to know why? Because baseball is America's game! It doesn't belong to the Japanese or the Koreans or the Italians or the Cubans. It belongs to the United States of America! We are not going 6,000 miles to lose!"

The tone had been set. Just as Tommy had let his expectations be known to his Dodgers teams, he had let his expectations be known to the young players on Team USA. Just as he had instilled confidence in his players from Ogden to Los Angeles, he did so with his Olympians.

For a bit of extra motivation, Tommy called in a favor. After his speech, the team huddled together around a phone. On the other end of the line was the Splendid Splinter himself, Ted Williams. Tommy had arranged a call with his old friend to reinforce the importance of their cause. Williams' historic career was interrupted twice when he served as a Marine pilot in World War II and Korea. "He told them how to conduct themselves, how to win, to play as a team and not as an individual," said Tommy. "I was going to take him over there with us but I couldn't get a plane that he could sleep on. He was willing to go."

"I couldn't believe that was him," said first baseman Doug Mientkiewicz. "We were all tremendously grateful that Tommy did that for us. He's like Gandhi—everybody loves Tommy. People in the world who have never watched baseball know who Tommy Lasorda is, and to say I had the chance to play for him is an honor."

When Team USA arrived in Sydney, the players had to clear customs and then board another flight for the Gold Coast. They would be there for 10 days, working out and playing exhibition games. The workouts and games gave Tommy a chance to see what tools his players had. In typical Tommy style, there would also be meals and walks around the hotel together. I would take Kurt Ainsworth and Ben Sheets out for a walk," said Tommy. "We would talk about baseball, about pitching, how to pitch, how to set up hitters, how to pitch to the count. All of those things become very important to a pitcher. It was a way for me to get to know my players and relate to them.

"I wasn't staying in the Olympic Village. I was at a hotel, but I would go over there early every morning, have breakfast with the team, have the workout or play a game, have dinner with the team, and then go back to the hotel around 11:00 PM and come back the next day at 6:00 AM. I wanted to be with them all the time."

For Tommy, the Opening Ceremonies was a moment he'll never forget. "I had tears in my eyes," said Tommy. "I had a pair of brand-new shoes on. They call you out in alphabetical order, so the United States was close to the end. I'm standing there for three hours with these shoes that are too tight, it was hot. But was it worth it? When we walked out there it wasn't just the baseball team, it was all the U.S. athletes, men and women who work hard for years to participate in the Olympics, and all the hours they put into it, the desire that they had, and when you put USA on the front of their shirt, it's a big deal."

Just two days before they were to play their first game, the United States Olympic Committee held a press conference for Team USA. Tommy was selected to speak on behalf of USA Baseball, along with a few of his players. Most members of the American media didn't give the team a chance to medal. Cuba was the favorite, followed by Japan and Korea. In fact, Peter Gammons, a renowned baseball reporter for ESPN, thought the United States was just the fifth-best team in the tournament.

While most of the questions and comments were customary, one in particular got the world's attention. Asked about a possible game against Cuba, Tommy said, "We would be playing that game for all of the Cuban Americans that have come to our country and who live in Little Havana, on the streets of Miami, and all across south Florida. That's who we would dedicate victory to." While the quote made headlines across the country, it did so especially in south Florida, where millions of exiled Cubans began their new lives years before. Many of those people had cheered for Tommy and Almendares back in Cuba in the 1950s, and Tommy had always had a soft spot in his heart for their plight.

"When I dedicated our victory to the Cuban exiles, it wasn't just to motivate my team but to motivate the people who suffered through that.

The people who were teammates of mine who lived in Cuba and had to go to Miami. I saw the country coming apart," said Tommy. "I felt bad for all the people who had to leave all their belongings, leave their homes, leave their families. But a lot of them were allowed to come to the United States and have a chance to live for something." Tommy had put his patriotism, his belief that the United States was the greatest country in the world, front and center for the world to see.

• • •

One of the players on Team USA's roster was a young first baseman from the Twins organization. Selected in the fifth round of the 1995 draft, Doug Mientkiewicz was a promising prospect. In 1994 he played for Team USA in the Baseball World Cup, and came back to Florida State in '95 to hit .371 with 19 home runs and 80 RBIs. In 1999 he made the Twins roster and split time at first with Ron Coomer. He struggled that year, and criticized his manager's style. He was sent back to Triple A for the 2000 season, which was a stroke of luck for USA Baseball, as he was then available to play in the Olympics.

"He was upset with the Twins," said Tommy. "I told him not to let it affect his play down here. 'You're a good ballplayer. You'll play in the big leagues with someone else if they don't want you. But I don't want you here with that attitude because we have to win this thing. I need you real bad.'"

Mientkiewicz had a reputation as an outstanding defensive first baseman, and also as someone a team could count on in the clutch. That was something he learned from his father in the backyard of the Mientkiewicz home in Toledo, Ohio. "My dad put me in that situation from day one, when I was five years old," said Mientkiewicz. "Every time we hit in cage or on a field or in our backyard, even with a Wiffle ball bat, it was always bottom of the ninth, two outs, second and third, tying run is at third, winning run is at second, what are you going to do?"

Another part of his makeup was his patriotism. Living in Toledo he shared his hometown with Mike Eruzione, "Pete Rose on Skates," the captain of the 1980 U.S. Hockey team that famously defeated the Soviet Union. "Before the Olympics he played for the Toledo Goaldiggers," said

Mientkiewicz. "We were season ticket holders. Here we are in a small town in Ohio and Mike's on the world stage, so when he scored the winning goal against Russia it caught our eye, and ever since then we were into the Olympics."

Just as Tommy's father had impressed upon him and his four brothers the importance of doing something for their country, Eruzione's goal impressed the same importance upon millions of Americans. Since Eruzione's goal, it had been Mientkiewicz's mother's dream to see her son play in the Olympics. When Doug turned professional in 1995, being a part of the 1996 team was impossible. Then, because of the rule change for the 2000 Games, he was given the opportunity that he and his mother both wanted so badly. "My mom really wanted me to play in the '96 Olympics because that was her end-all goal for me, and when I signed pro I kind of broke her heart a little bit," said Mientkiewicz. "The day I was able to call my mom and tell her I was on the [Olympic] team was one of the happier days of my life."

Even so, his spot on the roster wasn't always secure. During the preliminary games on the Gold Coast, Mientkiewicz was struggling during batting practice. "Reggie Smith, our batting coach, said to me, 'When are you going to start hitting?' I remember saying, 'Trust me, when the bell rings, I'll be ready.' I remember catching Tommy saying, 'Well, don't wait too long!'"

Tommy had more advice for his first baseman. "He believed in me probably more so than I believed in myself at the time," said Mientkiewicz. "I remember talking about it with my wife. I told her I needed this. This is made for me. This is what I'm really good at. I was built for a two-week series. Compared to a major league season, 162 games, at the end of the year my numbers aren't going to be anywhere near a Jason Giambi's, the great players I played against," said Mientkiewicz. "But for two weeks, in a winner-take-all, when the games really matter, numbers go out the window. I used to tell coaches and GMs that you might not want me from April through August, but in September and October you want me on your team because I catch it, I don't make stupid mistakes, and in the playoffs everybody is dangerous. I have always had the ability during condensed series to do whatever needs to be done in the moment. One hit can mean everything. It's not how many hits you get, it's when you get them."

Just as Mientkiewicz was built for a two-week series, built to perform in the clutch, to do whatever needs to be done in the moment, so too was Tommy. Managing as if there were no tomorrow was a hallmark of his managerial career. "That's why I think he was the perfect man for that job," said Mientkiewicz. "To him, it didn't matter who they gave him. If he could get 25 guys to believe in one common goal, it doesn't matter how talented they are, it doesn't matter who they are playing. If he could get them to believe they are going to do something, they are going to end up doing it."

Tommy was a master at getting players to believe in themselves, of building team chemistry, and treating his players like family. However, while managing Team USA his time was short, and camaraderie cannot be achieved on the fly. Luckily for Tommy, the team was involved in an off-the-field incident that would provide a perfect opportunity: Tommy and the players went to a hotel casino after beating South Africa in an exhibition game.

"I've never been a gambler," said Tommy. "I never wanted to use up my luck on the tables instead of on the field." Still, he wanted to be with his players and use every opportunity to get to know them. Mientkiewicz was there, along with Pat Borders and Brent Abernathy. The players sat down at a blackjack table and played a few hands, throwing chips on the felt and hoping to see an ace and a face.

"There were a few people behind us," said Mientkiewicz. "In Australia, people could stand behind players at the table and bet on their hands. One of the guys started to bet behind Pat, and he didn't like it. Pat politely asked the guy to stop. Pat went to the bathroom and came back to keep playing, and the guy kept betting on Pat's hand. This time though, he kind of bumped Pat with his elbow. Pat stood up and told the guy he didn't want any trouble. All of a sudden, Tommy comes over and gets in the guy's face."

"I'll paralyze you with this left hook!" yelled the skipper.

"The guy pushed Pat," Mientkiewicz said. "Pat picks the guy up and literally throws him across the table into the pit. The woman was hitting me with her purse because I was holding her boyfriend back. Brent had another guy in a bear hug on the ground, but he broke away. He bit Brent in the chest! He bit his nipple! The guy Pat threw across the table got away from him and Pat chased him across the casino floor. After the fight, Brent had to get a tetanus shot because the bite was so nasty. It left teeth marks in his chest."

After the melee, the casino contacted the USA Baseball officials. Bob Watson, the general manager for Team USA, met with Mientkiewicz and Borders. Tommy was there, too. "I was in Watson's room at 3:00 AM trying to explain what happened," Mientkiewicz said. "And Tommy kept yelling, 'I love these guys! I want these guys in the foxhole with me!' I didn't think Watson wanted to hear anything about foxholes, but it helped us understand Tommy. It helped us understand that he is not in this for himself. He is in this for us, and he cares. It just reiterated to us how bad he wanted to win this tournament. Tommy could have very easily either sent us home or not even heard our side of the story, but he stood up for us."

In David Fanucchi's book, *Miracle on Grass*, Abernathy was quoted as saying, "I really believe that the incident helped our team bond and come together even more. Doug, Pat, and myself didn't know each other very well yet, and we were hanging out just having a good time that night. And our reactions showed that we had each other's backs no matter what, because we all stuck up for one another right away. When the rest of our teammates heard about it, they supported us as well."

From the first team workout in San Diego, to the 17-hour flight across the Pacific, to the exhibition games on the Gold Coast, to the preliminary games in Sydney, Tommy kept roaring the team's motto: we did not come 6,000 miles to lose. As he roamed the aisle of the plane talking to the players, Mientkiewicz shuffled through his carry-on. He found a letter from his wife. "The gist of it was, don't you dare go 6,000 miles without doing something special," said Mientkiewicz. "She wrote, 'Do something grand.'"

In the first game of pool play, games that would determine which teams played for a medal, Team USA beat Japan 4–2 in 13 innings and in high fashion; Mike Neill hit a game-winning, walk-off home run. In their second game, against South Africa, USA won 11–1. In the third game, Team USA beat the Netherlands 6–2. Their fourth game was against South Korea, a team seen as a medal contender. The game was a pitcher's duel. Team USA's Roy Oswalt blew fastballs past the hitters while dealing a mix of changeups and sinkers. The South Korean pitcher, Tae-Hyon Chong, was a submariner. He was able to neutralize the Americans with sliders and curves that kept the hitters off-balance all night. Jin-Woo Song came on in relief in the eighth of the scoreless game. He got the first batter out, but Mike Neill lined a shot to right field and Ernie Young followed up with a walk. Song was pulled for Pil-Jung Jin, who retired the first hitter he faced but walked Mike Kinkade to load the bases. Up to the plate strode Mientkiewicz. It was his moment.

"I was locked in," he said. "We faced a lot of sidearm guys who weren't throwing real hard, and they brought this guy out. He was more conventional than most South Korean pitchers and he was throwing hard. The count was 3-2 and I remember taking a lot of close pitches that were just off the plate or just outside. I kept looking up at board trying to do the math of kilometers to miles per hour. It was 148 or 149, and I didn't know what that meant but it seemed really hard. Having the bases loaded helped, because the last thing I was thinking of was driving the ball out of the ballpark.

"I went back to what my father told me in the backyard. It was my calming factor. I didn't let the situation overwhelm me."

Mientkiewicz overwhelmed Jin as he crushed the 3-2 fastball over the right-field wall. Living up to his wife's request, he had done something grand, as his grand slam gave Team USA a 4–0 lead that would end up being the final score. The feat overwhelmed Tommy, too. Just as he did throughout the 1988 Dodgers season and postseason, he yelled out one of his favorite sayings: "How sweet it is, the fruits of victory!" He did so again that night in Sydney, and with all of Team USA's wins. "Mike [Neill] and I still text each other a lot and it always ends with 'the fruits of victory,'" said Mientkiewicz. "That saying will never die. It was something we always used."

Team USA beat the Italians 4–2 in its fifth game, which was played on Tommy's 73rd birthday. On hand to help Tommy celebrate was former Dodgers owner Peter O'Malley and Tommy's best friend, legendary USC baseball coach Rod Dedeaux. In their next game, they would face the mighty Cuba.

A full house of 14,010 was on hand to see the game Team USA had wanted to play since that first workout in San Diego, the game Tommy had wanted to play since he was named manager, the game he had wanted since Castro had ruined a country he once cared for.

Cuba threw a hard first punch, putting four runs on the board in the bottom of the first. In the top of the fourth, Cuban pitcher Jose Ibar plunked Ernie Young in the back with a blistering fastball. "They were trying to intimidate us," said Tommy. "That was their style." Young threw down his bat and stared at Ibar. Both benches cleared, but the umpires quelled the feud.

"I was never intimidated by Cuba," said Mientkiewicz. "I played against them in '94. We played three close games against them, and I think we lost all three 2–1 or 3–2. We played them in Nicaragua to qualify for the Olympics. We came out and lost 10–0, but I was never afraid of their great players. I respected them because they were that good. I kept going back to USA hockey coach Herb Brooks saying someone is going to beat these guys. I always felt like if I ever got a crack at it, when it really mattered most, I wanted to be on the team that does this."

"They try to intimidate the other team. That's their style," said Tommy. "My second baseman, Abernathy, said, 'Hey, Skip, are you backing down on these guys?' I said, 'Son, I've knocked more guys down than you've got hairs on your head. I've gotten in more fights than Mike Tyson. But I don't want you fighting. If you get hurt, your general manager is going to blame me, not you. So if you want to kill 'em, you want to beat 'em, beat 'em when we play them for the medal. That's the biggest whipping you can give them.'"

Cuba put up one more run in the bottom of the fourth to make the score 5–0. Later in the game, Mientkiewicz proved that he wasn't intimidated by Cuba. Miguel Caldes hit a grounder, and as he ran up the line toward first, Mientkiewicz, who was covering the bag, tripped the runner. "I was so mad that we weren't going to retaliate," said Mientkiewicz. "That guy was notorious for running up the line. He tried to kick me three other times, but he wasn't going to kick me on this one. If they were going to play dirty, here it is boys, right back at ya. I felt like someone had to make a stand. We were getting our butts kicked at the time, and they were doing their usual, really showboating, and I was sick and tired of it."

Cuba's 6–1 victory gave the Americans their first loss of the tournament and made Cuba 25–3 all time against the U.S. "We lost our focus for a day," said Mientkiewicz. "We got it back after that game, and realized that we have to beat them on the field. We can't try to beat them up. At the end of the day, if we were ahead we would win it respectfully."

Team USA would win the next game in pool play against Australia, their last, setting up a rematch with South Korea in the medal round. Cuba was slated to face Japan. "When they played Japan in the semifinals, I was saying please, please, please win this game," said Mientkiewicz. "We wanted Cuba."

The game was tied 2–2 as the Americans batted in the bottom of the ninth. Mike Kinkade was hit by a pitch, putting the winning run on first. Up to the plate came Mientkiewicz. Once again he found himself batting in the bottom of the ninth with the game on the line. Once again he was trying to get that one hit, the one that counted. Once again he was in the moment.

Tommy pulled Kinkade and put in Gookie Dawkins to pinch run. Although he had hit a grand slam earlier in the tournament, Tommy told Mientkiewicz he was going to bunt. "He said, 'Dougy, I gotta make you bunt.' I told him I didn't care, just find a way to get that guy home," said Mientkiewicz. "He didn't have to say that to me, but he was thinking three batters ahead, and I think his mind never stops. It's just the way he goes about every game."

The relief pitcher, Seok-Jin Park, missed with his first two pitches, so with the count 2-0, Tommy put on the hit and run. But before the next pitch, Park threw over to first, caught Dawkins leaning, and picked him off. Tommy and first-base coach Reggie Smith argued in vain with the umpire. While Tommy barked, Mientkiewicz collected himself. He went back to his father's backyard lessons, his calming place. As he dug back into the box, he was prepared for the moment. "I remember seeing the pitch come off his fingers," said Mientkiewicz. "When the ball came off his hand, all I thought was, *Game over.*"

Just as Kirk Gibson had done the impossible for Tommy in 1988, Mientkiewicz had done the impossible, too. He hit a game-winning home run, a shot that propelled Team USA into the gold-medal game. Just as Tommy had yelled during the 1988 World Series, he would yell again throughout Mientkiewicz's home run trot, through the dog pile celebration on the field and into the clubhouse, and throughout the Olympic Village: "How sweet it is, the fruits of victory!"

"Without the Olympics, I don't think I'd [have] had the confidence I had for the rest of my career," said Mientkiewicz. "Having a chance to play for Tommy was the best thing that ever happened to me. Tommy was the one of the first few guys I played for that really tried to get to know me. He really made an effort to get to know each and every one of us on a personal level.

"For us and the situation we were in, everybody kept saying we were a bunch of no-names, and for us to get notoriety we needed a larger-than-life figure, a stamp on our team. Tommy was the perfect guy for that."

The honor of starting the final game against Cuba went to Ben Sheets, the same young man who was drafted in the first round of the 1999 draft by the Brewers, the same young man who in his professional debut struck out eight batters in five innings, the same young man from Baton Rouge who grew up on jambalaya, crawfish etouffee, and baseball. He also had Tommy's confidence. "I knew Sheets had a great arm, and I knew that if he got into the right frame of mind he could beat the Cubans," said Tommy.

Tommy knew that although Sheets had found success in college and in minors, facing the seasoned and powerful Cubans was another matter. He would have to instill in Sheets the same self-confidence he instilled in Bobby Valentine and Mike Scioscia; that you gotta believe, that you had to compete, that you had to want it more than the other guys.

"He's a great motivator," said Sheets. "His big thing was believe in yourself, believe in what you do. Go out there and compete. He's big on competing. That's one of his big things—don't back down from nobody."

Before the first pool-play game against Japan, one Sheets started, Tommy spoke to him and the rest of the staff. "I knew I had to fire them up, to make them believe," said Tommy. "I said to them, 'Maybe you guys don't know this, but I would take this pitching staff right now in the major leagues, and within two years we would be in the World Series. You guys have all the talent anyone could ask for. You have the ability to perform right now in the major leagues. That's how good I think you are. There is no team around who could beat you guys.'"

Sheets and the guys knew winning Olympic gold would mean a lot to the country, and especially to their manager. "Tommy stressed not playing for stats but for our country," said Sheets. "That we had to believe in each other and had to rely on each other, and you gotta trust in each other to do the job."

Tommy sat down with Sheets at lunch the day before the final. "I said, 'Ben, you may go to Milwaukee, maybe win 20 games, maybe even win the Cy Young. But today, you are going to pitch the biggest game of your life. You are going to pitch a game and represent your country.' And he said, 'Who are we playing?' When he said that, we knew we had the perfect guy. We knew he wouldn't be intimidated by the Cubans."

In his final message to the team, Tommy appealed to their collective sense of patriotism. "We are playing the game for the gold medal," he told them. "We worked very hard in getting to where we are. We cannot give it away. We have got to get that medal. That medal belongs to us, America. We are not playing for the Dodgers or the Yankees or the Minnesota Twins, we are playing for the United States of America. You have to play for the name on the front of the shirt, not for the name on the back, and the name on the front of your shirt says USA. We did not come 6,000 miles to lose!"

"I knew it was an opportunity of a lifetime, and I was ready for it. I was fired up," recalls Sheets.

Team USA jumped out to a 1–0 lead when Pedro Luis Lazo left a 2-1 pitch over the plate that Mike Neill sent over the fence. "That first-inning homer was huge. It gave me a little more room for error," said Sheets. In the fourth, a Pat Borders double and Ernie Young's base hit made the score 4–1. "When we got four runs, I really just wanted to get back to the mound. I was in such a good rhythm," said Sheets.

As the game progressed, Tommy continued to support his players, even if he was confined to the dugout. "He was always talking smack to the other team," said Sheets. "He was awesome on the bench, because he would yell, 'Throw that over the plate so we can rip it! Throw that old watermelon curveball. We'll crush that thing!' Then he would yell it in a different language depending on our opponent."

Sheets was dominant. He refused to give Tommy any reason to consider going to the bullpen. "There wasn't no pitch count that was going to have him take me out," said Sheets. "They think they had a hard time with giving him pitch counts? I would have given him more fits than he would have given the brass. He would have had a hard time getting the ball from me."

"Bob Watson, our general manager, was sitting behind home plate and would holler at me in the dugout," Tommy said. "I would look over and he was flashing his hands with all 10 fingers extended. He was giving me Sheets' pitch count, indicating I had to take him out. I hollered back, 'Sit down, Bull! I ain't taking this guy out if God tells me to, let alone you!' The kid had never pitched nine innings in his life."

"Phil Regan, our pitching coach, had a pitch counter, and Phil's getting nervous because Sheets' pitch count is running up," said Mientkiewicz. "He's clicking the thing, and he tells Tommy that we had to get somebody up. Tommy looked over at him and says, 'Give me that damn thing.' He looked at it and threw it and it broke. He told Regan, 'I'll take the heat. This kid's not coming out of the game.' That was awesome. I felt like, *I love this guy.* He was going to take the heat from every organization, but at this moment this is what's right. Let this kid finish this game, for him, for us, for our country, for everything. He deserves this moment to finish this thing."

"It's what we trained to do," said Sheets. "I was living in the moment, and it was a special moment."

Headed to the ninth, Sheets had only given up three singles. No runners had reached second base. When Javier Mendez dug into the box to lead off the inning, Sheets cleared the dirt around the rubber and cleared his mind. "I was so focused that I couldn't believe it," said Sheets. "I was about to throw a shutout in the gold-medal game."

Mendez fanned, and so did Luis Ulacia. With one batter standing between Sheets and a gold medal, maybe he was thinking about all those walks and talks he and Tommy shared, about the confidence it would take to win. "He talked you into being braver than you were," said Sheets. "He brought a confidence and a certain air that made you feel like you were better than you were."

Maybe he was thinking about his teammates and how in just a short time they had formed a real bond. "Tommy can get guys to believe in the team," said Sheets. "Tommy makes a good player great. Tommy would find a way to make that .108 guy good. He puts the parts together and wins. What did Adam Everett hit? 0-for-17? But Tommy made him relevant. He made some big plays. Tommy believed in the sum of the parts. It didn't matter how we got there. This is what we've got and this is how we're going to do this."

Maybe he was thinking about his manager's will to win. "He thought no matter who they gave him he would go over there and compete and win," said Sheets. "He was there with a bunch of minor-leaguers and he was going to show the world he could win with them. To him it was the ultimate challenge."

Sheets delivered to Yasser Gomez, who sent a soft liner down the left-field line to Mike Neill for the third and final out. Sheets dropped to his knees and was engulfed by a group of giddy, gallant, glorious, and gifted ballplayers representing the United States of America. As Sheets and his teammates celebrated, Tommy cried. "I cried because I had done something for my country," he said. Then, in Spanish, he yelled at the Cubans, "*Oye! Tu va a Havana, Castro espera por tu a cortar cana!*" ("Hey, go back to Cuba and Castro will have you cutting sugar cane!")

"Nobody thought we could beat the Cubans," said Tommy. "But we believed it."

Tommy also played a part in another gold medal–winning team. The U.S. Olympic women's softball team had won 110 consecutive games headed into Sydney, then lost three of its first five in the tournament. Facing elimination, Lisa Fernandez and a few other players asked Tommy to speak to the team before their next contest. Despite priding himself on not using bad language in front of women or children, Tommy agreed to give the players the same

speech he would give to his own team

"Coming into the Games you had a 110-game winning streak," Tommy began. "You thought these teams were going to lay down for you, but then you realized they wanted to beat you a lot more than you wanted to beat them! Lose tonight, and you'll go back to America a disgrace to your country! How bad do you want it?"

The women went out that night and beat New Zealand, then won their next game against

Italy to qualify as the fourth and final team in the medal round. In a show of support, Tommy and his players came to their game and pulled for their fellow Americans. They ended up winning the gold, just as Tommy's team had.

Sadly, Olympic coaches and managers do not receive medals, no matter how big a role they played in their teams' success. "Everybody felt sorry for me, but I told them that I got my medal when they put the medal around my players. I got my medal when I saw them raise that American flag. I got my medal when they played our national anthem," said Tommy. "To me, it was bigger than managing the Dodgers. It was bigger than the World Series, bigger than the playoffs, bigger than anything I had done in baseball. If the Dodgers win, the Dodgers fans are happy but the Giants fans aren't. But when you win a gold medal, all of America is happy."

Especially happy were the Cuban Americans to whom Tommy dedicated the victory. To anybody who asked Tommy about his feelings or experiences in Cuba, he would say, "*Antes que yo muerta, yo quiero mira un Cuba libre!*" ("Before I die, I want to see a free Cuba.") Tommy had learned Spanish during his days in winter ball. "In Cuba, lying on the beach with the jai alai players, a girl would walk by. I would say *girl* and they would say *mujer*. A dog would walk by. I would say *dog* and they would say *perro*. That's how I learned a lot of words and I started to put them together."

He had also learned how important baseball is to people around the world. He learned how much good baseball can do, how it can bring foreign cultures together through a shared love of the sport, and how baseball's worldwide popularity can be a source of pride for Americans, because, after all, baseball is America's game.

The bond between Tommy and Sheets continued after the Olympics. Tommy went to St. Amant, Louisiana, to see Sheets get married. "I did everything in that wedding but marry them," he said.

"That was a big deal in our town," said Sheets. "It showed that he cared about us. For him to come to the wedding was special for a lot of people here. A lot of people grew up idolizing Tommy Lasorda here, or he was one of their favorite managers. Just to show up for me was special, because he thought enough of me to come here. The guests really enjoyed being a part of it. They still talk about it today."

They still talk about his performance in the Olympics, too. Hopefully they share Tommy's belief that baseball is America's gift to the world, as well as Sheets' sentiment about Tommy.

"Baseball doesn't change," he said. "Tommy is old school and I'm new school, but not as new school as some. There's one way to play it. Some people try to come in and change the game, but I'm sure that Tommy has always managed and played the game the correct way. And it doesn't change."

Neither will Tommy's love of his country.

• CHAPTER 9 •

LOVE FOR THE DODGERS

"I bleed Dodger blue."

Tommy has lived his life loving the Dodgers. He has been with the organization in one aspect or another for more than six decades. He has climbed the ladder from minor league player to major league player to coach to scout to minor league manager to major league coach and eventually major league manger. He has joined Jackie, Sandy, Duke, Pee Wee, Campanella, Drysdale, and a couple others in the Hall of Fame. Since donning the Dodgers uniform he has visited 28 countries on behalf of the team and Major League Baseball, spreading the Dodgers gospel, praising the Dodgers name, and enjoying the club's reputation that he and other pioneers work tirelessly to provide. He is baseball's goodwill ambassador, and his life's work in that regard proves true one of his most famous claims: that while Dodger Stadium was his address, every ballpark was his home.

While that description might be common, or even famous, these days, it has been around since the 1970s, well before the glory he found managing the Dodgers, well before he stood at the podium in Cooperstown.

"I used to tell my wife that when I'm buried I know what I want my tombstone to say," said Tommy. "I wanted it to say TOM LASORDA, A DODGER. Underneath it would say DODGER STADIUM WAS HIS ADDRESS BUT EVERY BALLPARK WAS HIS HOME. Mr. O'Malley, the father, heard about it. One

153

day during spring training he called for me. He had a group assembled, and he presented me with my own tombstone. It had a heart on it with a drop of blood painted blue. And the script said exactly what I had told my wife. In accepting it, I thanked Mr. O'Malley and told him that I was honored to be the only person still living with their own tombstone. I was so proud that I told him that I wanted to work for the Dodgers after I was dead and gone."

"I can understand your pride, but how are you going to work for the Dodgers when you're dead?" O'Malley asked.

"I want my wife to put the Dodgers schedule on my grave," Tommy said, "so when people are at the cemetery visiting their loved ones they can check to see if the Dodgers are playing at home or on the road."

It's easy to take pride in an organization that has won six championships. It is easy to take pride in an organization that broke the color barrier by signing Jackie Robinson. It is easy to take pride in an organization that built the first baseball academy in the Dominican Republic, in an organization that was one of the first to travel to Japan to play an exhibition series, in an organization that signed the first Japanese and Korean players to play in Major League Baseball, in an organization that has had the best broadcaster in the history of the game in its booth, in an organization that was the first to top 3 million fans in attendance in one season, in an organization that took care of its players like they were family, in an organization that was synonymous with baseball.

"When you tell someone you're with the Padres, they ask when you became a priest. When you tell someone you're with the Twins, they ask where your brother or sister is. When you tell someone you're with the Cardinals, they say work hard, next step is to be the Pope," said Tommy. "But when you tell someone you're with the Dodgers, they know immediately that you are with Major League Baseball."

The Dodgers logo is on Tommy's business card and stationery. It's on his luggage, his shirts, all over his home, his daughter's home, his brothers' homes, and his distant relatives' homes. It's on his picture that hangs in restaurants across the country, on his picture that hangs on youth fields that bear his name across the country, and on his plaque in Cooperstown. In fact, the Dodgers name may even be in the most of obscure places. "When I had my heart attack, the doctors who performed the surgery cut my chest open," said Tommy. "When they saw my heart, they looked closer and saw DODGERS tattooed across it."

That feeling is something he drilled into his players. "I certainly wasn't going to teach them to love another organization!" said Tommy. "The Dodgers gave me my life, made it possible for me to provide for my family, made it possible to achieve my dreams, so what did I owe the Dodgers in return? Loyalty, and love, and respect. I have said many times that if you really and truly love what you do that you have never worked a day in your life. That's how I felt about being with the Dodgers. I loved it, and I wanted my players to love it, too."

• • •

One of the players who felt the Dodgers love, who would also bleed Dodger blue, was a young man from Sacramento, California. Growing up in Giants country, being a Dodgers fan wasn't always easy for Jerry Royster. His father and three brothers were Giants fans; he and his mother loved the Dodgers because of Maury Wills' speed and Larry Sherry's windup. His loyalty paid off when the Dodgers signed Royster as an amateur free agent in 1970 at age 17.

The next spring he was off to Vero Beach and Dodgertown. That's where he met Tommy. "We had a relationship from the very first day," said Royster. "He introduced himself. I was so nervous but he told me not to be because I was now part of the Dodgers family."

Tommy was then managing in Triple A; Royster was just a rookie, and an undrafted one at that. Royster worked as hard as he thought he could, and while most of the coaches may or may not have taken notice, Tommy certainly did. "Tommy would come over to our practices and watch us," said Royster. "He saw I was working hard and invited me to do extra work with him and some other players. He would take the best five or so third basemen out for extra grounders, and although I was younger than the other players, Tommy included me."

From then on Royster would buy anything Tommy was selling, especially when it came to the value of extra work. "One of Tommy's favorite lines was,

'There are only four more hours of daylight,'" said Royster. "He worked me harder than anyone else ever did. He would work on my strengths because he told me that would get me to the big leagues quicker. It was a real lesson in hard work."

Royster also bought into how Tommy preached about loving the Dodgers. He found Tommy's love for Dodgers blue infectious. "He taught me how to love the Dodgers because he constantly talked about it," said Royster. "He would let me sit at his table for dinner at Dodgertown with all the old time Dodgers—Don Drysdale, Maury Wills, Don Newcombe— people I would never have [had] the opportunity to be with. When they would leave, he would sit there and talk about them. He would talk about the history of the Dodgers and what it meant to be a Dodger. What Tommy was teaching about what was loyalty and dedication. These days, players dedicate themselves to their profession, but in those days Tommy taught us to dedicate ourselves to the Dodgers. To be a Dodger meant dedication. It meant pride."

After two more seasons in the minors, Royster returned to Vero Beach for his third spring training, by then prepared for the hard work that was expected of him. He was more confident in his ability, more dedicated to the organization, and more determined than ever to become a Los Angeles Dodger. "It was ridiculous," said Royster. "Tommy would have us fielding grounders, diving all over the place, throwing the ball all over the field, and taking batting practice as he threw his curve. We would hit it and he would get mad because he was competitive, but he was also proud that we were getting better."

Royster would spend the 1973 season in Triple A; his .302 batting average earned him a callup to Los Angeles that August. That winter Tommy was the third-base coach in L.A. and was slated to manage in the Dominican Republic, and he wanted Royster on his team. "He was the one who got me down there," said Royster. "I was underage and underexperienced to play in winter ball, but I had all the abilities he needed to win. He talked me into going and staying. He told me if I came down there and played for him, he would have me home by Christmas, and I would make the major league team." Steve Garvey was scheduled to join that team before the holiday, so Royster could be back in Sacramento for eggnog and carols. However, Tommy convinced Royster to stay. "He is just full of enthusiasm. He can talk you into doing anything," said Royster. "I was leading the league in hitting and Tommy told me, 'This is how you make it to the big leagues.' All of a sudden it's January 28." But true to his word, Royster joined Tommy in Los Angeles the following spring.

"I'm on the Dodgers plane heading back to L.A. sitting where the rookies sit and here comes Lasorda and all the other coaches, and Walter O'Malley," said Royster. "Tommy says, 'What are you doing here?' He did the old joke on me. 'I'm not sure you're supposed to be here. You need to go talk to Walter Alston.' He had the whole coaching staff in on the joke. It went on for some time, and here comes Alston and he says, 'No, you sit right here, son. You worked your butt off. You deserve it.'"

Although he had made the major league roster, he spent most of the season back in Triple A. However, Tommy was as determined as he was to see him back in Los Angeles. "He would back me up in meetings, and when there was a need he would mention my name. He told Walter Alston to bring me up when Ron Cey needed a rest. Walt didn't know me from the man on the moon. I was in the lineup that same night. I got to play two days in a row. He gave me an opportunity. He already had a backup at the time, Ken McMullen, but Tommy thought I could give the team some energy. I wasn't going to take Ron Cey's place, but that's the determination part that Tommy taught. Don't settle for being second-best. Get after it every day. You have to work your way out of the minor leagues. He used to say that when we got to the major leagues, you want to outplay the guy who's playing in your position. You focus on that guy and make sure you do more than he did."

• • •

One night, Tommy was with his old friend and baseball broadcaster Joe Garagiola. The two attended a party at Joe Ferguson's house. While there, Garagiola saw something that he had never seen before in all of his years in baseball. With a jaw that dropped lower than a sinker in the dirt, Garagiola asked Tommy is he could get his players to replicate what he had just seen on Garagiola's television show. "I can get them to do it on Fifth Avenue in Manhattan during rush hour," said Tommy.

What Garagiola saw was proof positive that Tommy loved the Dodgers and taught his players to love them, too. The scene opens with Tommy talking to his players.

"Okay, fellas, it's spring training and we gotta get that spirit going. You play for the greatest organization in baseball and you gotta believe it's the greatest organization in baseball! Tell me something!"

The camera pans to the right and there assembled in a half circle, in full uniform, are Ron Cey, Charlie Hough, Tom Paciorek, Davey Lopes, Joe Ferguson, Jerry Royster, Bill Russell, and Willie Crawford. In unison the players yell, "I believe!"

"What would you give for the Dodgers?" yelled Tommy.

"My life!"

"Get down and show me how much you love the Dodgers!"

At that point the players kneel to the ground, and with hands extended to the Big Dodger in the Sky, they yell, "I love the Dodgers!"

"And the Dodgers love you!" yelled Tommy back, pumping his fist like he had just won the pennant.

Each player stood up, then knelt back down and reaffirmed their love for the Dodgers. Each player, that is, except Willie Crawford, who yells, "I love the O'Malleys!"

"Why do you love Peter O'Malley?" asks Tommy.

"Because he signs our checks!"

"Oh yeah!" yells Tommy.

"Tom, this is something you started. Do you believe all this?" asks Garagiola.

"I believe it and passed it on to them when they played for me."

At this point in the scene, Tommy tells Garagiola the story about the tombstone, and as the camera pans the players standing around the tombstone with their hats over their hearts.

"It was a fun thing to do," Royster said. "We took pride in being a Dodger. That's what people who don't know him or just see him from across the field think—that he's full of it. But it was never that for us."

While playing for the Dodgers was a fulfillment of his dreams, Royster's dream was about to come to an end. After the 1975 season, Royster was in Mesa, Arizona, playing for Tommy in the Instructional League. He had heard a rumor that he was being packaged with Tom Paciorek, Jimmy Wynn, and Lee Lacy in a trade with the Atlanta Braves for Dusty Baker and Ed Goodson.

"I knew I was being traded, but I didn't want to leave the Dodgers," said Royster. "So I hid. Campanis couldn't find me for two days. Tommy found me and said, 'Hey, all this work you've done, now you have an opportunity to play every day.' I didn't want to leave the Dodgers and go to Atlanta, but Tommy convinced me that I was the main piece of the trade, and that they wanted me over all the other Dodgers prospects. What Tommy told me meant so much, because we had worked hard and he instilled in me how much I wanted to be a big-leaguer. That's when I became a starter and played for 16 years. I have 1,000 stories of him being good to me, making me a part of something. I was just a backup infielder but he treated me like he treated Garvey and Penguin. This story means so much to me because when he convinced me to go to Atlanta, he convinced me that this was the best thing for me, and nobody else was able to do that."

All of Tommy's lessons about making it to the big leagues, and loving the Dodgers, had worked on Royster. That became apparent after the trade. "When I left the Dodgers, I found out more about what it meant to be a Dodger because of the dedication to work, watching how the other organizations worked. Nobody treated me like Tommy treated me when I left and went to these other teams. Nobody did that but Tommy. When I got traded, I was still one of Tommy's guys, I still bled blue. The Braves knew that in my heart I was still a Dodger."

Over the course of his career, Royster would play for the Dodgers, Braves, Padres, White Sox, and Yankees. But 13 years after the trade, Royster was still in the hearts of the Dodgers, and the team made inquires about his future plans after he retired. "I left the field and went right into coaching young Dodgers," said Royster. "As Tommy has said many times, once a Dodger, always a Dodger. I'd do anything for him. He's like a father to me. Even today, I still bleed Dodger blue."

• • •

Drafted by the Dodgers in the fifth round of the 1968 draft, Tom Paciorek was an all-around athlete. He played football and baseball at the University of Houston before being drafted, played for Tommy for four years in the minors, three winters in the Dominican Republic, and with the Dodgers full time for three years while Tommy was their third-base coach.

When he reported to Ogden in '68, it was his first brush with professional sports. He didn't know anyone or anything. "I really didn't know what it meant to be a professional," said Paciorek. "When I met Tommy I loved him, and I thought that everybody in pro ball would be like him. It's been 47 years since we've met, and I still waiting to meet someone like him. I'm waiting for the second coming of Lasorda!"

Paciorek's roommate on the Ogden team was Bobby Valentine. "Tommy picked him up at the airport because he's Italian, but I had to take the bus because I'm Polish," Paciorek jokes. Despite the different modes of transportation, Paciorek, Valentine, and the rest of the players were all enrolled in Lasorda University. "It was like you *played* baseball, you didn't work baseball," said Paciorek. "A lot of coaches, especially at the lower levels, don't understand that. They work on all these drills that don't mean anything, but Tommy would put us in game situations and we would have fun playing baseball. That's how the love of the game is produced. We used to go out in the morning and just play. We would have hitting competitions. We would go to the Chuck-A-Rama to eat, go back to the hotel, and then go to the ballpark to play the game. It was fun."

Tommy wanted to win, and he wanted his players to have fun doing it. He wanted his players to wear the Dodgers uniform with pride, and to embody what being a Dodger meant. Part of that was hating the Giants, or any other team they were playing. "I never told my players to play any harder against the Giants than any other team we played," said Tommy. "But I did tell them to hate them more. We taught that throughout the system—we were Dodgers, and they were the enemy."

"He indoctrinated us. We bled Dodger blue. That was it. He taught us to hate the Giants. It seemed like every year there was a Giants team in our league and we were supposed to hate them," said Paciorek. "We used to have to fight our way out of town, especially in the Rookie League. We were getting bottles thrown at our bus on our way out of town. We were always involved in knockdown wars. We thought we were going to have to fight our way through life."

Those knockdown wars, those fights, were all a manifestation of the competitiveness that Tommy was trying to foster. Peter O'Malley once came to visit Tommy while he was managing in Ogden, and asked him about all the scuffles.

"Peter, I don't like it one bit," Tommy said. "These guys want to win and that's how they do it. God almighty, I can't stop them."

O'Malley turned to one of Tommy's catchers and asked him what Tommy would do when fights broke out.

"He's hollering, 'break it up, break it up,'" said the catcher.

"Do you?" he asked Tommy.

"Oh, no," said the catcher. "When the season started, he told us there would be times when we had to fight and he would be hollering to break it up, but to keep fighting."

Tommy believed that the Dodger Way applied to all walks of life, even friendly get-togethers. "We used to go bowling every Saturday night in Vero," said Paciorek. "Lasorda and Penguin, Buckner and Valentine. The losing team would have to buy bowling and beer. Lasorda never had to pay until one day he loses the match. We couldn't wait to see this. We find out that he went up to the manager and said, 'Hey, buddy, I bring in all these guys and we bowl and drink beer and spend a lot of money. You'd think at least one time you'd pick up the tab for the bowling.' And he did the one time Lasorda lost.

"He was the greatest motivator ever. One time we were playing lousy and Tommy held a team meeting and went up and down telling all of us a thing or two. 'Wimpy, you stink! I don't know who ever signed you. You should be playing football! Garvey, you don't have a hair on your butt. You were horrible. Buckner, you're so arrogant you don't care about anybody else! Valentine, you're the cockiest Italian I've ever seen in my life!' He goes on and on, just getting on everybody. There's one guy on the team who's a devout Mormon, Gary Pullins. He never cussed, never did anything. We were all wondering what Tommy was going to say to Pullins. He finally gets to Pullins and says, 'Pullins, I was just like you before I got into this game!' We all busted out laughing and everything was okay. One thing about Tommy is if you messed up he would never carry it over to the next day. That's the way it should be."

Paciorek was doing so well in Ogden that he was called up to Bakersfield in the middle of the '68 season. While he was happy with the promotion, Paciorek hated leaving his new Dodgers family. "I was in tears when I had to leave Ogden," said Paciorek. "We were in Caldwell, Idaho, and I had to catch a flight. I didn't have a suitcase with me because it was an overnight trip. The only clothes I had I put in a brown paper shopping bag. Tommy looked at me and said, 'Hey, Wimpy, what is that, your Polish Samsonite?' I was crying getting on the plane."

In 1969 Paciorek hit .318 with 15 home runs in 91 games, earning him a spot in Spokane in 1970, where he was reunited with Tommy and other colorful characters. "In Spokane, we had a Jesuit priest named Father Tom Mulcahy," said Paciorek. "We called him the 'Hoodlum Priest' because he was tough. He used to come to the ballpark every night and pitch batting practice. He was an ex–minor league pitcher and he was a mean guy. If you hit a home run off him he would drill you on the next pitch. On an off day, Tommy and Father Tom took us to the fights at the Spokane arena. When the first fight was getting ready to start, one of the boxers got down on one knee and made the sign of the cross on his forehead. I asked Father Tom if that would help him in the fight. He said, 'Yeah, if he can fight it'll help him. But if he can't fight, he is going to get his butt kicked.'"

In 1972 Paciorek played for Tommy in Albuquerque, where the team went 92–56. However, at one point during the season the team lost five in a row. That kind of performance was unbefitting a Dodgers affiliate.

"Salt Lake was coming in to pay us and they were hot," said Paciorek. "Tommy was the greatest motivator in the world. He could kick you in the butt or pat you on the back, but we had played for him for so long that we thought he had used up all his motivation skills."

"I don't want you hanging your heads," Tommy told them. "Yeah, you lost five in a row but they were close, tough games. Did you know that just a few weeks ago, the sportswriters took a poll on who was the greatest team in the history of baseball? They chose the 1927 Yankees. That team had Lou Gehrig, Tony Lazzeri, and the Babe. Well, the '27 Yankees lost seven in a row, and you guys only lost five, so don't worry about it. Let's go out and win tonight."

They won that night and went on to win 10 in a row. "I had told my wife about that meeting after it happened," said Tommy. "About a month later, after the winning streak, she asked me if the 1927 Yankees really lost seven in a row. I said, 'How the heck do I know? That was the year I was born, but it sure sounded good to those guys!'"

Paciorek was with Tommy in the Caribbean that winter. During one game, with the score 2–0, the opposing batter hit a shot over the head of center fielder Von Joshua. Even though the ball hit the fence and stayed in play, the umpire called it a home run. The umpire claimed Joshua pulled a ball out of his pocket, and that the real ball had gone over the fence.

Tommy argued with the umpire and was ejected. Instead of making a calm exit, he took off his shirt and spikes and threw them into the stands, then retreated back into the clubhouse. He showered and got dressed in street clothes, and as he was leaving the clubhouse after the game two policemen were waiting for him. He was taken to jail and spent the night there. "There was a woman in my cell and she was crying and screaming," said Tommy. "The soldiers came in and hit her in the face. All I could do all night was recite the Mass." When he was released the next day, he was told that he was charged with indecent exposure. (Also, General Javier had bet on the other team to win.)

Some of their experiences in the Dominican Republic were more glamorous. "While we were down there they were filming the *The Godfather Part II*," said Paciorek. "Al Pacino and Robert Duvall and those guys were at the ballpark on a regular basis. They offered us a speaking role in the film. We were supposed to be soldiers. Tommy, of course, was going to be a colonel, and Buck and I were going to be sergeants. We go down there and they give us these ridiculous haircuts. They shave down the sides of our heads and we looked like woodpeckers when we came back to the hotel. We looked horrific, but we were in the Dominican, so we didn't care. We were going to be in *The Godfather Part II* and be famous. After we spent all day there getting fitted for uniforms and getting our hair cut, they called us and told us that our parts had been cancelled. I asked if we could keep the haircuts.

"Later, Tommy, Buck, and I were going deep sea fishing. Buck wanted to get in the film and they were filming that night, so we went back. The scene they were filming was when Michael Corleone finds out it was Fredo. We are in that scene. We didn't actually get our faces in the scene, but my right arm is!"

Paciorek played for the Dodgers until 1975 when he was traded, with Jerry Royster, to the Braves. As well as playing in Atlanta he played for the Mariners, White Sox, Mets, and Rangers. In 1981, Tommy was tasting the fruits of victory as his Dodgers won the World Series against the Yankees, with the title-clinching game in New York. Bobby Valentine and Paciorek decided to pay their old skipper a visit.

"Amidst all the chaos, Valentine and I went into Tommy's office and took his uniform, his pants, his hat, and Dodgers jacket," said Paciorek. "We took it back to Valentine's house and Tommy is looking all over for it. He's calling us, 'I know it was you two!' We start sending him pictures of us in his uniform, anonymously. He's calling us every night, 'I want my uniform back!' He has a function in Norristown where he is being honored for the 9,000th time as Italian of the Year or something like that, and he invites us. After we stay out all night we go to Mass, and Valentine takes Lasorda's uniform and puts it on. We are sitting in the back of the church and Valentine walks all the way to the altar with Tommy's uniform on. Lasorda is watching this and wanting to cuss the whole time. We are watching him and just laughing so hard.

"I always had loyalty to the team I was playing for, but there will always be a special place in my heart for the Dodgers because they were always a first-class organization. They always did things the right way, and from Dodgertown on it was a family. The O'Malleys created that, and Tommy perpetuated it. I loved playing for Tommy. Something happened every day.

It was hysterical. We just had so much fun. I think he's in a world by himself. There's only one Lasorda. A lot of people thought they could have made it to the big leagues sooner, but I don't think I'd trade those years with Tommy for anything. I'm sure there were other great managers that I played for that were great tacticians but no one that could handle personalities like Tommy did. He made you love the game, made you want to go out there and play every day, whether you were going good or bad, if it was hot or cold, or whatever the heck it was."

As a student at Lasorda University, Paciorek learned well. He learned about the fundamentals of the game and the characteristics required to be a great player, but he also learned to love the Dodgers, just like Tommy. "He really, truly loves the Dodgers. He is the face of the Dodgers. He is still at every game, too, which I think is amazing. He acknowledges everyone that comes up to him," said Paciorek. "I always considered Tommy my second dad. I just love him to death. He probably had more influence on me than anyone. It's been 39 years since I've been a Dodger, and still, my love for the Dodgers revolves around my love for Tommy. He is synonymous with the Dodgers. I'll always have a soft spot in my heart for the Dodgers, but that doesn't come close to the sentiments I have for Tommy."

• • •

Drafted by St. Louis in the second round of the 1967 draft, Jerry Reuss had an overpowering fastball. Standing 6'5" with a plough of blond hair—characteristics that would earn him the nicknames Big Bird and Q-tip in the big leagues—he spent three years in the minors before making his major league debut for the Cardinals at the end of 1969. He was traded to Houston in 1972 and then to Pittsburgh, where he pitched for five seasons. As the 1979 season opened, he thought Pittsburgh would remain his home. Then he was shipped to the Dodgers on April 7 for Rick Rhoden.

Pittsburgh and Los Angeles are about 2,500 miles apart, and so were the two organizations philosophically and culturally. During Reuss' years with the Pirates, the club won its division twice and otherwise finished second. Like the Dodgers, the Pirates wanted to win, but that's where the similarities ended.

"Pittsburgh was like a frat party 30 minutes after the keg was tapped," said Reuss. "Guys were yelling and screaming in the clubhouse, cutting up. Thirty minutes before the game they got serious and went out and played. With the Dodgers, it was like a Fortune 500 company. Everybody gets there on time, very businesslike." Tommy had rules for his Dodgers: no long hair, no facial hair under the upper lip, coat and tie on travel days, no jeans. "The fans look up to the players," said Tommy. "And as long as they do, by golly, you better look good. They represented the Dodgers."

"When I first joined the ballclub, I still had my Pittsburgh bag and put it in my locker," said Reuss. "Nobi, the clubby, came up to me and said the manager wanted to see me. I figured it was a welcome to the club. I sit down in Lasorda's office and the first thing he tells me is, 'I love the Dodgers!' and he went into that speech. Then he went into this thing about when he dies he still wants to work for the Dodgers. I'm getting the $10,000 speech, and I just joined the ballclub. As he's going on, it dawned on me that he really believes this. He was sincere."

Not long after that first meeting, Reuss received the first of many Lasorda hugs. "I never had a manager prior to Lasorda do that and I never had one after Lasorda to do that. He was the only one that was like that, to outwardly show affection to the players with a hug, but that all kind of played into who he is," said Reuss. "The hugging became a big issue amongst the players on other teams. They thought it was phony, but it wasn't phony with him because he did it all the time. With him it was genuine. He wasn't afraid to show it anywhere. It may seem like some theatrics, but he got his point across. The interesting thing about it was that everyone bought into it, and they believed him.

"Tommy brought excitement to the game of baseball during his time there. His personality, his passion, his enthusiasm for baseball and for the Dodgers carried him through his career as a player. Eventually he made it as the manager of the Dodgers, all the time showing passion and desire for baseball, for winning, and for the Dodgers."

Tommy would show his passion for the Dodgers anywhere, even on the most popular television shows. He once appeared on *The Tonight Show*

Starring Johnny Carson while wearing his Dodgers uniform. "What he did more than anybody else in baseball was talk about his players and the Dodgers whenever he had the chance. He was good," said Reuss. "When he talked, people listened. When he talked, he wasn't talking *at* them, he was talking *to* them. He was getting them to share that enthusiasm. People wanted to be a part of it. They started coming out to the ballpark. The people were excited."

Tommy would also appear on national and local magazine covers, and almost always in the famous Dodgers uniform. "Now, Tom has become the darling of Los Angeles," said Reuss. "Every time you saw a picture of him he was wearing the Dodgers uniform, talking about the players, talking about his experience with the Dodgers."

Not only did the players respond to Tommy's love of the Dodgers, the fans in Los Angeles did, too. When Dodger Stadium opened in 1962 the team drew about 2,750,000 in attendance. That number would stay about the same for years, even during the 1974 pennant-winning season, when they drew only 2,630,000 fans. After all of Tommy's appearances and promotion, after all his chances to share his love of the Dodgers with the people of Los Angeles, the numbers picked up. The attendance in 1977, Tommy's first year as manager, was 2,950,000. After winning the pennant that year and again in '78, attendance went over 3 million for the first time in the history of baseball.

"He became the face of the Dodgers," said Reuss. "Vin Scully was the voice of the Dodgers, but Tommy was the face. He was up front, personal, and you saw attendance increase as a result. With the people coming out to the ballpark, the players responded. The guys started playing to the crowd, and suddenly there was a different kind of excitement at Dodger Stadium. Guys who had pretty good careers in some cities but had reached a standstill would join the Dodgers, and with the enthusiasm of the crowd and the whole thing of Dodgers baseball, they raised their game to another level. I was one of those guys."

If there is one man who understands what a unique manager Tommy was, it might be Reuss, who played for a variety of skippers. With the Cardinals it was the great Red Schoendienst, often described as a player's manager. "What Tom did was let everybody be themselves," said Reuss. "Red was inward and quiet, whereas with Tommy everything was out there. He was promoting the club."

Reuss' Astros team was managed by Harry "The Hat" Walker. He won the National League batting title in 1947 and was considered by many players to be a hitting guru. As he wrote in his book, *Bring in the Right Hander*, Reuss said of Walker, "Harry had a lot of baseball to offer, but he was his own worst enemy. Respect and trust from the manager were missing ingredients for the talent-laden Astros of 1972, and Harry Walker couldn't and didn't provide either."

Walker was fired and the Astros brought in Leo Durocher as manager. He and Reuss clashed; Durocher called his pitcher "the a-hole of all time." When it came to players, he was authoritative to say the least. "Leo was always right, and everybody else was wrong," said Reuss.

Reuss played for Danny Murtaugh with the Pirates from 1974 to 1976, and then for Chuck Tanner after Murtaugh retired. "Chuck liked to spin a yarn as well as anybody and he liked to stay positive," said Reuss. "Tommy was more real in dealing with the press. With Tommy there was a bit more depth. Chuck kept it on an even keel and never revealed too much about himself or got too down on a ballplayer, whereas with Tommy, if something was bothering him, you knew it. Plus, Tom related more to the fans and got them involved. Chuck didn't do that."

Although Reuss went 7–14 during his first season with the Dodgers, his performance improved the following season. "I made some adjustments in my training and in pitching, trying to get someone out in the first three pitches as opposed to pitching for the strikeouts" said Reuss. "As a result, I started winning ballgames, pitching games with fewer pitches."

Los Angeles was always somewhere Reuss wanted to pitch. "Part of the reason I accepted the trade to the Dodgers in 1979 was because of the excitement and enthusiasm around the club, much of which can be traced back to Tom," said Reuss. "I also liked Los Angeles because the field was grass, not turf like in Pittsburgh. Also, the weather was cooler, and at night a fly ball that would normally be hit for a home run was caught on the warning track. I thought L.A. was the perfect place to play. I was playing where I wanted to play, I was doing well, and I was pitching as well as I'd ever pitched. I thought I had died and gone to heaven. Every day was a fun day. How does it get better than playing where you want to play, you're doing well, and the team has a chance to win every year? In 1980 we had a playoff against Houston. In '81 we won the World Series. In '82 we got beat the final day by the Giants. In '83 we made it to the playoffs. Every day in September meant something all four of those years."

Reuss had a tremendous run with the Dodgers. Of his 22 years in the big leagues, his time with the Dodgers was his best. He pitched two games in the 1981 World Series—which the Dodgers won—was the winning pitcher of the 1980 All-Star Game, and threw a no-hitter. As a reward for his no-hitter, Peter O'Malley gave Reuss a big-screen TV. It didn't fit in his house, so O'Malley bought him a smaller one as well as a VCR. (The big-screen stayed in Tommy's office.)

Fun, winning, and family: that was the Dodger Way and part of why Tommy loves the Dodgers so much. "Tom expected us to win. That was a foregone conclusion," said Reuss. "Every manager said that, but they didn't say it quite the same way he did. They didn't deliver the message like a preacher with brimstone and fire. He would deliver those speeches in spring training. I was in the corner of the clubhouse, and Tommy was going. Me and a few other guys started humming 'The Battle Hymn of the Republic.' Tommy got a lick of what we were doing and went along with it. We got louder, so he got louder. He stood on a picnic table and yelled, 'Now get your butts out there and have a day!' He liked it so much that he pulled me aside and told me that was great.

"The point I'm making is the impression Lasorda had over all of Los Angeles. So many fans have told me that they started loving the Dodgers in the 1970s. In fact, one person said they used to get near the water cooler in the morning when there was a coffee break, and they used to talk about different people in the office. But suddenly conversations turned to what the Dodgers did that weekend and how they could get tickets. It was all about the Dodgers, and it was all over Los Angeles, and the reason was the passion and the excitement and enthusiasm that Tom brought to the table. He became the face of the Dodgers, and he still is that to this day. He bleeds Dodger blue. That phrase belongs to him."

While that phrase belongs to him, Tommy has shared it as openly as his hugs. When he has a group of Little Leaguers assembled at his feet, at the end of his speech he asks the kids for a favor. "Tilt your heads back and look up to the Big Dodger in the Sky," Tommy will say. "Now, on the count of three, repeat after me. One, two, three: I love the Dodgers!" As the kids holler and grin, Tommy will holler back the same way he did to his own major-leaguers: "And the Dodgers love you!"

• CHAPTER 10 •

DODGER ROYALTY

"The Dodger Way is a way of life."

It has been said that the true mark of a gentleman is someone who considers others before himself. Such is the perfect description for Peter O'Malley. Son of the man who brought the Dodgers to Los Angeles, Peter assumed the presidency of the club in 1970 while his father, Walter, remained chairman of the board. In doing so, Peter assumed control of one of baseball's crown jewels, one of America's most beloved sports franchises. Not only did he control the direction of the organization, he was the steward of the Dodger Way, a way of playing baseball but also a way of sharing the Dodgers with the people of Los Angeles.

O'Malley was the embodiment of respect. He respected the organization his father built and was determined to sustain its legacy. He respected any player who wore the Dodger uniform. He respected the team's employees, both the people with big titles and the ones who punched the clock. He respected the players' families and the employees' families. He respected the fans. They were all part of the Dodgers family.

The grand contributions the Dodgers made to the game while his father was president, as well as during his tenure, are notably profound. The franchise brought Major League Baseball to the West Coast, broke the color barrier with Jackie Robinson, and built the first baseball academy in the

Dominican Republic. However, to those who knew O'Malley, he was known for the simple gesture. Everyone who wrote to O'Malley received a reply. Everyone who saw him walking to his seats and asked for a picture or an autograph was given one. Through an unprecedented policy, ticket prices did not increase between 1958 and 1976 because the O'Malley family wanted tickets to be affordable.

In 1982, O'Malley cut off season ticket sales at 27,000 accounts so that everyone was able to walk up to the box office to buy tickets if they wanted to.

"I was talking to Peter one day," said Tommy. "I told him that he should put luxury suites on the Club Level. He told me that he could never do that because he didn't want to move all the existing season ticket holders."

O'Malley was equally generous and inclusive to the Dodgers employees. Whenever the team would gain ground or move into first place, he would treat everyone to ice cream. After the Dodgers won the World Series in 1988, O'Malley invited employees to an all-expenses-paid trip to Rome. One of O'Malley's secretaries was leaving the organization because she was getting married. He hosted a going-away luncheon for her at his home.

"In the front office, everyone played a role in our success," said O'Malley. "We wanted everyone to realize that their role was significant." He fully embraced the mantra of once a Dodger, always a Dodger. "According to newspaper reports, that phrase dates back to the Brooklyn Dodgers days in 1934," said O'Malley. "I am very happy that players and those who worked in the front office are proud of their Dodger days and look at that period of time in their career with good memories."

One of O'Malley's favorite ways to foster those memories was hosting reunion luncheons and games for retired greats. "Inviting former Dodgers to our old-timers' weekend was very important, as we wanted them to feel a part of the organization they played for in the past," said O'Malley. "We wanted the luncheons to be private, with just the old-timers catching up and reminiscing."

The reunions were special to the Dodgers players and to O'Malley. "All the old-timer weekends were enjoyed by everyone. These gatherings connected the current team with former Dodgers who established the Dodger tradition," said O'Malley. "Leading the Dodgers organization for my dad and myself was not difficult. Common sense was important, and we both wanted everyone in the organization to feel they had a meaningful responsibility."

Once a Dodger, always a Dodger.

Leo Durocher managed the Dodgers for nine seasons as part of a 24-year career. He was on the Hall of Fame ballot for years, but waited years for induction. After one such missed opportunity, O'Malley asked Joey Amalfitano to invite Durocher, as O'Malley's personal guest, to Dodgertown so he wouldn't feel bad.

Roy Campanella's career was cut short by an auto accident that left him paralyzed. O'Malley made sure that Campanella had a role in the organization for as long as he wanted. "When I became manager, I asked Roy to be one of my coaches," said Tommy. "I told him that although his body was paralyzed there was nothing wrong with his mind. He worked with Yeager, Piazza, Scioscia, and all the hitters. When I asked him, his eyes were as big as baseballs. I knew Peter appreciated that." O'Malley also had Campanella serve in the community affairs department and asked him to make appearances on behalf of the organization.

When Don Newcombe fell on hard times, he sold his World Series ring for extra cash. "When Don Newcombe placed his World Series ring in a pawn shop, he was going through a very difficult time," said O'Malley. "When I heard it was for sale, I bought it and kept it for Don, giving it to him years later. He appreciated that. And fortunately with the help of close friends, he completely turned his life around and is doing many positive things for various charitable organizations throughout Los Angeles." O'Malley gave Newcombe a job in the front office, making him the head of the community affairs department.

O'Malley also took great care to keep widows close to the Dodgers family. He would send them clippings regarding their late husbands, notes on special anniversaries, and promotional items, programs, and schedules. They too would be invited to reunions. Joan Hodges was taken care of as well as Gil would have been. Roxie Campanella was able to see as many games after Roy's passing as she would have while he was still alive. After Jackie Robinson's passing, the O'Malley family, especially Peter, went out of its way to keep their relationship with his widow, Rachel, intact.

"Our family had the greatest respect for Rachel Robinson, and it was natural to keep in touch with her after Jackie passed away," said O'Malley. "When she asked me to join the board of the very vibrant Jackie Robinson Foundation in New York, I was honored and pleased to accept. That foundation has helped fund more than 1,450 scholarships. Rachel also deserves a tremendous amount of credit for Jackie's success and support in difficult times."

When Don Drysdale unexpectedly passed away while the team was in Montreal, O'Malley personally called Ann Meyers-Drysdale to give her the heartbreaking news. "Peter had to track me down," she said. "Don and I usually talked five or six times a day. I called Don twice that morning but couldn't reach him. I took the boys to the beach and we were there all day. We usually had the game on, because Don would do the pregame and the boys would always go to the TV and kiss their daddy. Well, the TV wasn't on, and then we got the phone call. Peter told me that Don had a heart attack, and my first question was, 'Which hospital is he in?' He said, 'No, Annie. I'm sorry to say he didn't make it.' I just went blank.

"Peter and his sister, Terry, both were the class of the organization. Peter took care of everything: having Donnie brought back from Montreal, the funeral, the doctors, the service at Dodger Stadium afterward. I had no worries. He handled everything.

"Even after Donnie had passed away, and Campy had passed away, Roxie and I were always treated like queens. Peter would always invite me into his box and he told me that I had four tickets to the box for life. He would have Christmas in March in Vero Beach. He would bring in fake snow and had presents for all the players' kids. I never felt like I wasn't part of the family."

• • •

While O'Malley took care of Dodgers, he also took care of fans throughout the world. He built Campo Las Palmas, the Dodgers' academy in the Dominican Republic, which was regarded for years as the best academy in the

Dominican Republic. He also built the Dodger Friendship Field in Tianjin, China, Dodger Little League Field in Managua, Nicaragua, and the Dodger Baseball Field and the O'Malley Little League Field in Dublin, Ireland.

"I was introduced to international baseball at an early age, when my parents included my sister Terry and me on the Dodgers' trip to Japan in the fall of 1956," said O'Malley. "That experience, together with going to Cuba and the Dominican Republic with the Dodgers for spring training in the late 1940s and visiting our Triple A farm team in Montreal, made a profound impression on me. It was clear that a tremendous amount of goodwill could be generated by our players who enthusiastically connected with the fans, and the fans graciously responded."

In December 2008, Tommy received the Order of the Rising Sun, Gold Rays with Rosette. It is a prestigious honor bestowed on behalf of the Emperor of Japan to those who have made distinguished achievements in various fields. Tommy's medal was draped around his neck by Junichi Ihara, then Consul General of Japan, for Tommy's contributions to Japanese baseball, and for continuing to build a special friendship between the people of Japan and the United States. After being awarded with the honor, Tommy said, "When you honor me, you honor the Dodgers."

The Dodgers also have a long association with Japan. After the '56 season, then-owner Walter O'Malley sent his team there to play a 20-game exhibition series throughout the country. That trip was a grand success, as the streets of Japanese cities and towns were lined with fans welcoming the Dodgers. It set the stage for further visits and exchanges, for decades of friendship built around the mutual love of baseball.

"The Dodgers' 1956 goodwill tour to Japan was the first time our family visited Japan," said O'Malley. "I was surprised that the fans were so knowledgeable about baseball and the Dodger players. The team enjoyed the trip and realized they were making a significant contribution through sports to the important relationship between the two countries. The fans throughout all the stadiums in Japan expected the Dodgers to win every game and we did not disappoint them, winning 14 and losing only four games."

Tommy has been working to improve baseball in Japan since 1965, when Walter O'Malley sent him to Tokyo for two weeks to work with the Tokyo Giants. "I taught them all aspects of the game," said Tommy. "I worked with the manager and coaches and players on hitting, pitching, fielding, base running, defense, everything. Scouting and player development, too." After Tommy left, the Giants went on to win nine consecutive championships.

In a letter dated January 30, 1965, that Tommy wrote to Walter O'Malley on Tokyo Hilton stationery, he talked about the regard the Japanese people had for the O'Malley family, the Dodgers, and for baseball. The feelings of respect and admiration they held stemmed from the Dodgers' 1956 trip, as well as the team's continued success over the following years. Speaking of Matsutaro Shoriki, the founder of the *Yomiuri Shimbun* newspaper and "father of Japanese professional baseball," Tommy wrote, "We met yesterday with Mr. Shoriki and it was a real thrill to sit and talk with him. He is a wonderful man, he thinks highly of you, and sends his regards." The letter later noted, "These people are great lovers of baseball."

What the letter didn't say was how hard Tommy worked to secure another trip by the Dodgers to Japan. "I would sit with Shoriki every night and talk to him about the Dodgers," said Tommy. "We would drink whiskey all night, and the only thing he knew in English was the song 'Home on the Range.' We would sing that over sips of whiskey till 3:00 or 4:00 in the morning."

The Dodgers returned to Japan in 1966 for another goodwill tour. "My dad was awarded by Emperor Hirohito the Third Class 'Order of the Sacred Treasure, Gold Rays with Neck Ribbon' on November 15, 1966," said O'Malley. "He appreciated this high honor, established in 1888 for both civil and military merit, at the prime minister's office, where he was decorated by Kiyoshi Mori, director general for prime minister Eisaku Sato, in recognition of fostering United States–Japan friendship through professional baseball and the second of two Dodger goodwill tours to Japan. Tommy and my dad have appropriately been honored by Japan, and I know this recognition was appreciated for everything they did in support of baseball in Japan and goodwill. They both enjoyed this role."

Tommy and Peter met in the 1950s, when Tommy was a player-coach in Montreal. "His enthusiasm and ability to communicate very directly was obvious," said O'Malley. "I saw that Tommy was completely at ease talking with someone young as well as adults. Tommy and I bonded early on, and I am happy that our relationship is like two close, personal friends. Over the years we have occasionally differed on a few things but that never got in the way of my admiration and respect for him."

"Peter means everything to me," said Tommy. "He gave me the opportunity to manage the major league team, and I will be forever grateful to him and his family for the friendship and loyalty they showed me. He wanted someone in the position who would represent the Dodgers to the highest degree of class, dignity, and character. I loved his mother and father and his sister very much, and I loved him and his family."

On September 28, 1976, Tommy was wrapping up his fourth season as Walter Alston's third-base coach. Everybody knew that Alston was retiring, but nobody knew who would replace him. "Peter told me that day to make sure that nobody was on the phone the next morning at 9:00 AM," said Tommy. "When I went home, I told my family to stay off the phone. Sure enough, the next morning at 9:00 AM he called me and told me that he wanted to see me in his office. I was there at 10:00 AM sharp, right on the nose. The whole drive in, I couldn't stop thinking about what he was going to tell me. Would it be that he decided to go with someone else? I never thought it would be me because of all those great Brooklyn Dodgers that would have done the job. I sat down and he said, 'Congratulations. You are the new manager of the Dodgers.' It was the greatest thing that ever happened to me. I told him I would do the job for nothing, but I needed something to live on."

"I thought the Dodgers would be in good hands," O'Malley said. "Tommy would follow Hall of Fame manager Walter Alston and I was very confident he was the right man for the job. While watching Tommy manage in Ogden in the mid 1960s, Tommy's leadership skills, ability to inspire and encourage young players, and his unique communication style were all very impressive. Communication was an important thing for me and the Dodgers organization, and I wanted everyone to know what was important and how we were trying to accomplish our goal. Those days were before e-mail, and a phone call or brief note served this important purpose. Something as small as a Christmas card kept everyone in touch and included."

After Tommy suffered his heart attack in 1996, he and Jo met with O'Malley to discuss his managerial future. "We talked to him for a bit, and Jo was crying, thanking Peter for all he had done for our family over the years," said Tommy. "Jo and I asked Peter for a few moments alone and we went outside to talk. I was worried that I wouldn't be the same manager as I was before. I was worried that I would end up like Drysdale and that I would never see [my granddaughter] Emily graduate college. We went back in and I told Peter that if I continued to manage, he wouldn't be getting the same Tommy Lasorda. After all he had done for me and my family, I couldn't do the job the way it should be done, and he deserved that. So I resigned.

"He accepted my resignation and immediately said, 'Congratulations. You are now a vice president of the Los Angeles Dodgers.'"

"Tommy's health was our number-one concern, and his retirement after managing the Dodgers for 20 years was the right decision, but he didn't want to take off the uniform," said O'Malley. "It was important to me that all our employees, both in the front office and the dugout, be proud of being a member of the Dodgers organization. Tommy truly bleeds Dodgers blue and always represents the organization in a most positive way."

The next year Tommy was inducted into the Hall of Fame. It was a proud day for the Dodgers family, including O'Malley. He was in attendance to see Tommy's plaque installed, and to see the manager he hired, the manager who brought his team so much success, the manager who captivated the fans, the manager who was also his friend immortalized in Cooperstown along with all the great Dodgers of years past.

"After my induction, my hometown threw a dinner for me, and Peter was invited," said Tommy. "He couldn't attend, but he sent a telegram that they read from the podium. It said, FROM OGDEN TO COOPERSTOWN. CONGRATULATIONS ON YOUR INDUCTION INTO THE HALL OF FAME. I still have that telegram in my desk."

"Tommy taught us all that being a Dodger and major league player, coach, or executive is a 24-hour, seven-days-a-week, year-round, full-time responsibility, and to cherish that opportunity," said O'Malley. "It was a privilege to work in Major League Baseball representing the city and millions of fans. Many people underestimate the hard work, commitment, and talent it takes to be a successful major league manager. Tommy possessed all those ingredients together, with a true love for his job."

• • •

Just as O'Malley had envisioned Tommy's future success, he must have had the same notion with another legendary Dodger, one who has made contributions to the organization far beyond some of the home runs, stolen bases, and saved games.

That man is Vincent Edward Scully, a name synonymous with the Dodgers. He has been broadcasting Dodgers baseball since 1950. When the Dodgers moved to Los Angeles, Scully made the move with them. When the team played its first game at the Coliseum, while Dodger Stadium was being built, Scully welcomed the new fans to the Dodgers family, and in return the fans have felt as if he was a part of their family, too.

In a city based on fiction, on transience, on novelty, Scully has been the antithesis, a mark of permanency more enduring than stars on the Hollywood Walk of Fame, more lasting than a Los Angeles sunset in July. His calls have fortified the fans' love of the Dodgers like the San Gabriel Mountains anchor the west side. His audience has been anyone who has tuned in to listen or watch the Dodgers; he has also broadcast numerous World Series and All-Star Games, and relayed countless moments of greatness in the game. Whether you are a Dodgers fan or not, if you've listened to Scully you have probably heard some of the most precious lines uttered about the game.

> Robinson, kind of shaking up the ballpark a bit as he dances
> down off third. Robbie's coming to the plate. The
> throw, the tag, he steals it!

Never have I been asked to make an announcement that hurts me as much as this one. And I say it to you as best I can with a broken heart.

If you have a sombrero, throw it to the sky.

So when he wrote his name in capital letters in the record books, that K stands out even more than the O-U-F-A-X.

It gets through Buckner!

High fly ball into right field, she is gone!

Tommy and Scully have been together for more than 60 years, together in sharing their love for baseball and the Dodgers with their respective audiences. To Scully, that's anyone listening or watching a game. To Tommy, that's anyone he's talking to.

"The first time I ever heard the name Tommy Lasorda was in Vero Beach," said Scully. "I was talking to Buzzie Bavasi, the GM of the Dodgers. We were chatting and he said, 'Oh, I've got to leave. I have to stop a kid from killing himself. There's a kid who has bet me that he would pitch batting practice to every player in camp.' In those days, we had 26 farm teams, so if you were going to pitch batting practice, with free agents, we're talking 600, 700 players. I asked what his name was, and he said, 'Tommy Lasorda. He's a left-hander on the Montreal roster.' That was the first time I heard his name, and I realized that whoever it was had to had a terrific spirit to even think he could do such an undertaking. To pitch batting practice to 600 guys would kill you, but not Tommy."

"Buzzie called it off," said Tommy. "I made the bet and I was serious. Buzzie found out about it. He said, 'No way. That guy will die before he quits.' But I could have done it."

Scully's career in the Dodgers booth was the culmination of a boyhood dream. "I would come home to listen to a football game," he said. "There weren't other sports on, and I would get a pillow and I would crawl under the radio so that the loudspeaker and the roar of the crowd would wash all over me, and I would just get goose bumps like you can't believe. I knew that of all the things in this world that I wanted, I wanted to be that fella saying, whatever, home run, or touchdown. It just really got to me."

Scully has had many opportunities to indulge, to become again that eight-year-old boy, and let the roar of the crowd wash over him. He is a master at letting the indelible moments that baseball provide speak for themselves. "It is my trademark I guess, but it is pure selfishness on my part," he said. "I love to hear the roar of the crowd. I try to call a play as quickly and accurately as possible and get out of the way."

Scully once said, "It's a mere moment in a man's life between the All-Star Game and the Old-Timers Game." He was probably talking about some veteran on the verge of retirement, or perhaps he was talking about himself. "My life has been the fulfillment of a dream," said Scully to *Los Angeles Daily News* reporter Tom Hoffarth. "I wrote for the nuns an essay when I was eight years old on what I wanted to be when I grew up. The boys were all about being policemen and firemen and doctors and lawyers, while the girls were about nursing or ballet dancers or becoming mothers. There was no TV and just a few things on the radio, maybe a Saturday afternoon football game between Ohio State and Notre Dame. So when I said I wanted to be a sports announcer, that was way out in left field. So when I eventually got that job with the Dodgers, It really was the fulfillment of a dream. That's rather remarkable in itself. I have a great deal to be thankful for."

While he never had to be successful on the field, he did share the doubts of a pitcher struggling to keep his ball down in the late innings, or to get his ball to break over the exact corner of the plate where the bat wouldn't reach. He needed a boost of confidence, but his couldn't come from a manager. When Scully was in his early years behind the mic, he would partner with Red Barber and only worked the third and seventh innings. Like a father passing a family tradition to the next generation, Barber would turn the mic over to Scully and say, "Okay, young fella. It's all yours." Barber believed in Scully and so did their boss.

"In 1953 I was doing my first World Series, and I was pretty frightened because I hadn't done any TV," said Scully. "One or two innings the whole year, and now I'm sharing the microphone with Mel Allen to do the World Series. It was a big moment. I was 25 years old. The day of the first telecast, Mel came into the booth and said, 'I just saw your boss [Walter O'Malley]. He said, "Mel, take care of my boy." That was a wonderful feeling.

"The first word that comes to mind when I think of the Dodgers is *family*. The reason I think that more than anything else was Walter O'Malley, Peter O'Malley, and Terry O'Malley almost made me feel like I was part of their family. Mr. O'Malley was either a second father or a Dutch uncle, whatever you want to call him. I was younger, impressionable, emotional, insecure, and they made me feel a part of the family. That was the greatest single feeling I had working for the team."

After the official announcement was made that Tommy would become the Dodgers manager, Scully interviewed him. "You are replacing a man who has been here for 24 years. You are replacing a future Hall of Famer. You're replacing one of the greatest managers in baseball. Don't you think there will be a lot of pressure on you?" asked Scully.

"You want to know something Vinny?" Tommy asked. "I'm worried about the guy who's going to have to replace *me*."

Scully once said, "Good isn't good when better is expected." Tommy always wanted more from his players, and would rest at nothing to make it happen. "Tommy was a great motivator. He had a remarkable skill," said Scully. "When they were playing for him, they played 100 percent up to their abilities. I think that was the greatest gift Tom brought to the ballclub. His ability to motivate, to get the players personally involved; it's not just a job going to the ballpark every day. If you were around Tommy, his spirit was definitely contagious."

When Scully was behind the mic during Sandy Koufax's perfect game, he blessed the audience with one of his most eloquent observations of that passion, of that love for the game, that Tommy and all the Dodgers shared: "A lot of the people in the ballpark are starting to see the pitches with their hearts." Tommy saw every pitch, hit, catch, run, win, and loss with his heart, too. "When you have been with him all those years, you realize that he couldn't wait to get to the ballpark, and he relished every single moment as the manager," said Scully. "He loved it from the minute he was in the clubhouse before he even got dressed."

Tommy loved few moments as much as his run in the 1981 World Series. "He had gone through '77 and '78 and come up a buck short, and now he was going to be so close to winning it in '81. I'm sure that was a pressure-packed moment in Tommy's career," said Scully.

• • •

For Tommy, being inducted into the Hall of Fame was overwhelming. It started with a phone call from a friend.

"We were in Vero Beach and Derrick Hall comes to me and tells me that I had a call," said Tommy. It was from Ted Williams.

"These guys I'm meeting with here think the world of you, and I think the world of you, too," Williams said. "I thought I was the only guy who loves you, but we all do. So they asked me if I would call you to let you know that you have been inducted into the Hall of Fame."

"I knew that although he could never make it the way he wanted as a pitcher, by coming back as a very successful manager and motivator of men, he had fulfilled his dream," said Scully.

When Scully was inducted into the Hall of Fame, his speech was predictably eloquent and indicative of a man who personifies gratitude. He asked the rhetorical question that so many of us who have been befuddled by life's blessings asks: "Why me?" For the millions of fans who have been blessed by Scully's brilliance, the answer is an easy one. The game's story cannot be told without the man Jim Murray once described as, "the Fordham Thrush with a .400 larynx." The National Baseball Hall of Fame's motto is "Preserving History, Honoring Excellence, Connecting Generations." It is thus fitting that Scully be included. While talking about baseball, he once said, "It's a wonderful feeling to be a bridge to the past and to unite generations. The sport of baseball does that, and I am just a part of it."

In Scully's induction speech, he told a story about an Indian chief who wanted to test the mettle of his younger tribesmen.

The chief wanted to test them by making them climb up a mountain as far as they could in a single day. At daybreak on the appointed day, four braves left the village. The first came back in the late afternoon with a sprig of spruce to show how high he had climbed. Later that afternoon, another came with a branch of pine. Much later in the day, the third came with an alpine shrub.

But it wasn't until late that night, by the full moon, with the stars dancing in the heavens, that the fourth brave arrived. "What did you bring back? How high did you climb?" asked the chief. And the brave said, "Where I was there was no spruce nor pine to shield me from the sun. There was no flower to cheer my path. There was only snow and ice, and barren rocks, and cold, hard ground. My feet are torn and bloodied. I'm worn out and exhausted. I'm bare-handed, and I have come home late." And then a wondrous look came into his eye, and he said, "I saw the sea."

For 33 years the Good Lord has allowed me to do what I've always wanted to do: broadcast my favorite game. He has allowed me to climb my mountain. And today, thanks to the Ford C. Frick Award, I thank you for sharing this moment with me, because believe me, today I saw the sea.

Tommy has said many times that people who really and truly love what they do have never worked a day in their lives. Tommy has also said that if you are ever feeling deprived or denied, look over your shoulder and see how lucky you really are. Tommy and Scully are both wealthy men who have never had to punch the clock, and they know it.

"If I have one overwhelming feeling, it's one of deep gratitude and thanksgiving to God for everything that I have," said Scully. "I also know that I could lose it in a blink of an eye, so I cherish every moment."

Certainly both Scully and Tommy cherish their friendship. "We get along very well. I understand Tommy. Tommy wears his emotions on his sleeve. We have never had a cross word, and I have known him over 60 years," said Scully.

"He is the greatest announcer ever," Tommy said. "He has always set a good example for people. He was always friendly, whether he liked you or not, and he was a very personable man, a tremendous family man. And, like me, we had that second love of the Dodgers only behind our families. I'm thankful for his friendship."

During many of his broadcasts, when baseball reveals itself as unpredictable and sometimes silly, Scully has said, "If you want to make God smile, tell Him your plans." The irrationality of baseball is part of the reason the game is so beloved. So is its difficulty.

"The most important part of it, my love for it, came because I tried to play it," said Scully. "I was good enough to play it in high school and good enough to play varsity college ball, but I knew once I got to college. I knew then I could never go on, and I knew how difficult the game is. I have always been fascinated how these players make a very difficult game appear to be so easy. They catch those towering pop flies and foul balls, they make dazzling plays on line drives, and until you've been down there and tried to play, you just can't appreciate the artistry of these men, and that's the thing that has intrigued me more than anything else. I just can't believe how good they are."

Although Scully did hit one home run playing for Fordham University, he never played past college. The closest he came to being a Dodger on the field came courtesy of his friend. "Tommy had asked me if I had ever been in a Dodger uniform," Scully said. "I said no. He said, 'Why don't you come down? You're not televising the game, you're not working.' I told him I would only come in if he asked the umpires a day before for permission, because I don't want to just go in and get kicked off the bench. Tommy asked for permission and I was allowed, and I thought no one had any idea. I crept into the dugout at the end of the anthem, and I had the hat pulled down over my eyebrows, arms folded at my chest. At the bottom of the first inning, John Vukovich, the first-base coach for the Cubs, ran by our dugout and hollered, 'Vinny!' I was startled. He tossed a ball to me, and on the ball it said, *If a fight breaks out I want you*, and it was signed by Don Zimmer. I looked over and all the Cubs were falling down laughing."

Joe Posnanski, for *Sports Illustrated*, asked Scully about the meaning of baseball. He said, "Dreams and escape. Children dream about this game, and when we grow older, the game provides our escape from the troubles of day-to-day life."

Dodgers fans, and baseball fans in general, must surely thank God for Vin Scully. He once told sportswriter Steve Rushin, "The sweetest thing is when people come over to me and say, 'When I hear your voice, I think of summer evenings in the backyard with my dad.'"

Of course, the sweetest thing Dodgers fans ever hear is when the Voice of Summer, baseball's poet laureate, says, "And a very pleasant day to you wherever you may be. It's time for Dodger baseball."

And how, Mr. Scully.

• CHAPTER 11 •

DODGER REALEZA

"Yo soy Liceista!"

While Vin Scully is the voice of the Dodgers, there is another voice that echoes throughout the Southland, past Mexicali, down Central America, and into the Southern Hemisphere. That voice belongs to Señor Dodger, La Voz de Oro, Jaime Jarrin. Just as Scully has defined Dodgers baseball to generations, so too has Jarrin; he has been broadcasting Dodgers baseball in Spanish since 1959. He has broadcasted more than 10,000 games, 25 World Series, 19 All-Star Games, 20 no-hitters (including three perfect games), and five of the Dodgers' six World Series championships.

In May 2013, his 55th season with the Dodgers, Jarrin threw out the ceremonial first pitch at Dodger Stadium, another way of honoring his legacy and thanking him for his service. While he stood on the mound before tens of thousands of fans—a small audience in comparison to those of his radio broadcasts—he must have felt just a bit nervous, despite his family helping him practice the throw in their backyard that afternoon before the game.

On hand to salute Jarrin was his old friend, Tommy. The two first met at the Los Angeles Memorial Coliseum when Tommy paid Jarrin a visit in the radio booth. "He came with a prospect of the Dodgers, and he spent a few minutes in our booth," said Jarrin. "Of course, he started talking right away about Charlie Hough and Steve Garvey and about Bobby Valentine and

189

those players that will someday come to the major leagues. I remember when he was a coach with the Dodgers, a third-base coach, and then of course in 1977 he became manager. He was always extremely nice with me. We used to spend lots of time together. He distinguished me with special signs of friendship. He would invite me to go to dinners outside of the baseball circle. I have gone to many dinners with him when he has been honored. One time he took me to a clothing store. He said, 'Choose anything you want. Choose this, choose this, choose anything. Choose a suit, choose a tie, choose a shirt, anything.'"

Just as Tommy treated his players like family, he did the same with Jarrin. The meals and the gifts were Tommy's way of showing his affection for those he loved. So too was sharing his stories. "That's part of the sessions with Tommy," said Jarrin. "He would always talk about his experiences in the Dominican Republic especially, and in Cuba. You know, his stories are precious. I have heard the stories hundreds of times and still enjoy them."

"Jaime is a true and great friend," said Tommy. "He has been for many years, and I have always looked up to him with respect for what he has done for the Dodgers. I am very appreciative to him for our friendship and I love his family just as much."

Another special friend of Jarrin's was also on hand to salute him during his first pitch. That player was Fernando Valenzuela, one of the greatest pitchers in the history of the Dodgers. For the first few years of Valenzuela's major league career, Jarrin was his interpreter. When he debuted for the Dodgers in 1980 he was only 19 years old, and he didn't speak the language. To make matters worse, the media intimidated him. Those years became the foundation of a true friendship. Valenzuela holds a special place in his heart. "When Fernando came on in 1981, it was very special. It is one of my favorite moments of Dodgers baseball," Jarrin said.

The press may have rattled Fernando's nerves, but the hitters in the National League did not. He made his major league debut for the Dodgers on September 15, 1980. To end that season he pitched in relief in 10 games, won two of them, and in the 17.2 innings he pitched he only surrendered eight hits and two unearned runs while striking out 16. On April 9, 1981, he was scheduled to start the Dodgers' home opener. When Fernando took the mound in the top of the first, Jarrin saw a lot of himself in the young pitcher. The two Dodgers had a lot in common.

Jarrin emigrated from Quito, Ecuador, and sailed through the Panama Canal on a German ship carrying countless bananas but just 40 passengers. He already had experience in broadcasting. "When I was very small—12, 13 years old—I had a cousin, Alfredo Jarrin, who was a very well-known radio announcer in Quito," said Jarrin. "He used to take me to the station with him, so I had a chance to be, practically on a daily basis, at the radio station visiting and learning. I started on radio when I was 15 years old. I became a very well-known announcer there doing news and special events. I was only 17 years old when I was named the announcer for the Congress of Ecuador's senate."

"When we came to this country as immigrants as Fernando and I did, we came here looking forward to a better life, better chances, better opportunities," said Jarrin. "I came without the assurances of work or anything like that. In 1955, when I came to this country, we had only one Spanish radio station, KWKW, but there were no openings. So I had to wait until my turn came. I was trying to get into radio because I came to this country to work in radio, nothing else, so I tried and I tried and I tried.

"I went to school for eight years taking English in Ecuador, and I was working at the radio station with many American people. When I came to this country, I thought I knew English but really I was lost. It is very different to be in a classroom and being on the streets listening to the English language. That's why I went to school here to learn English."

While he waited for his break into broadcasting, Jarrin worked for six months in a factory that made fences. Finally, he got his chance. "At the end of 1955, I had my opportunity on KWKW," said Jarrin. "I started working on weekends, three hours on Saturday, three hours on Sunday, until a few months later I got a full-time job in news."

Six months after getting his job at KWKW, Jarrin was promoted to news and sports director. His hard work was paying off. William Beaton, the owner of the station, secured the broadcast rights for the Dodgers for the 1958 season, the team's first in Los Angeles. Jarrin was given another opportunity, an opportunity that would change his life. "William came to me and said he needed two announcers, and I had to be one of the announcers," said Jarrin. Prior to Jarrin getting the job to broadcast Dodgers games, the only sporting events he had called were boxing matches.

Jarrin didn't know anything about baseball. He asked Beaton for one year to learn the game. "I saw in October of 1955 the World Series being played in New York between the Brooklyn Dodgers and the Yankees," he said. "I saw so many people around a television watching the game in New York. In the restaurants in Los Angeles, in the stores, there were television sets tuned to the World Series. I started asking questions about baseball and started to go to watch the Triple A teams in Los Angeles at Gilmore Field and Wrigley Field. That's where I learned and fell in love with the game."

For the first six years, the Spanish-language announcers did not travel with the team. Instead, they would re-create the games on radio while listening to Scully broadcast the games. "Vin was very helpful to me," said Jarrin. "He knew how tough our job was, so he would give me as much information and facts as he could in advance, and that was very helpful."

Not only did Jarrin get help from Scully, he got help from another one of baseball's favorite sons, Roberto Clemente. "Roberto was very unique. He was very helpful to me and to us. He understood our situation when we came," said Jarrin. "In the late '50s and early '60s, very few Spanish-speaking ballplayers were playing. He understood that and was always willing to help us. He took the time to really help us. He was just great."

Eventually, Jarrin covered special events of the highest significance. He reported from New York on the Pope's first visit to the United States. He reported from London as Winston Churchill was buried. He reported live from the nation's capital after the assassination of John F. Kennedy.

Just as Jarrin worked hard and made the most of every opportunity he was given, so too did Valenzuela. A native of Etchohuaquila, Mexico, he hailed from a place where children grow up playing soccer, not baseball. He had to work hard to develop his screwball in the Dodgers system, a pitch that dives away from right-handed batters, something that took the young left-hander a couple years to master. After working his way through the Mexican League, Valenzuela's opportunity to start for the Dodgers on Opening Day came because Jerry Reuss and Burt Hooton were both injured.

He was starting against the Astros, the team the beat the Dodgers the year before in a one-game playoff for a ticket to the postseason. The Astros came into the '81 season a pennant favorite. Just as Beaton gave Jarrin the opportunity of lifetime despite Jarrin's lack of baseball knowledge, Tommy gave the inexperienced Valenzuela the opportunity of a lifetime. Valenzuela was set to duel Joe Niekro, the very pitcher who beat the Dodgers in that one-game playoff.

The game remained scoreless until the bottom of the fourth. Steve Garvey tripled and scored on a sacrifice fly by Ron Cey. In the bottom of the sixth, Pedro Guerrero gave Valenzuela some insurance with an RBI double, giving the Dodgers a 2–0 lead. By then, the young Fernando was cruising. Mark Heisler of the *Los Angeles Times* quoted Dodgers catcher Mike Scioscia as saying, "He started off a little slow, stuff-wise. As the game progressed he got stronger. From the seventh through the ninth he had awesome command of everything. He wasn't one bit nervous. He was cool out there. I don't think he even broke a sweat."

In the ninth, Valenzuela gave up a base hit with two outs. As he worked the next hitter to two strikes, the fans rose to their feet and raised their cheers to the heavens. He threw a screwball for his fifth strikeout, for his first win as a starter, for a complete-game shutout, for the start of Fernandomania that lit the hearts of Latin fans afire and drew them to the Dodgers, to baseball, in record numbers.

"That was unbelievable, the way he pitched," Jarrin said. "Everything clicked. It was Opening Day, so the ballpark was full of people, not because of Fernando, because he wasn't supposed to start the game. But he came on and it was a jewel he pitched that night."

After that first win Valenzuela went on to win his next seven starts for an 8–0 record. In those eight starts he was magnificent, throwing seven complete games, five of them shutouts. He only surrendered four runs in 72 innings, giving him an ERA of 0.50. He finished the year with a 13–7 record and a 2.48 ERA while leading the league in complete games (11), shutouts (eight), and innings pitched (192.1). He was an All-Star and won the National League Rookie of the Year award. More impressively, he won the Cy Young Award.

Of course, none of that would have been possible without the help of his skipper, Tommy. "It was a perfect marriage because of Tommy's personality," said Jarrin. "And on the other hand you had this kid from Mexico, 19 years old, a little bit chubby, long hair, not a single word of English. Tommy helped him a lot. He understood him because he spoke the language."

"I tried to help him with the press, tried to give him some privacy," said Tommy. "I also got him his first suit, and once in a while I would translate for him."

One time, Valenzuela was being interviewed by Stu Nahan, a Southern California sports broadcaster. While Tommy stepped in to translate, he thought he'd have some fun with it. "Everything Stu asked Fernando, I repeated something different," said Tommy. "Valenzuela wanted to punch him out right there but I told him he was just kidding."

The fans responded to Valenzuela's success. "Because of Fernando and the coverage the Dodgers had in Spanish, we had 86 radio stations carrying the Dodgers games," said Jarrin. "Because of that there were so many new baseball fans, and especially Dodgers fans. Fernando meant so much to the Latin people. He was unbelievable. I don't think that any president, any diplomat, any politician, any civic leader did what Fernando was able to do. He opened the doors to many Latin American players to come to the U.S., particularly from Mexico. Before Fernando, there were very few Mexican players in the major leagues. Baseball was a very foreign sport for them, and thanks to Fernando they started listening to the games, they started watching the games, and they became involved in baseball and they really started learning about the game and became fans. The success of the Dodgers attracting so many Latinos to the ballpark, it's thanks in part to Fernando. Now it's 46 percent of the fan base. Fernando did what no other baseball player did for the good of the game, that's why I think he should be in the

Hall of Fame. The Hall of Fame is not only about numbers, it is about what you have done for the game of baseball, and Fernando did so much."

If Valenzuela ever did get into the Hall of Fame, he would join his skipper, Tommy, and his friend, Jarrin. In 1998, the Ecuadorian immigrant stood at the podium in Cooperstown to receive the Ford C. Frick Award, just as Scully had years earlier. "My longevity in baseball is thanks to the feedback I get from people," said Jarrin. "I think they appreciate my work and I think that we have created in our broadcast here so many new fans, and it is very satisfying for me to be the tool that gives the fans so much enjoyment about baseball. I will always be very thankful to this country, because this country opened its arms to me and gave me the chance to do what I love to do and broadcast baseball. I will always be in debt to this country for the opportunities I have had.

"I hit the jackpot when I found a job with the Dodgers. It has been a privilege to be working with the best organization in baseball. There's no question about it. Tommy is so right when he said the Dodgers are unique. They have been extremely nice, and in my case the Dodgers have always paid all the respect and all the attention that my community deserves. You come to Dodger Stadium and go to the bleachers, go upstairs to the fourth level, and you hear more Spanish than English.

"Many times, especially in New York after a defeat, Tommy would say, 'Come on, walk with me.' We would walk until 2:00, 3:00 in the morning. He would remember the game. We should have done this, we should have done that. Always speaking about the game, nothing else. That was Tommy. Being close to him and listening to him, he sounds like a professor, like a teacher. He is so colorful and has so many stories and anecdotes. It's never-ending sessions with Tommy. I have always enjoyed that very much.

"The Latin people love Tommy, just like everybody. His personality comes across great with the Latinos, because they understand very well that Tommy tries to speak Spanish. He speaks a very special kind of Spanish, very colorful. He mixes the past tense with the present tense with the future tense, and he speaks and people understand him. We Latinos, if you are trying to speak and you come up with a word or two, we try to understand the meaning of your thoughts. He loves the Latino people and the Latino people love Tommy.

"I am extremely proud to be his friend. I will always remember him as a great friend. My wife, Blanca, adores Tommy. He was always very nice to her, with my whole family. He loves my son Jorge a lot, and also my son Mauricio. Tommy is like a part of the family."

In turn, millions of Dodgers fans feel Jarrin is a part of their families. They treasure him for his eloquence, for his instruction, and for his five decades with the Dodgers. They will always remember his poetic calls like, "*La pelota viene como una mariposa*" ("The ball moved like a butterfly"). Or "*Es el momento del matador, el momento de la verdad*" ("It's time for the matador, it's the moment of truth"). Of course, they will always remember his signature home run call: "*Se va, se va, se va, y despídala con un beso!*" ("It's going, going, going, and kiss it good-bye!")

For Jarrin, one thing he will always remember happened away from the ballpark. During spring training in 1990, Jarrin was involved in a serious car accident. He was trapped in his car, barely able to breathe. He remembered doctors telling him that he was lucky to be alive. As he struggled to hang on to life in the smoldering wreck, he saw the faces of Blanca, Jorge, and Mauricio. He remembered crying, thinking he was going to die. The Jarrin family, the Lasorda family, the Dodgers family, and the millions of fans who include Jarrin in their families thank La Dodger Gran en el Cielo that he didn't.

• • •

Just as many have thanked God for Jaime Jarrin, many have thanked God they have survived an argument with Tommy Lasorda. It takes a strong person to stand up to Tommy, but he respects those who take a stand, those who don't hide their feelings, those who have an opinion. One of the people who has stood up to Tommy, who has had countless arguments with him, and who has earned his respect and love is Ralph Avila. "I am his Cuban brother and he is my Italian brother," said Avila.

If you ever have the privilege of sharing a meal with them at Sal's, an Italian trattoria in south Florida, you would have the opportunity to experience the love between the two—even as they argue about just about everything. You would also learn that some of Avila's core values and characteristics are strikingly similar to Tommy's, characteristics that make him Dodger royalty.

Avila was born in Camaguey, Cuba, in 1930. Like most of the country, Camaguey is surrounded by sugarcane and mills. Today it is one of Cuba's largest cities, but when Avila was a child it was mostly rural. "We had horses and mules," said Avila. "We also had cows, pigs, chickens, and turkeys, including me." All kidding aside, the Avilas were not running a petting zoo. Ralph, like the rest of his family, had responsibilities on the farm. "When I was eight years old I wanted to learn how to milk the cows," said Avila. "My father gave me two cows and told me I had to milk them for our home and for my grandmother's home. Then I walked two miles from our farm to the school."

Avila wanted to follow in his father's footsteps. The senior Avila was a catcher in a semipro league in Cuba, and his son was by his side. "As a kid I was a batboy most of the time, hanging around with him, until I started to play baseball when I was 12 years old," he said. When Avila turned 14, his father moved the family to Havana so his son could go to the Cuban equivalent of high school. "He wanted me to be a doctor, an engineer, whatever. That's why he sent me to school," said Avila. Of course, he wanted to play baseball. "I was so big and strong at 14 that if I played with kids 14 years old I'd kill somebody, so I played with the 18-and-under team. When I started to play baseball my father realized I wasn't a major league player. He said I had some tools but I'd never play in a high level. That's the reason he didn't want me to play baseball."

Baseball is part of the national identity in Cuba. So is politics. Avila joined a group that included Che Guevara, Camilo Cienfuegos, and Fidel Castro that wanted to oust president Fulgencio Batista. As the revolution was under way, Avila led a convoy into Havana. Leading Guevara and the other revolutionaries in his column, they arrived at La Cabana, an 18th century fortress located on the eastern side of the harbor in Havana. "I was the first person to go inside La Cabana. Che Guevara and the rest of the group followed me," he said.

As Castro came to power and conditions worsened in Cuba, Avila became convinced that Castro and his regime were not good for Cuba either. He became involved in the Bay of Pigs attempt to oust Castro, and fled to the U.S. after its failure. He and his family set up life in Florida and he got a job as a sheet metal mechanic. He also followed his passion. "When I moved to Miami I organized the Liga de Cubanitos [Cuban Little League]," said Avila "I also managed. We organized a semipro team with all the professional players who weren't able to play. The Latin players protected on the 40-man rosters could not play in winter ball. We had a lot of Cubans living in Miami, also people from Venezuela and the Dominican Republic, and we organized a tournament. Charlie Hough used to play for me while he was in high school. We had major league players in our league but we didn't have enough players. We had to get high school and college players. We had Hough, Bobby Ramos, Kurt Bevauqua, amateurs playing against professionals. That league was organized in 1963. I met a lot of good scouts in those years, like Max Macon and Billy Herman. All the great scouts in those years came to our league before the draft."

He also came across a man who would change his life. "I met Al Campanis in Vero Beach," said Avila. "Campanis was raised in Brooklyn with my cousins. My cousin insisted I go to Vero Beach to see Campanis and the Dodgers. He remembered when Campanis was managing in Cuba, that he spoke Spanish, and that he was a nice guy. He invited me to see the ballclub and have dinner with him. Three days later, he called me and told me he needed to go to Miami. I agreed to pick him up at the hotel and drive him to the University of Miami to see three premium prospects. On the way to the university, he told me the names of the three players. Two of them were Cuban. I knew both kids well. I told him that whoever said those two guys are major league prospects didn't know what he was doing. Then Campanis got mad. He said he had a good scouting report from professional scouts, and I had never been a scout and I was trying to tell him about players. Campanis had a quick temper, but I had a quick temper, too, so we got in an argument in the car. Finally, after three or four innings he said, 'Ralph, you are right, they are not prospects. They are good college players, but that's it.'"

That was the start of Avila's apprenticeship with Campanis, the start of his career with the Dodgers. "In 1967 Campanis told me that if I wanted to recommend any ballplayers that he would listen to me," said Avila. "He said I could be a bird-dog scout. He told me he would give me $1,000 a year, but no expenses. I had to cover from West Palm Beach to Key West. I did it because I loved it."

It wasn't long before Avila found a promising prospect. "I saw Rick Rhoden play in high school when he was a freshman," said Avila. "I followed him for three years until he could be drafted. I fell in love with him." Excited about his find, Avila told Campanis about Rhoden. Campanis already believed in Avila as a scout. He remembered their first encounter at the University of Miami, as well as Avila's report on another prospect he wanted the Dodgers to draft: Bucky Dent. "I couldn't sign Dent because the cross-checker didn't like him at all," said Avila. "I told him I didn't care if he didn't like Dent and that I wasn't going to change my report. That's why Campanis had some confidence in my judgment."

The Dodgers drafted Rhoden in the first round of the 1971 draft. "I agreed with his father to sign him for $35,000," said Avila. Unfortunately, Rhoden's father changed his tune and told Avila his son wouldn't sign for less than $50,000. Avila's blood was boiling; like another Dodgers legend, he highly valued a man's word and his loyalty. Eventually a deal was struck, which impressed Campanis. He decided that he wanted Avila to be a Dodger, and to learn the Dodger Way. Campanis had Avila move to Santo Domingo to cover most of Latin America. It was there that he met another Dodger who would change his life.

"The first time I met Tommy was in Santo Domingo," said Avila. "I knew of Tommy when he was playing in Cuba, but I'd never met him." Like most Cuban baseball fans, Avila was probably well aware of Tommy's altercation with another player, Chiquitin Cabrera.

"In 1952 I was pitching for Almendares against a big Cuban first baseman I didn't like, Chiquitin Cabrera," said Tommy. "He comes to bat and I lowered the boom on him. I did it again on the second pitch. On the third pitch he came out after me with his bat. He started to swing at me with the bat and I threw my glove in his face. It distracted him, and I got underneath him and picked him up over my head and slammed him down. When he was on the ground I was punching and choking him. He was only a few seconds away from saying adios.

"After they broke up the fight, they took us to see a judge. We were still in our uniforms. He asked me if I wanted to press charges, and I told him all I wanted was to pitch to him again. The next day some soldiers came to get me. They took me to President Batista's house. He apologized to me. I told him not to worry about it because if they didn't break it up, they would have been going to his funeral. No Italian will ever run from a Cuban!"

That story is one of Avila's favorites. When he met Tommy in person, the two laughed about it. Not long after, Avila took over responsibility for building the roster of Tommy's team, and he made sure Tommy would manage the club while he served as the assistant manager and pitching coach. That is when Tommy and Avila became friends for life, when they became brothers. That's also when they started to argue.

"Nobody argues with Tommy more than I do," said Avila. "We disagree on just about everything. Sometimes I give up, sometimes he gives up, but when we argue we are trying to get to the best decision for the Dodgers. That's the reason we were honest with each other. That's the reason we love each other like brothers."

Their first real argument came that winter, while the two were running the Licey team. "It was the first game Rafael Landestoy played for Licey. Tommy played Landestoy in left field that day," said Avila. "Peter O'Malley was in Santo Domingo and he invited everybody to dinner after the game. In the fifth inning, Tommy pinch hit Rico Carty for Landestoy. I got pissed off. This was the first game the kid was playing, and he was going to pinch hit for him in the fifth inning? I walked away, took off my uniform, took a shower, got in my car, and drove away. I went crazy. I forgot about the dinner with Peter O'Malley. I was close to San Cristobal when I realized that I forgot the dinner. When I came back the dinner was over. That was the first real argument."

Besides his first argument with Tommy, that first year with Licey was an eye-opener for Avila. The lack of organization gave him the idea of building

a baseball academy. Unfortunately, despite the team's working agreement with the Dodgers, any major league team could scout and sign players at the academy. Avila, loyal to the Dodgers, wasn't interested in developing players for other clubs. He was a Dodger.

Campo Las Palmas was Avila's crowning achievement. For years it was considered the crown jewel amongst academies in the Dominican Republic. It was a place where Avila could continue to show his loyalty to the Dodgers, and to Campanis. Sadly, Avila's champion was fired that very same year. "The Dodger Way was the Campanis way," Avila said. "You play for the name on the front, not the name on the back. Campanis got the best teachers in baseball. They taught us how to play the game, and that's what I did at Campo Las Palmas. It's funny when I hear managers in the major leagues say they don't know about catching because they were a shortstop. That's baloney! A manager in the major leagues should know every position! That's how Campanis did it. That was the way Tommy and I learned about the Dodgers."

Avila didn't just teach baseball fundamentals at Campo Las Palmas, he also taught his youngsters another important part of being a Dodger. "I taught them how to live life. I taught them about family. Be honest. You cannot fake it," said Avila. "Number one, the family. Number two, baseball. You have to realize you represent the Dodgers, but also your country. I'm proud of that."

Avila made sure that each player at Campo Las Palmas took courses in English. He also taught them about hygiene. "Most of the kids we had in camp had never taken a shower. They only took baths at home, or bathed in the river. Ramon [Martinez] had 21 cavities. I sent him to the dentist and we paid the bill. Players I developed were not just players but people. I taught them how to survive in this jungle, which is Major League Baseball. I taught everything from *A* to *Z*."

Though Tommy and Avila argued about seemingly everything, Avila was also Tommy's biggest defender, his champion in the court of public opinion. He has always been loyal to his Italian brother. When the press criticized Tommy for overusing Fernando Valenzuela, Avila stood up for him. When Tommy was criticized for overusing Rick Rhoden while pitching for him in Caracas, Venezuela, Avila stood by him. "We won the first three games in a best-of-five," said Avila. "Then they proposed to play two more games. Tommy used him twice more. In those years we didn't count the pitches. A lot of people complained, but I know Rhoden well and he never overused him."

Avila's support may have been most needed when Tommy was criticized for his treatment of a young pitching prospect, Ramon Martinez's younger brother, Pedro. "Pedro came to Campo Las Palmas when he was 13 years old carrying Ramon's duffle bag," said Avila. "He was a very hyper kid, and finally I signed him. He was a healthy, strong kid but not too tall. He also had an average arm, nothing like an arm on the major league level."

Avila saw something special in Pedro. He sent his scouting report to farm director Charlie Blaney. "My report said we have to take care of him. In my opinion, he was the best prospect I ever signed, but he's a special person. He's like a diamond—if you polish him well he will be great. If you don't polish him we will lose him."

Martinez was in the majors by 1992. During batting practice, Martinez and the other pitchers would play a game to see who the best hitter was. When Martinez stepped into the cage, he took a swing that took him out of his shoes and injured his non-throwing shoulder. The Dodgers sent him to see legendary doctor Frank Jobe. "Dr. Jobe said he needed surgery," said Avila. "Dr. Jobe sent his medical report and said this kid is good but very weak. The way he throws takes a lot of effort, and that pretty soon he would have problems."

Of course, Avila would defend Tommy to Martinez, too. "Tommy was the manager, and I got in an argument with Pedro because he thought Tommy didn't trust him," said Avila. "He was wrong. Tommy was following the instructions of the doctors. That year [1993], Pedro won 10 games and lost five, but Tommy didn't use him as a starter. He would let him pitch three, four innings, because that was the recommendation from Dr. Jobe."

By 1993, his second year in the big leagues, Pedro had real value. But Dr. Jobe's warning about his potential for future injury led some in the Dodgers organization to believe it would be better to trade him then, while interest was high. Felipe Alou, manager of the Montreal Expos, wanted to trade for Pedro. Despite Dr. Jobe's report, Tommy and Avila loved Martinez. "We didn't want to trade Pedro," said Avila. "We offered Valdes, Ramon, Astacio—all the pitchers except Pedro. [Dodgers GM Fred] Claire knew we didn't want to trade Pedro, but Felipe insisted on Pedro. We needed a second baseman, so Fred traded Pedro for Delino DeShields on the recommendation of Dr. Jobe. Tommy didn't want to trade Pedro and neither did I. But he did it anyway, and the rest is history." Ever since, Tommy has been blamed for recommending that the Dodgers trade Martinez, who went on to win three Cy Young Awards while pitching for the Boston Red Sox.

Tommy and Avila carried on nonetheless, continuing to find and develop future Dodgers stars. Avila knew his friend would get the most out of any prospect. "Tommy took care of not only the Latin players, he took care of all the players, but you had to produce," said Avila. "If you're not a prospect, get out of here! If Tommy saw some tools in a ballplayer, he didn't care if he was Chinese, or Korean, or African American. He took care of tools. Our teacher was Campanis. We didn't care about religion or race, we cared about tools, period."

Even when one of Avila's prospects didn't make it to the big leagues, they were still thankful for his effect on their lives. "I'm very happy because I signed good players, but I had to release a lot of good ballplayers," said Avila. "I'm very proud because the kids I released sent me letters telling me how much they appreciated what I did for them, what I taught them, how to survive in this world out of baseball. Every year I receive phone calls, letters, Christmas cards, on my birthday, on my anniversary, from the players that I released."

Those letters are a reflection of Avila's efforts to help people, to make boys into men, to pass along the loyalty that he and Peter O'Malley shared. They are a reflection of Avila's efforts to pass along the Dodger Way. "Originally I wasn't a Dodger fan, but then when I started to work for the Dodgers I made great relationships with Campanis and Peter O'Malley. Peter came to Santo Domingo and gave me all the resources to build Campo Las Palmas. He named me the first Latin American vice president of a major league organization. I started as a bird-dog, but then I became vice president in charge of Latin American operations. I won't work for any other organization. When I resigned as a Dodger, I got a lot of offers from different organizations. But I was born a Dodger and I will die a Dodger. To me, to this day, the Dodgers are Peter O'Malley, Al Campanis, and Tommy Lasorda. That's the way I think."

Avila and Tommy had tremendous success in the Dominican Republic partnering with Licey and with Campo Las Palmas. Over the years, the two became well known in the area, much to Tommy's delight. "One of the members of the board of directors for Licey had a farm up in the mountains of San Francisco de Macoris, and he invited us to spend a few days up there," said Avila. "We went there and had a good time, and on the way back there were very narrow roads going down the mountain. Tommy was saying that everybody around the world knew him, and when we came down the narrow street there was an old man, hunched over, pushing a cart in the street, and I had to stop to give him a chance to pass. Epy Guerrero was with us, and he said, 'Nobody here will know you, Tommy.' The old man looks in the car and says, 'It's Tommy Lasorda!'"

"I flew from New York to Santo Domingo, but I didn't have my passport," said Tommy. "When I landed in the Dominican, they let me right through because they all knew me."

For as legendary as Avila is throughout the Dominican Republic, he should be equally legendary throughout baseball. Even if he never receives the credit he so richly deserves, he will always be a legend to anyone who played for him, and especially to his Italian brother, Tommy Lasorda.

"Ralph has produced more major league players than anybody in any organization," said Tommy. "You look back on all the players that came through the academy and you'll see what Ralph has meant to the Dodgers. He's been like a brother to me. We have been together many, many, many times. He helped so many American players, took care of them when they came down to play. His dedication and loyalty to the organization are second to none."

He, and Jarrin, and Tommy will always be Dodgers royalty.

CHAPTER 12

LOYALTY

"You play for the name on the front of your shirt,
not for the name on the back."

In 1994 the Dodgers were in Montreal for a three-game series against the Expos. It was the early part of the season, and despite talks of a possible players strike, the teams carried on with their business. As usual, Tommy was throwing BP before one of the games. As usual, he was challenging the hitters with hollers of motivation mixed amongst loopy curveballs. As usual, after BP, he called Mike Piazza and Eric Karros into his office for a father-son chat.

"I remember like it was yesterday," said Karros. "He said, 'You guys, I know you think the grass is greener on the other side, and sometimes you think old Tommy is full of it. Mark my words, you're going to be sorry when I'm not here.'"

As usual, Karros and Piazza laughed it off as another joke, another of Tommy's outlandish fables. "I remember thinking it was just Tommy being Tommy," said Karros.

Tommy being Tommy can be funny. Tommy being Tommy can also be outlandish. It can also be prophetic. To most of the guys who played for him, Tommy being Tommy was a mixture of all of those descriptions. What was undeniable was that Tommy had his own way of doing things, of teaching the game, of getting the best out of his players, of having them play up to their capabilities and beyond, of managing a major league team.

Karros was no stranger to hard work. He didn't start in high school until his junior year and walked onto the baseball team at UCLA. After being selected by the Dodgers in the sixth round of the 1988 draft, he was a valuable prospect until then Dodgers GM Fred Claire let Eddie Murray go and pinned his hopes for a first baseman on Kal Daniels and Todd Benzinger.

As a boy, Karros would lie on the floor of his father's office in San Diego listening to Vin Scully call Dodgers games. Karros' father, George, was a die-hard Dodgers fan, a Brooklyn bleacher bum. The son of a Greek immigrant, he was one boy amongst four sisters. While his father worked tirelessly, he thought George would be better served being raised in a Masonic home in Utica, New York, because his wife was seriously ill. Growing up in Utica taught George some valuable lessons. George's father would visit every now and then, but without direct parenting, he learned to be independent. "You received no special attention, no pats on the back, so you did everything for yourself," he said. "I learned to adapt to whatever situation. I learned that just because somebody tells you 'no,' that doesn't mean you have to accept it."

From the moment his first son, Eric, was born, George was in love, and like most fathers he was determined to pass along the lessons he learned in life to his son, as well as his passions, including loving the Dodgers. This self-made man, wrought by hard work, forged by perseverance, would not take no for an answer when it came to giving his son all of the loyalty and love he never had as a kid. "He made the decision early [on] that nothing would be more important to him than being a father," said his wife, Karen.

The Karros family settled in San Diego. George and Karen built a house of love, and George was always there for his family. When Eric signed up to play Little League baseball, George signed up to be the coach. Although his work constantly kept him busy, his first priority was his family. He would leave work early and finish in his home office late into the night so he could keep his commitment to the team. He also made sure Eric worked to develop his competitiveness; the two played chess almost nightly. "There was no discussion, just full-on competition," said Eric. "He was going to beat me. He would never let me win."

They didn't have a meeting set up with Gary Adams, the head coach at UCLA, when the duo went to visit the campus. Father and son waited for Adams and almost ambushed him. Adams agreed to give Eric a shot. It was yet another lesson about determination, about not taking no for an answer. Karros enrolled at UCLA not only because he wanted to play, but because he wanted to leave home. "I left home because I just wanted to see what I could do on my own, and so did my dad," he said. "It would make me stronger. My mantra was, if you don't think I can do it, I'm going to show you I can and get you to believe in me."

Karros struggled through his freshman year, but it was no struggle for his father to continue to be there for his son. While he rarely played, George still made the three-hour drive just in case his son was in the lineup. He never even missed batting practice, probably because he knew it was his only chance to watch Eric swing the bat. But during his sophomore and junior years, Karros showed Adams he could do it; he got his coach to believe in him. Batting in the middle of the Bruins lineup, he hit 25 bombs and drove in 111 runs in those two seasons.

The scouts believed in him, too. But when the first several rounds of the draft went by without his name being called, Karros was livid and decided to stay in school. "Then I get a call [that] of all teams, the Dodgers had drafted me," said Karros.

George visited Eric in Great Falls, Montana, where Karros lit the Pioneer League on fire. After the season, he went to Arizona to play in the instructional league, watched the Dodgers win the World Series, then went home to San Diego and prepared for his first spring training. When he reported to Dodgertown, he was given what every rookie in the organization got: a room assignment, equipment, uniforms, and a motivational address from the manager of the reigning World Series champions. "Tommy spoke to me amongst a group of minor-leaguers," said Karros. "You think, *Holy cow, this is Tommy Lasorda.* I thought he was larger than life. My dad loved Tommy and thought he was great before he even knew him."

Now that larger-than-life personality was telling him about the Dodgers, about baseball, about what it would take for the young players to succeed, about life. Karros wondered if it was part of his act. "It just didn't seem possible that this man could have done all these things, that this man could have been in all these situations, handled all these situations the way the stories go," he said.

As Karros walked around camp, he would see the retired players whom his father had told him stories about. "You go to spring training and Koufax was there, Newcombe was there, Duke was there, Drysdale was there, Campanella was there in his wheelchair," said Karros. "The tradition and history was there. I could tell you the history of the organization, who played where, everything going back to the '50s. Then to get drafted by the organization, to having Tommy Lasorda motivating me..."

At Double A in San Antonio, Karros again posted big numbers, hitting .352 with 18 home runs and 78 RBIs. "He realized he had to try to hit more line drives instead of hitting home runs," said John Shoemaker, his manager. "He realized that he was going to have to work hard, to persevere, to have good numbers in that league. He was really competitive. He talked a lot of times about winning and being on winning teams and always wanting to win. Some players don't battle with the umpires. They let it go. Eric was one not to like to get a bad call called against him, and if he felt like they called a bad one on him, he would tell them about it."

Back at Dodgertown for his third spring training, Karros was on the verge. While he was still competing with fellow prospect Henry Rodriguez for playing time, he was also looking up at Kal Daniels and future Hall of Famer Eddie Murray. Before he could make the Dodgers' 40-man roster, he would have more indoctrination into the Dodger Way and hear more speeches by Tommy.

"I was fortunate because Mike Scioscia was still there. Orel Hershiser was still there," said Karros. "Scioscia and Orel absolutely respected Tommy. They recognized that buying into Tommy's stuff was why they were at where they were. They knew what we were going through, the tutelage, the schooling, the education we were getting, and they were supportive of it."

Although he made the 40-man coming out of spring training, he spent much of the year at Triple A. He hit a low point while the club was in Las Vegas; he was benched and facing the doubt that every ballplayer faces. As usual, he called his father. As usual, his father was there for him. "I had heard his voice. It sounded like he was down. I just wanted him to know that he should not question himself," said George.

"All of a sudden he shows up," said Eric. George took his son to lunch and then made the six-hour drive home.

That drive wasn't the only one George would make that year to see his son play. Karros made his major league debut for the Dodgers on September 1, 1991. In the bottom of the eighth the Dodgers were beating the Cubs 12–3. With two out, Mike Sharperson drew a walk. Tommy put Karros in to pinch run. "I always kid Tommy about that," said Karros. "My first appearance in the big leagues, I came in as a pinch runner for Mike Sharperson. I'm slow, and I go in to pinch run for a speedster. That was always the joke, that a Hall of Fame manager had me pinch run."

After the season Karros went back to Venezuela. "I didn't want to go back," said Karros. "But it was the price I had to pay. I had heard Tommy's saying about paying the price and the avenue of hard work so many times. I answered that question by going out and playing, going out and working. I felt like I was answering the question differently than a lot of people, and those were the people I was competing against."

Karros was in the mix to replace Eddie Murray at first base during spring training in 1992. Tommy took him under his wing. "It was nonstop," said Karros. "It was myself and Mike Piazza. He would throw to us nonstop. Every day, after we'd be done playing our games, he'd have people cart out the L-screen and he would just throw and throw and throw. It's one of those things where he's putting in the time, he's working, and he's got no interest in anything other than trying to develop the young players and give us opportunities. You see that at a point in his career where he's already won the World Series. What more did he have to prove? But he genuinely cared about his players. There's no question about it.

"The amount of work he does, you have to be willing to put in that work, too. He instills that in you, not just by talk. And that's the thing—it's one thing to say this is what you have to do, but he walked the walk as well. You see that and it gets ingrained in you. You probably don't realize it at the time but as an individual you start working harder, you pursue your goals, you know the line about the avenue of hard work. You hear all that stuff and you're going, *come on, really?* But it's every single day and that's the way he lives his life. The amount of time he spent with me in spring training, I think that's when he started to take a liking to me. That's when he started to get to know me as a person. He saw something in me."

"He just worked so gosh darn hard," said Tommy. "That's really what impressed me. Phil Regan had him in Venezuela and he didn't hit much down there. Regan was in Vero [Beach] one day and he was standing behind the cage. He said, 'That's not the same guy that played for me.' I said, 'His name was Karros down there, wasn't it?' The difference was in Venezuela he couldn't hit the ball from the middle of the plate in, but after our work during the spring, he could."

Tommy believed Karros was ready, that he would play in the big leagues, and was determined to make Karros believe it, too. He was determined to have that effect on Karros, to have his lessons become part of the way he approached the game. In the end, Karros made the club coming out of spring training. "Fred wanted to send him out, but I fought for him to make the club," said Tommy. "He had given Kal Daniels a lot of money and didn't want a high-priced player on the bench."

"I believe that Tommy fought to keep me on the roster," said Karros. "He has always been there for me, been in my corner. Tommy has had my back every single day. For that I'll be forever grateful."

The Dodgers opened the season at home against the Giants before hitting the road for San Diego. On the mound for the Padres in the opener was left-hander Craig Lefferts. "I get my first start against San Diego, my hometown," said Karros. "I'm on deck. I have the adrenaline going. I'm nervous as heck, and Tommy starts screaming at me from the dugout to come back over. I'm thinking to myself that there's nothing he could tell me right now because

I'm so fired up. I walked back over there and he puts his arm around me and says, 'Look, you've been hitting off me all spring. They are going to try to throw you inside, and you know I have better stuff than he does.' He's giving me some advice but he's also trying to calm me down with the humor. I don't think he was joking. I think he was serious about it, but in my mind I was laughing."

"I told him that the Padres went over him in their meetings and thought he couldn't hit the inside fastball," said Tommy. "I told him that the first fastball he saw would be in on his hands, and to attack it."

"I'll be darned. The very first pitch he threw was an inside fastball. I turned on it and hit a home run. So when I'm running around the bases I'm thinking, *No way did this just happen, and no way did Tommy just call me over and say it*," said Karros. "It's one of those things that you can work and work and work, but there's got to be some sort of reward. And the reward is you see the hard work come to fruition, you see all that stuff we worked on hitting against left-handers, him coming inside during spring training, and he called it. He legitimately called it in the first at-bat. It goes along with all the stories you hear, whether it was from Orel or Garvey or any of the former players. You hear these stories and you go, there's no way. But I just had a first-hand experience of a story. It validates all the things you've heard, and you say, 'You know what? I believe.'

"When I got to the big leagues, I really started to take pride in being a Dodger. I always respected the organization and was grateful they signed me, but after being around Tommy in Vero, seeing him, seeing the way he lived, that's when I think I started buying into the whole Dodger Way. I would go back to the amount of time and work we spent together in the spring of '92, not only physically but it mentally prepared me for anything. No matter what I was going to be faced with, Tommy had always preached about putting in the time and hard work. What that does is prepare you physically and mentally. I felt like I had done everything I could do to be prepared for this situation. At that point, it was making the team and proving I belonged in the big leagues."

Karros began as a platoon player; Daniels would play against right-handers and Karros would play against left-handers. However, Tommy was loyal to Karros, he appreciated all of his hard work, and he liked his bat. In a game in May, the Dodgers were trailing the Pirates in the bottom of the ninth, down by two runs, with two on and one out. The Pirates went to the bullpen and brought in Stan Belinda, a right-handed sidearmer. Tommy pinch hit Karros in the pitcher's spot. "I must have fouled off 10 pitches and just ran into one," said Karros, who hit a bomb deep into the left-field pavilion for a walk-off home run.

"That week I was just waiting for someone to come off the disabled list and my butt was going back down to Albuquerque," said Karros. "Being ready, not giving up, and continuing to fight, fight, fight—I think going through what I went through in the spring with Tommy and his building me up and getting me to believe, I subconsciously used the determination he taught to get through that week. Instead of just giving up, it was one of those things where Tommy had worked with me, had prepared me. Then, after that, I started every single day. That was that."

Karros finished the '92 season batting .257 but slugged 20 home runs and drove in 88 runs. Those numbers earned him the 1992 National League Rookie of the Year award. Tommy's examples had become ingrained in Karros, and they paid off.

"I was so proud of him," said Tommy. "When I saw him work so hard in spring training and saw how he could play, I thought he was going to be a heck of a ballplayer."

Karros was well aware of how much loyalty Tommy felt toward his players. As time went by, he also began to see more and more examples of Tommy's competitiveness. During BP at Busch Stadium in St. Louis, Karros was in the cage while Tommy was roaming around third base. Karros smoked a ball that nailed Tommy in the shin, but Tommy refused to show any weakness. "When I hit it and it hit him, I was scared," Karros said. "He said, 'It didn't even hit me.' Everybody saw the ball just smoke him. He refused to acknowledge that it hit him. Three days later his shin is so swollen that he has to get it drained, and has a legitimate hole in his shin. The point was he

was not going to let on, he wasn't going to limp, and that's just like Tommy. He was sixty-something years old, and he was so tough, such a competitor, that he would never admit defeat. The next year, I'll be darned if he's not over at third base at Busch Stadium in St. Louis during BP. I crushed him again almost in the same place."

That wasn't the only example of Tommy's competitiveness. "We were in Cincinnati. There was a 20-pound watermelon. He said he could eat the whole thing in three days," said Karros, "No way can this man possibly eat this 20-something-pound watermelon. He ate the watermelon in three days, but ask him how many times he had to go to the bathroom. I guess what he was showing was his competitiveness, and that if you believe it, you can achieve it. Mind over matter. If he tells himself something enough times, he'll actually believe it."

Tommy reinforced Karros' self-confidence the following year, when the young first baseman hit an extended slump. "I just couldn't hit a thing. I would get to the field early and go down to the cages for extra work," said

Karros. "To get to the cages you had to walk by his office. I've got the tee in my hand and I'm walking down to the cages and he calls me into his office. He says, 'You got two choices: you can go down and hit off that tee all day long if you want but I'm not going to play you. If you want to play tonight, go sit in the clubhouse and just relax. You're good enough to hit. You're going to kill this guy tonight. Don't worry about it. Get in there and I'll play you tonight. You go down there to work off the tee and you're not playing.' He took all the pressure off me. This is a guy who preaches hard work and he's telling me I'm fine. Whether he believed it or not, he made me believe I'd be fine that night. That night, I hit a home run. You can call it all a bunch of BS, but the point of it is there were results. I know what happened. I know what Tommy did. I remember it like it was yesterday, and it worked.

"He could get players to play to their potential. How he did that was by getting players to believe. His personality is infectious. The beauty of him is that you start doing these things without even realizing you're doing them. Being around him, getting to know him, it's almost like you take on a little bit of him. You do it unknowingly."

"Karros was, above all, a tremendous example of what a Dodger should be like," said Tommy. "His character, his personality, his disposition were excellent. And he could hit."

"The Dodger Way was a legitimate way of life," said Karros. "There used to be a Dodger Way of doing things. You were taught a certain way to play the game, to handle yourself in the media, to treat the fans. People call BS on it, but it's true. I kid Tommy about it, and I tell him that baseball was his vehicle, but [he] taught me a lot about life, loyalty, the family aspect. You are going to get out of it what you put into it, and with Tommy, whether it's relationships or his affiliation with the Dodgers, he's the greatest example of that. Just look at how he treated my parents. He was great to them. My parents used to fly on the team plane and Tommy would invite them to dinner. To this day, my parents send him birthday and Christmas cards because they know the impact he's had on my life."

"They were good people," said Tommy. "Eric was raised right. They taught him about love and respect, and he was an outstanding young man. Those were the kind of guys I loved to have play for me."

Karros hit 270 home runs for the Dodgers, more than any other player in the history of the franchise since the team moved to Los Angeles. "Never in my wildest dreams did I ever think I would set that record," said Karros. "It's bizarre. Growing up in a Dodgers household, there's one picture of myself and my brother. I'm five and he's three. I've got a Wiffle ball bat and a Dodgers hat on."

Karros learned to be independent and loyal from the example his father set, lessons that Tommy reinforced. "There is something to be said about that, the loyalty factor," said Karros. "Tommy was the same way. I definitely learned loyalty. Also, the whole idea of just work, work, work, that is something that my father taught me. Whether it was on a baseball field, whether it was just believing, whether it was just undying determination to get to where you wanted to go, you saw that every single day in Tommy. He has used baseball to create relationships, to motivate people, to inspire people. He has been there for me. Always, for anything. Not only is he a friend, he's a father figure. Tommy spoke at my wedding. If I needed anything I could call him and he would do it for me, and there's never been a time when I called him that he didn't do whatever he could. He has had as big an impact on my life as anybody outside my parents."

"I like a guy to be loyal to his teammates, loyal to his team, loyal to his organization, and loyal to his family," said Tommy. "It was part of the Dodger Way."

As previously noted, Tommy retired in 1996 after suffering a mild heart attack following a Sunday game against the Astros. "I thought that Tommy was indestructible," Karros said. "He was still swimming, still throwing BP, and you didn't see it coming at all. Even then, I thought it would be just a couple weeks and he'd be back. Never in a million years did I think that his health would force him to make a choice. I don't think anyone thought it was permanent. Tommy was going to be down, but he would be back. Nothing was going to knock him down because he's this indestructible force."

When Tommy decided to retire, it was the end of an era. It was a sad day for the Dodgers and for baseball. "That day sucked because there was some finality there. I thought, *This is really happening. Tommy is not going to be managing any longer.* The energy, the enthusiasm, the stories, the spring trainings. They were legendary.

"I go back to that conversation in Montreal. He was right. You take for granted all the things he does. After Tommy, it wasn't the same. He made you feel a lot better about yourself as a player than you probably were. You missed that. He's worth a handful of games, not because of the strategic moves but because of the environment and the atmosphere. It sounds corny but you actually start to think you're that good.

"Tommy is the last of the great teachers of the Dodgers' tradition and lore. There were so many along the way that had different impacts within the organization, but there were none like Tommy. You get indoctrinated into the Dodger Way, and if you adhere to it, if you go by it, whether it's in baseball or outside of baseball, you are going to be successful. That's what Tommy taught."

When asked to describe his relationship with Tommy, Karros said, "Lucky. Not proud—lucky. I've had a lot of great fortune in my life. Outside of having a wonderful wife, my kids, my brother, and my parents still being alive, crossing paths and having my life touched Tommy made me very lucky."

Aren't we all?

• CHAPTER 13 •

MY FAVORITE TOMMY STORIES

"I believe that God put me on earth for a reason."

By the time Tommy was 14 years old, he had sold potatoes out of the back of a truck, played countless baseball games at Elmwood Park, and had gained a reputation as one of the hardest-working boys in his neighborhood. He had also joined the Boy Scouts. "I heard about them around the neighborhood and thought it sounded good," he said. "I learned how to take care of myself in case of an emergency, and they taught me how to act. If you wanted to be a scout, you had to be good."

By the time Tommy he was in his midthirties, he was scouting for the Dodgers in Los Angeles. In addition to finding players, he was also responsible for representing the franchise. An opportunity to do just that came via an invitation to speak at a benefit dinner. "The first speech I had to make was at the Huntington Hartford Hotel," said Tommy. "During that time I smoked cigarettes, and I was about to light one because I was nervous. I looked up at the TV and the surgeon general was saying that cigarettes were harmful to your health. I looked at the pack and said, 'Who's stronger, me or you?' And I put the pack away. That's how I quit smoking.

"The dinner was for Eagle Scouts. A scout would write a letter to a person in the profession they were pursuing, and in turn that professional would escort them to the dinner and act as a mentor. The first speaker

219

on stage was a retired admiral in the U.S. Navy. They read his bio about graduating from Annapolis and leading fleets throughout the world. The next speaker was a judge who graduated from Yale and enjoyed a successful legal career before joining the bench. I was next, and all that was said abut me was, 'And now, our featured speaker of the night, Tom Lasorda, a scout for the Dodgers.' I don't know what possessed me, but when I got to the podium it hit me: 'On my honor I will do my best to do my duty to God and my country, and to obey the Scout Law; to help other people at all times; to keep myself physically strong, mentally awake, and morally straight. A Scout is trustworthy, loyal, helpful, friendly, courteous, kind, obedient, cheerful, thrifty, brave, clean, and reverent.' Needless to say, I had their attention."

Since that speech in 1963, Tommy has held the attention of thousands of people throughout the country and around the world. He has given countless commencement addresses. He has given speeches to more than 40 military installations on behalf of the Hall of Fame, Major League Baseball, and the Dodgers. He has spoken to teams, coaches, players, businesses, charities, schools, civic organizations, elected officials, appointed officials, students, teachers, doctors, lawyers, and just about anyone else you can imagine.

"I gave a speech to a morticians convention," said Tommy. "I told the story of the widow who wanted to have her late husband buried in his Dodgers-blue suit. When she got there he was wearing a brown suit. The undertaker said, 'Don't worry. We'll take care of it.' 'How are you going to take care of it when the ceremony is about to start?' At that moment the undertaker picked up the phone and said, 'Hey, Charlie, switch the heads on seven and eight.'"

All kidding aside, Tommy's speeches are filled with similar lessons to those he taught his players. "When my mother passed away, Cardinal O'Connor said a memorial Mass for her," said Tommy. "After it was over, he told me that whenever he hears me speak I am always talking about motivation. He wanted to know why ballplayers making millions of dollars needed to be motivated. I told him that everybody in this country from the president of the United States to the lowest job in the country, needs to be motivated, because we think we are doing our best, but we can always do better."

It has been this author's distinct privilege and honor to accompany Tommy to at least 1,000 of his speeches during my career with the Dodgers. At one point, I tried keeping a running count of the standing ovations he received, both before and after his speeches, but it was a futile effort. You think Babe Ruth hit a lot of home runs? Try counting the number of teary eyes in Tommy's audiences. You think Pete Rose had a lot of hits? Try counting the number of lives Tommy has touched through his words alone.

"I always felt that if I could make just one person happy then it was all worth it," said Tommy. "If that person is happy, their husband or wife is happy. If they are happy, then their kids are happy. If the kids are happy, their friends are happy, and so on. My father used to tell us that if we couldn't smile then borrow our brother's. He would also tell us that it doesn't cost a dime to smile."

Over the last half century, Tommy has shared his smile with anyone who treats him politely, a number that would fill all of the major league ballparks to capacity. He receives bags of mail, both at home and at Dodger Stadium, full of thank-you notes for his motivational messages, full of promises to live by his lessons, full of love for all that he has given.

My favorite Tommy story, one that he tells in most of his speeches, is about his first visit to the United States Air Force Academy, a place where he has now spoken at 13 times.

"General Scott asked me to go there and motivate the cadets. I was honored to do this," Tommy said. "When my wife and I arrived in Colorado Springs, there was a young lieutenant who was assigned to take us around. He told me he wanted to be a pilot but could never fly. He said, 'I was a pitcher on the baseball team. I got hit on the head with a line drive that knocked me unconscious. I spent three weeks in the hospital. I just took my physical and the doctor said I could never be a pilot.' I asked him the name of the doctor who told him this. 'Was it God?' He said, 'No, sir.' I said, 'Well, the only person who can tell you that you cannot fly is God, and don't you ever forget that.'"

After Tommy had made his speech to 4,600 cadets, the lieutenant told him he had been struck by hearing about the advice Tommy's father had given him, that every time one door closes, another opens, and that just because God delays does not mean that God denies. The lieutenant told Tommy he would follow his dream and become a pilot.

"Two years later, I received a letter from Lieutenant Bob Wright," Tommy said. "In the envelope, there was a picture of him standing next to his jet getting ready to go to battle in Desert Storm. On the bottom of the letter he wrote, BECAUSE GOD DELAYED, GOD DIDN'T DENY. Later, I was asked by Harvey Schiller to speak at a luncheon in Colorado Springs to raise money for the U.S. Olympics, which I was honored to do. At that luncheon, a colonel walked up and said he wanted me to know that one of the most prestigious honors bestowed upon an alumnus of the Air Force Academy was given to Captain Bob Wright, who had shot down three enemy planes in Bosnia.

"General Kelly asked me to go to Montgomery, Alabama, to Maxwell Air Force Base to speak to the graduating class. As I got off the plane and was walking toward the baggage claim, someone ran toward me. I looked and it was Major Bob Wright, the youngest major in the U.S. Air Force. He was hugging me like I was his long-lost father. He said, 'If it weren't for you, none of this would have happened.' I said, 'Major, don't ever say that to me again. It was because of you that it happened, not me. The moment that you believed you could fly, you were on your way to becoming a hero.'"

"You always have setbacks, but I was so focused on becoming a pilot," now-Colonel Wright said. "The way to do that was to do well where I was assigned and never lose focus. Continue to improve. *What can I do now? What should I do now?* Continue pressing it, be persistent. I think athletics taught me to be persistent, and Tommy is the one who enforced 'don't take no for an answer.' Essentially he is the one who says don't give up on yourself. Other people will give up on you, but don't give up on yourself. It meant a lot, especially coming from someone like Tommy Lasorda. The stories he told me made him more human. Instead of being the icon Tommy Lasorda, Dodgers manager, he got down to the human level. That's what struck and impressed me the most. Here's someone so famous that would take time out for a young kid, which I was, and to invest time in me, that meant so much to me. I admire Tommy, and am proud of everything he's done. I feel very lucky to have been considered a friend. Every time I see him it's just an inspiration, and everything he did…as far as I'm concerned, the man walks on water.

"I'm surprised by the fact he tells our story, because I don't think I've done anything special. I just followed my dreams. I was just a kid that had a dream and a great opportunity. There were a few challenges, but I luckily crossed paths with the great inspiration and motivation of Tommy Lasorda. Based on the words he gave me, I was able to live my dream."

• • •

Another of my favorite stories is about a ballplayer. Not a famous Dodger or All-Star or even a high school phenom. This story is about a 10-year-old first baseman from Crowley, Louisiana. It has nothing to do with the Dodgers, but everything to do with baseball, and everything to do with who Tommy is and what he means to people.

If you have ever been to Crowley, you haven't been there long. The town is only about five square miles. The population is less than the Reserve Level at Dodger Stadium, about 13,000. Perhaps the town's most famous residents were Tommy Casanova, a four-time All-Pro defensive back for the Cincinnati Bengals, and Jim Gueno, a linebacker for the Green Bay Packers.

But you might also hear people in Crowley talk about Alyson Habetz, and her uncle Tom. The youngest of eight children, Habetz and her four older brothers loved to play baseball. "I was seven years old when I started playing," said Habetz. "I grew up on a baseball field. We were always playing, and Daddy was our coach. I was a Yankees fan, because of [Ron] Guidry. I liked watching him on TV and he was from Louisiana, the Louisiana Lightning. It was cool to have a fellow Cajun playing for the Yankees."

When Habetz was 10 years old, her father took her to a baseball clinic at the University of Southwestern Louisiana, which is now the University of Louisiana at Lafayette. The featured speaker was Tommy Lasorda. "I knew him as the Dodger manager who would always kick dirt on the umpires," said Habetz. "The cool thing was me and a bunch of kids were waiting for Tommy to arrive. I was first in line." The kids waited for quite a while. Unfortunately, Tommy's plane was late.

"We hit the storm hard. I felt like I was on Charlie Hough's knuckleball," Tommy said. "There were two servicemen in front of me and they were both upchucking in the bags. I thought if this flight wasn't going to make it, the best thing I could do was to say my prayers and fall asleep. That way if the plane goes down, I won't know it. I could hear the hail hitting the plane. When I woke up, we were landing. I was woozy and the two servicemen were white with fright."

"The people in charge were trying to get him in quickly because they were trying to get him on the live broadcast," said Habetz. "I said, 'Mr. Lasorda, will you please sign my glove?' He stopped and said sure, and I still have the glove. He asked me my name, and he was signing the glove. They were in such a hurry that they pushed him along and he messed up his signature."

"Hey, pal, hold it," Tommy said in his stern, managerial voice.

"It made him really mad," said Habetz. "He turned the glove over and sat there and talked to me as he signed his name properly. I told him I played baseball and that I was the only girl on the boys team. He gave me his business card and told me to write him. That night there was a banquet and I followed him around all night. After that he was my hero."

"I was on the dais and she stood next to me the whole night," said Tommy. "We got to be friends, and when I left she wrote me a letter and I wrote her back." Habetz never thought Tommy Lasorda would write her back, but he did. The two became pen pals. "I would tape the letters to my wall," said Habetz. "I had a whole wall that had letters from Tommy Lasorda. After a few letters he started to sign them Love Your Adopted Uncle, Tom Lasorda, so I started calling him Uncle Tom."

"When I got into high school, there was a rule that girls weren't allowed to play on boys' teams," said Habetz. "The rule was from the Louisiana High School Athletic Association. My high school coach wanted me to play, the principal wanted me to play, but it was the association's rule. We took a trip with the coach and principal to Baton Rouge and told them my story, that I had been playing baseball since I was seven, and asked for an exception to the rule. They said no. I cried the whole way home from Baton Rouge. My dad said if I wanted to play that bad, we could always go to court. For two years I was in the courtroom battling to do something I loved to do, because, you know, I was going to play for the Dodgers!"

During those two years of courtroom battles, Tommy would send his young pen pal, his future first baseman, more letters of encouragement for her wall. He implored her to keep playing, to keep following her dream. "It was awesome," said Habetz. "Finally they changed the rule, and I got to play my junior and senior years."

After graduating high school she enrolled at the University of Southwestern Louisiana, the same place she met Tommy, and joined the softball team. While she was there, Tommy came back to speak at a USL fundraiser. "When my mother found out he was coming to speak to the team, she wanted to cook for him. We're Cajun," said Habetz. "I told him it would be immediate family only. I'm the youngest of eight and my father was from a family of nine, so there were about 50 people at our house. He sat at the head of the table, and for three hours told story after story and had my family laughing, and then crying, and then laughing again. I wish I had a tape recorder that night. We ate every kind of Cajun food there is."

"I thought I was at an Italian wedding," said Tommy. "I shook more hands than the mayor of Crowley."

As it turned out, she wouldn't need a tape recorder, because she and Tommy were well on their way to a lifelong friendship. But there was one thing Tommy told her that she would never forget. "I was riding in the limo with him and I told him I didn't know what I wanted to do after I graduated," said Habetz. "I was majoring in communications, and was probably going to go to law school. He said, 'I know what you are going to do. You are going to be a coach.' I'll never forget that."

Habetz graduated college in 1995 but wasn't ready to hang up her cleats just yet. "My last year of college I heard about this team, the Colorado Silver Bullets," said Habetz. "Phil Niekro was the manager and they barnstormed the country and played against the guys. It was baseball. They already had their roster for spring training, so I called up Uncle Tom. 'Uncle Tom, do you know Phil Niekro?'"

As a matter of fact, he did, and gave him a call.

"Hey Phil, remember when I selected you for the All-Star Game?"

"Yeah, Tommy, I appreciated it very much."

"Remember when I put you in the game when you had never pitched in an All-Star Game before?"

"Yeah, I remember."

"Well, I'm calling in my markers. I want you to take care of my adopted niece."

While playing for the Silver Bullets, Habetz spent time training in Los Angeles, which gave her plenty of time to watch the Dodgers and hang out with her uncle Tom. One of her favorite Tommy stories is about the hours after a tough loss to the Phillies during a pennant race. "We went into his office at around 11:00 at night. He's not saying a whole lot because he doesn't like to lose," Habetz said. "I'm sitting there watching him, and he has this box of letters next to his desk. He's responding to fan mail. I noticed off to the side they had a spread of food. He told me to fix something to eat, which I did, and he had two plates fixed next to his desk. I figured they were for him and Jo. Well after midnight, we were the last people to leave Dodger Stadium. We walked to the parking lot and my car and his car were the only two left. He forgot the two plates, and I told him I would get them for him. They were constantly on his mind. I got back to the car and he told me to follow him out. We stopped at the gate and there were two guards there. He talked to them for a bit and then handed them the two plates of food. They just lost a game in the pennant race, and he was thinking about the two guards at the gate and fixing them a plate of food. Who does that?"

What that taught her is that everybody matters, just as she mattered to Tommy. Many people have asked, "Who does that?" after Tommy did something special for them. Habetz asked it after he delivered the food to the guards. She asked it again the following spring.

"He invited me to spring training. Raul Mondesi was having trouble hitting the curveball. After the game, he stays and throws curveballs to Mondesi. I went to the outfield to shag. Reggie Smith and Bill Russell would go to the golf course to pick up the balls and bring them back in.

After a while, all the balls were in the outfield and Smith and Russell weren't bringing the balls in. Tommy was hollering, 'Bring me the balls!' After a while he just throws down his glove and walks to the clubhouse. I went in and asked Reggie why they didn't bring him the balls. 'If we keep bringing him the balls, he'll pitch until midnight. He won't stop. He'll keep pitching, so we have to shut him down.'"

Another evening after she arrived in California, Habetz received a phone call from Tommy after midnight. He invited her to a karaoke bar. "I go and he's singing 'My Way.' He closes down the karaoke bar and it's 2:00 AM. Then we went to the Waffle House. People are asking for autographs, and he's signing, wide-eyed and bushy-tailed, even at 4:00 in the morning. It was a Saturday night. We are leaving and he says, 'I'll meet you for Mass at 8:00 AM. It's on the field.' They had Mass in left field at the stadium in Vero Beach. He was there and I was there, too. My goodness, he does not sleep."

The Silver Bullets folded in 1998. Habetz was still living in Los Angeles and playing for a women's team in Long Beach. "When I played softball in college, Patrick Murphy was the assistant coach," Habetz said. "He got the head coach job at the University of Alabama. He called me and told me to hang up my cleats and come coach."

With that call, Tommy's prediction of Habetz becoming a coach became a reality. She packed her bags and was off to Tuscaloosa. During her first year as a coach, she called Tommy often for advice, and she also got personal instruction anytime she was back in Los Angeles. Once, the power went out in Tommy's daughter's house. Habetz went over to help. "Sure enough, Tommy shows up," said Habetz. "It's midnight and the candles are lit. He says, 'Okay, Alyson, it's the bottom of the seventh, tie game. Your team is getting ready to hit. What are you telling them? What are you telling them? Stand up, stand up, and tell me what you're going to tell them!' I started saying, 'You have to believe. You have to…' 'No, no, no. It has to come from your gut! You have to believe it! If you don't believe it, your players won't believe it! You have to be passionate about it! It has to come from down deep! Let me hear it!' He made me give him a motivational speech."

Tommy never stopped impressing her as the years went by. After he led Team USA to the Olympic gold medal, Habetz asked him to speak at a University of Alabama fundraiser. "It was called an Evening with Tommy Lasorda," said Habetz. "I didn't want him to come in through the crowd so I took him in the back way. I was trying to get him through the people and hurry him along, but there is no hurrying with him. He's behind me, and I'm rushing. All of a sudden, I don't feel his presence behind me anymore, and I hear, 'Alyson!' with that stern voice. I turned around and he's not talking to our athletic director, he's not talking to the big money men—he's against the wall with all the people who were going to be serving the meals that night. He's talking to one of the guys, Jose, and says, 'Alyson, come meet Jose. He's going to be serving your meal tonight. You better meet him.' He didn't grade people on how much money they made, or how popular or powerful they were. They were just human beings. It seems like his greatest joy is making others feel good, feel special. It's not about him, it's about helping others feel good, regardless of who they are."

Habetz is still an assistant coach for the Crimson Tide and has asked Tommy to speak to her team many times. Tommy calls the players his "Bama girls." Habetz also incorporated Tommy's lessons into her own coaching style. "I always make it about the fans, and about other people, and that's how Tommy is," she said. "I also feel like I coach like him because he was always a lover of his players. That was something that was fun about him, because everybody said you couldn't have a relationship with your players, but that wasn't Tommy. He would hug his players, he would celebrate with his players. When I'm coaching, I think about him a lot and try to do that. You could continually tell that he cared about his players because their joy was his joy, genuinely. I also take the power of the mind. Believing, making them believe, because that's the biggest thing. I learned that from him as well, the power of the mind and believing."

She also makes her players sign autographs, just like Tommy made his. "Oh my gosh, yes, and I always, always, always think of Uncle Tom when I have my players sign after our games. I told our players over and over and over again about him."

When she does, she isn't lying. Tommy will always sign autographs, will always take care of people, will always love the fans, will always make people feel special. "Just last year I went to Dodger Stadium. Before the game he introduced me to everyone from the janitor to Vin Scully, and he would tell all of them about our story. He always made me feel like I was part of the family," Habetz said. "After the game we are coming out of the stadium well after midnight. Outside there are fans about 30 yards away. They were blocked off because Tommy was leaving to go to Chicago at 6:00 the next morning. He turns around and tells the security guard to let them through. They tell him he has an early flight the next morning. 'I don't care. They're Dodgers fans,' with that stern voice. I was just so proud. You just have to be proud to know someone like that. He didn't have to do that, but he went above and beyond to serve them. It was about them. Those fans stayed there, so he was going to make sure they were taken care of."

"All of that just because I signed her glove," said Tommy. "Can you imagine that?"

• • •

In 2006 T.J. Simers, writing a column for the *Los Angeles Times* sports section, made a bet with Tommy. If the Dodgers did not win their division that year, Tommy had to buy $1,000 worth of toys, dress as Santa Claus, and pass them out to patients at the Mattel Children's Hospital at UCLA. Although the Dodgers finished the regular season with the same record as the Padres, they lost the division on a tiebreaker. The Dodgers got a ticket to the playoffs as a wild card team and Mattel Children's Hospital got a Santa Claus.

Tommy traded in his Dodgers uniform for a Santa suit, traded his baseballs for foam snowballs, and traded his lineup cards for wish lists. While Tommy was busy spreading holiday cheer to those who needed it the most, Heather Buchanan and her fiancé, Mike Spohr, were putting the final touches on their wedding plans. Like most couples about to be married they were probably dreaming of their life together, of their honeymoon to Fiji and Australia, of starting a family. Unlike most couples, however, they might have been teasing each other about whose team would win the National League West the following year, Mike's Giants or Heather's Dodgers.

Buchanan-Spohr grew up in Thousand Oaks as a Dodgers fan and as a softball player. Self-described as "scrappy," she played the hot corner and racked up knocks as a contact hitter for the Newbury Park Panthers. Her two favorite Dodgers were Eric Karros and Mike Piazza. "We would pick where we sat based on who was on the team and who was playing," she said. "I liked Karros and Piazza, so we would sit on the first-base side even though it was the visitors' side of Dodger Stadium, because we could be closer to Karros and see Piazza. Going to Dodgers games was a treat. I thought I was going to be their first female first baseman for a long time. I either wanted to be on the team or go to the games. It was amazing. It was like a dream."

Her dreams were answered in 2005. She was working in New York and saw a job opening with the Dodgers. "They were starting a new inside sales department, and I applied. I had no sales experience. I sold them on me. Pulling into the stadium on my first day, I sat in my car and said, 'Oh my gosh, I work here. I work here!' That was pretty crazy. Our sales room was on the eighth floor, and that's where the players entered the stadium. There's Fernando. There's Vin, all these legends, Sweet Lou, Don Newcombe, the Penguin just walking around."

Another person she met as he walked by, someone she grew up watching at games and on television, was Tommy. "I remember hearing his voice booming, saying, 'Who's this, Haak [Casey Haakinson, an account executive for the Dodgers]?' He wanted my whole history, where I went to college, how I got the job with the Dodgers. Then to welcome me to the Dodgers he took me to eat lunch in the press box. I sat next to him, which was an experience."

She and Tommy became friends. Tommy always took an active interest in the rank and file of the organization. He would always stop and talk to the employees, holler motivational sayings as he walked through the offices, sign things for them, and invite them to lunch. Buchanan-Spohr quickly became a staple of the lunch group. "Then there were lunch invitations to go out to Paul's Kitchen, Buca di Beppo, South Street for Philly cheesesteaks. I thought that he was still larger than life, but you saw this much kinder side of him than you would have expected from the tough old Dodgers manager. He was much more human."

Buchanan-Spohr, Haakinson, I, and anyone else who worked for the Dodgers who had a chance to get closer to Tommy could easily see the more human side of him. He was quick to share his smile with us. He was quick to tell us things he thought would make a difference in our lives. "He would stop and talk to you, ask you about sales, tell jokes, and it actually seemed like he was listening," said Buchanan-Spohr. "He wanted you to be good at your job. He motivated everybody, not just the players."

He also wanted to know about your family. "Every time I saw him he asked how my husband was," said Buchanan-Spohr. "He was always very considerate, and he always remembered what was going on with my family."

Fortunately for the Spohrs, the couple did not have to wait long to expand their family. After a difficult pregnancy, Madeline Alice Spohr was born on November 11, 2007, at 28 weeks old. Maddie, as she was known, was a patient in the NICU at the Mattel Children's Hospital for almost 10 weeks. "They told us a million times that she wasn't going to make it another hour," said Buchanan-Spohr. One day of that is enough for a lifetime; 68 days of that is a nightmare worse than an Angels-Giants World Series.

As the holidays neared, the Spohrs didn't know when their time in the NICU would end. Tommy was preparing to be Santa once again for the Mattel's holiday party, just as he had a year earlier. But this year, Santa Tommy had something special in his sack. He heard that Buchanan-Spohr and her husband were in the NICU with baby Maddie. After the party, he decided to deliver them some holiday cheer.

"It was the quietest I had ever seen Maddie," said Buchanan-Spohr. "She gripped on to his gnarled finger with her hand, and he sang 'Daddy's Little Girl' to her. It meant so much to me that he was there for another event. He was done and could have gone home, but he came over not only to see her but also to say hi to all the doctors and nurses. It meant so much to me because these doctors and nurses had saved my daughter a million times, and by extension they saved me and my husband and our families. He thanked them all profusely for the job they were doing and for taking good care of Maddie, and for all the babies, and thanked them for what they did and the sacrifices they had to make. I didn't really invite anyone else to come see her, but he was the only person from the organization to come see her."

Tragically, Maddie passed away on April 7, 2009. By then, Buchanan-Spohr had left the Dodgers. But that didn't break her connection to Tommy. "Tommy reached out and made a donation in her name to the Association of Professional Ball Players of America," she said. "It meant a lot to us, because at that point it had been six months since I stopped working for the team, but the fact that he remembered Maddie and me when he didn't have to, it really meant a lot to me. That's the side of Tommy that a lot of people don't see."

• • •

As Logan White sat at home in Portales, New Mexico, watching Kirk Gibson dig into the box in the 1988 World Series, he was imagining what his life would have been like if he had made it to the big leagues, imagining where he would be pitching if he hadn't needed shoulder surgery. What he could never have imagined then was meeting, befriending, learning from, and loving Tommy Lasorda.

White joined the Dodgers in 2001 and was their vice president of amateur scouting through the 2014 season. He met Tommy on his first trip to Los Angeles. "I was real nervous," said White. "He was in his office with Hideo Nomo and his agent. He was talking to them and he brought me in as if I was royalty. He asked me if I had kids, and he brought out a Tommy key chain for Little Logan [White's son]. I couldn't believe it. From that moment on it was a real special relationship."

That didn't mean they didn't bump heads on occasion. Early on they had passionate disagreements over keeping young pitchers on pitch counts. "I wouldn't give in, but I was respectful," White said. "I think that was a key moment with Tommy. If I would have conceded, I don't think he would have ever respected me like he does." White spent that spring training driving across Florida, scouting amateur players. One night he was driving back to Vero Beach from Tampa, and his phone rang around midnight.

"Where in the world are you?" hollered Tommy. "Get your butt out here! We're jogging to the beach!"

"He was jogging for a hundred feet and then would walk. Jog, walk, jog, walk," said White. "It's about five miles from Dodgertown to the beach. He calls Dodgertown and has someone come pick us up. We get back and he says, 'Meet me for breakfast at 7:00!' His energy was ridiculous. I've never seen a person with that much energy, that much drive, that much passion. It's true when people say it; there's only one Tommy. I've never met anyone like him, and I don't think I ever will again."

When Tommy invites you to eat, when he invites you to do anything, it means he likes you. It means you are becoming part of the family. If you reciprocate with love, respect, and loyalty he will give you the shirt off his back. In White's case, Tommy offered something even better: he offered to be one of White's scouts.

"I was shocked," said White. "He always told me that he would do anything for the scouts. I think at first he did it because he genuinely loves and respects and cares about scouts. It is a love and a passion he has for them. I was honored and excited. He was a huge help to the staff and me. He gave me credibility, but he made me earn it."

White put the wealth and depth of Tommy's experience to work. In return, Tommy would go see more players, and more importantly, would also work with White's son, Logan Michael White, affectionately known as Little Logan.

During spring training in Vero Beach, Tommy would work with Little Logan's throwing mechanics. "Tommy would take him to the side field to throw and I would catch him," said White. "After throwing he would take us to dinner, and Tommy would be talking to him, telling him life lessons. That blew me away. To see how much my kid loved Tommy, and to see how much Tommy loved Little Logan, to see a Hall of Famer take time to work with my son?"

Tommy would also work with Little Logan on his hitting. "In the back of the cage you have the pitching machine behind a net with a hole in the middle where the ball comes out. Logan was eight years old at the time. Tommy says, 'I'll give you $50 if you can hit a ball through that hole.' The second swing, Logan hits it through. Tommy never thought in his wildest dreams he could do it. He had to give him $50. Tommy told him not to tell anybody, and Logan said, 'If you give me another $50, I won't.'"

Tommy also worked on his toughness. Tommy would tell him, "I see a lot of me in you—the smart part, the tough part, the good-looking part." Little Logan was listening. "Once, Logan had two buddies with him," White said. "They are riding in Tommy's cart and one of them got a little smart with Logan. And Logan looked at him and said, 'Don't forget who got you here, pal.'"

"That made me laugh, boy," said Tommy.

"Before I met Tommy, my impression of him was as a fiery competitor," said White. "After getting to know him, I see that he has a heart for kids and people that's second to none. He always signs autographs, he treats everybody [the same], no matter what walk of life they come from, and he is always very gracious and good to people. It amazes me how good he is. Once, we are eating dinner at Del Frisco's, an outstanding steak house. The food just got to the table and his steak was sizzling. A guy walks up to the table and tells Tommy that his brother was in the hospital dying of cancer. Tommy hands the guy his cell phone and tells him to call his brother. The guy called his brother from Tommy's phone, and Tommy spends 10, 15 minutes talking to this guy from the hospital and trying to pick up his spirits.

"He taught me about the game, but he also taught me about people and about life. My father died when I was young, and I had a tough upbringing. I think Tommy and I had a lot of things in common. We hit it off. I always looked up to him like a father, like the dad I didn't have."

White decided the best way to show his love and respect for Tommy was by starting a youth tournament and scouting combine called the Tommy Lasorda Elite Games. Dodgers scouts invite the top high school prospects from the western states to play in a four-team weekend series at Dodger Stadium, hosted by Tommy Lasorda. Not only would the scouts get another chance to see the kids play, but it gave Tommy a chance to do what he loved to do most: work with the players.

"Get the head of the bat out in front of you!" he would holler. If a player didn't get his bat out far enough, Tommy would stop BP and show him how to utilize the player's power.

"Snap it!" he would scream. He instructed hitters to snap their belly buttons around to generate bat speed.

"Chop that tree!" he would yell. He wanted players to swing on a downward plane, creating backspin on the ball that makes it carry farther than it normally would.

And when a ball sailed over the fence, perhaps for the first time in the player's life, Tommy would bellow, "Take a ride on that one! It would cost you $10 in a taxi to go that far!"

"He stood at the cage all day long and he would get so excited when a kid would hit one out by using something he taught him," said White. "He would also address all of the kids and teach them what it would take to succeed. He would take pictures with them, talk to their parents. The majority of the players I knew would never be big league players, but I knew most of them would become coaches, teachers, whatever, and their memories of the Dodgers and Tommy would always be great, and their influence on others would be great, too.

"To me, Tommy is a treasure. It's easy for us who are around him all the time to take it for granted, but if we could give these kids and families a taste of what we got to experience, it would be special."

When Little Logan was 12 years old, White and a few other dads started a travel team. The original name of the team was the Mission Surf Dogs. "I saw Lasorda University on a shirt he gave me years before," White said. "I pulled that T-shirt out and thought, *Oh my gosh, this is brilliant.* I called Tommy and told him I wanted to call Logan's travel ball team Lasorda University.

"Tommy comes out and talks to the team, signs balls, watches them play. How many of these kids are going to play in the major leagues? Probably not many. How many of these kids are going to play in college? But you know what? Every one of them will be able to say they played for Lasorda University. They will be able to say that their team was named after a Hall of

Fame manager, that they got to meet Tommy Lasorda, that he came to watch them play, that he signed a ball for them."

Lasorda University made Tommy proud. It also gave him a chance to work with kids again, and to teach them the game, teaching the same lessons he taught his players decades earlier. And just as he would scream from the dugout at Dodger Stadium in joyous celebration after a Dodgers victory, he would scream the same from the stands in Gilbert, Arizona, where Lasorda University plays: "How sweet it is, the fruits of victory!"

"He always yells that after we win," said Little Logan. Playing first, third, and catcher, Little Logan has been on Lasorda University since its inception. Of course, the lessons he and his teammates learn from Tommy have been drilled into him since his days riding around Dodgertown with Tommy on his golf cart.

"It's amazing to play on Lasorda University, because you put on that jersey and you're representing Uncle Tommy, and that means a lot because of all he has done in the game," said Little Logan. "The main thing was, I learned hard work. I've also learned that you owe your parents love and respect, that I've got to believe in myself, that I have to want it, that there are three types of players. I want to be the one who makes it happen.

"My goal is to play in the big leagues. When I'm practicing, working out, playing, that drives me. Sometimes when I'm playing, I can hear Tommy in the back of my mind hollering at me, and when I'm not doing my best I think, *Man, Uncle Tommy would not be proud of you right now*."

"Tommy told me once, 'I wish you would have pitched for me. If you would have pitched for me, you would have pitched in the big leagues,'" White said. "He was sincere. He believed it. He almost had me believing that, and I know I didn't have the ability to pitch in the big leagues. But Tommy really believes he can get that ability out of anybody. And that's what I love about him."

"I believe that God puts you on earth for a reason," said Tommy. "I think He put me on earth to help other people. To do everything I can to help."

ACKNOWLEDGMENTS

There is so much for which to be thankful and I have so many people to thank. I would like to thank my mother and father for giving me the gift of love for reading and writing, and for all of their selfless sacrifices to give me every opportunity in life. I would like to thank my wife and son for giving me the gift of unconditional love. I would like to thank Papa for giving me the gift of inspiration. I would like to thank the Gunderson and Hanks families for giving me the gift of pride. I would like to thank the Nave family for giving me the gift of acceptance.

I would like to thank Josh Rawitch for giving me the gift of respect.

I would like to thank Howard Sunkin and Peter Wilhelm for giving me the gift of compassion.

I would like to thank the great Steve Brener for giving me the gift of mentorship.

I would like to thank Acey Kohrogi for giving me the gift of brotherhood and Andrea MacCord for giving me the gift of sisterhood.

I would like to thank Camille Johnston for giving me the gift of mercy.

I would like to thank Chris for giving me the gifts of honesty, courage, and perseverance.

I would like to thank the Dodgers clubhouse staff for giving me the gift of fellowship.

I would like to thank Mark Langill for giving me the gift of laughter.

I would like to thank Mark Walter and Guggenheim Baseball Management for taking care of Tommy, our national treasure.

I would like to thank all of Tommy's players and friends for their participation in this book, specifically Peter O'Malley, Vin Scully, Jaime Jarrin, Ralph Avila, Ann Meyers-Drysdale, Bobby Valentine, Mike Scioscia, Ron Cey, Steve Garvey, Rick Monday, Bill Buckner, Eric Karros, Mike Piazza, Orel Hershiser, Kirk Gibson, Charlie Hough, Burt Hooton, Tim Wallach, John Shelby, Glenn Hoffman, Steve Sax, Kenny Howell, Steve Yeager, Rick Rhoden, Mickey Hatcher, Lenny Harris, Doug Mientkiewicz, Ben Sheets, Jerry Royster, Jerry Reuss, Tom Paciorek, Dave Righetti, Joe Garagiola, Bob Wright, Alyson Habetz, Heather Spohr, Casey Haakinson, Logan White, and Logan Michael White.

I would like to thank George Randazzo and the Italian American Sports Hall of Fame for connecting me with Triumph Books. Their commitment to helping others is an outward sign of the caring spirit within.

I would like to thank the Dodgers PR department, the Library of Congress, Josh Suchon, Jeff Idelson, Paul Seiler, and Dave Fanucchi for all of their help.

I would like to thank Triumph Books for their gift of partnership, especially Mitch Rogatz for taking a chance on a first-time author and my editor, Adam Motin, for the gifts of guidance, tutelage, and hard work. I am filled with gratitude for his outstanding effort, and humbled by his unwavering attitude.

I would like to thank the Lasorda family for taking me in and sharing with me all of the love they share between themselves. Specifically, I would like to thank Jo and Laura Lasorda for loving and taking me into their hearts. I would like to thank Tommy's brothers for taking care of me.

Lastly, I would like to thank Tommy for taking me under his wing, for giving me the gift of self-confidence, for teaching me how to live a life of purpose, for helping me shape my dreams and giving me my own pair of wings to pursue them with all the drive and desire I have in my heart. I thank you, Tommy, for all of the love and respect you have given me over the years. I only hope I have given them back to you each and every day I have had the privilege and honor of being in your life.

Sources

Books

Fanucchi, David. *Miracle on Grass: How Hall of Famer Tommy Lasorda led Team USA to a shocking upset over Cuba, capturing the only Olympic gold medal in USA baseball history*. CreateSpace Independent Publishing Platform, 2012.

Garvey, Steve. *My Bat Boy Days: Lessons I Learned from the Boys of Summer*. Scribner, 2008.

Hershiser, Orel. *Out of the Blue*. Wolgemuth & Hyatt, 1989.

Piazza, Mike, and Wheeler, Lonnie. *Long Shot*. Simon & Schuster, 2013.

Plaschke, Bill, with Lasorda, Tommy. *I Live for This! Baseball's Last True Believer*. Houghton Mifflin, 2007.

Suchon, Josh. *Miracle Men: Hershiser, Gibson, and the Improbable 1988 Dodgers*. Triumph Books LLC, 2013.

Newspapers and Periodicals

Atlanta Journal Constitution
Los Angeles Herald Examiner
Los Angeles Times
Miami Herald
New York Daily News
Pittsburgh Post Gazette
The Sporting News

Online Resources

Baseball-Reference.org
Baseballhall.org
Dodgers.com
Giants.com
Npr.org
Si.com